THE
SECRET FIRE

THE
SECRET FIRE

*A New View of Women
and Passion*

✾ ✾ ✾

ROSEMARIE SANTINI

PψP

A Playboy Press Book

The facts related in this book are all true. I have changed names, places, descriptions of all who have requested anonymity.

Rosemarie Santini

FIRST EDITION

Playboy and Rabbit Head design are trademarks of Playboy, 919 North Michigan Avenue, Chicago, Illinois 60611 (U.S.A.), Reg. U.S. Pat. Off., marca registrada, marque déposée.

Library of Congress Cataloging in Publication Data
Santini, Rosemarie.
    Secret fire.
        1. Women—United States—Sexual behavior. 2. Women—Psychology. I. Title.
HQ46.S334   301.41'76'33   76-25076
ISBN 0-87223-474-6

This book is dedicated to
Sidonie-Gabrielle Colette

"My darling, one day you will understand all this. You will understand that I must not belong to you or to anyone, and that in spite of a first marriage and a second love, I have remained a kind of old maid, like some among them who are so in love with Love that no lover appears to them beautiful enough, and so they refuse themselves without condescending to explain; who repel every sentimental misalliance and return to sit for life before a window, bent over their needle, in solitary communion with their incomparable vision. Like them, I wanted everything; a lamentable mistake punished me.

"I no longer dare, my darling, that is the whole trouble, I no longer dare."

COLETTE
The Vagabond

I wish to thank Mrs. Helen Barrett of the William Morris Agency for knowing what I wanted to write even before I did, and for encouraging me in this project.

Also, my editor at Playboy Press, Robert Gleason, whose dialogues with me about being a man in today's society helped me enormously in my perceptions of male/female relationships.

CONTENTS

It seems to me that even in this era of Masters and Johnson information, women are functioning as they always have. Trying to free themselves to be sexual, sometimes bewildered about modern events, women still discover that they are turned on by the remnants of the romantic courtly behavior of men. Flowers, perfume, and graciousness are often preferred by women as a prelude to a sensuous and pleasurable evening.

Yet, modern women are often guilty about these preferences. Many modern women are discovering that with the giving up of manipulative demands upon men, much of the fun and romance is disappearing from their sex lives.

What can women do about this?

Because I believe that this modern dilemma is not answered in laboratory experiments, I asked women themselves. Traveling from coast to coast on various journalistic assignments, I had the opportunity to meet many different kinds of women, with different kinds of needs. After interviewing over a thousand women, I am startled to see a similarity emerging. This sampling reveals something important, something I have not as yet seen recorded in the many books about women.

I am writing this book to explore what modern women really want from love and sex, and how they go about getting it.

Rosemarie Santini

INTRODUCTION

I

Recently, an attractive man I had known for several years, through his marriage and mine, phoned me to find out how things were. I was very sad, I told him, because I had just ended a relationship of long duration which, although it was an off-and-on relationship, had given my life a kind of schizoid blend of passion and reality, fantasy and platitudes, which I had been trying to balance. But this day, realizing that too much energy was being used on what was, realistically, a wasteful relationship, I had put an end to it.

Thus, I was feeling depressed and sorrowful, almost soap opera-ish in my thinking that something romantic had not turned out for me. It was no longer a matter of who was at fault, as it had been during my young marriage. Now, it was a matter of modern times/zeitgeist—men and women changing—what was to become of us all?

Nick, my friend, showed a surprising amount of compassion for my situation. While we had known each other for years, we had never been intimate friends. Yet, I had felt close to him because of his heritage, my friendship with his family, their holiday celebrations which are very much attuned to my Italian heritage, plus the fact that he was in a profession quite close to mine.

"Don't let it get you down," he said. "Why don't you come up to my new digs for dinner? I've sublet a lovely penthouse apartment. You can see the river from there, and there are predictions of a snowstorm."

Immediately my mind flashed to those 1940s films starring John Garfield on *The Late Show*, that sense of glamour, of romance, of virility—the sensitive strong man who could love you and care for you at the same time. Then I thought, no, I should suffer a while.

After all, the breakup had just happened last night. So I said I was too sad, planning instead to use the weekend to read, eat diet foods, and pine away.

"Okay," he responded casually, "but think of what you're doing. There is no need for a funeral. I'll call back later."

There is no need for a funeral. Those words stuck in my mind. Yes, why the burial? The memorial service? The epitaph for the dead lover? This was 1976, the year of change, the year of sexual freedom. It was nonsensical to be romantic and sad with nostalgia. Nick was right. He was offering me his company in a situation which we had both been through before. (My sadness on this day was only ten percent of my desperation when my marriage had failed.) So when he called back, I accepted his invitation.

We met an hour later and drove to his lovely penthouse where anyone could be happy. It was astonishingly beautiful. A grand foyer greeted me as I entered a ballroom of elegance, with a marble tiled floor. Large potted ferns trimmed it, bordered by a terrace from where Manhattan's skyline could be admired.

Through the foyer was a large living room filled with unusual antiques and a fireplace. Then a dining space, facing the again exciting skyline. The apartment was like a breath of fresh air in a city where everyone's economic situation curtailed their imagination of living quarters. "They should have been very happy," I commented, referring to the couple who had lived here before.

"Yes," he said, quietly. "Instead, they are getting a divorce."

We looked at each other in a tender way, the look of two who had known that ordeal; his divorce had been painful, so had mine. Forgetting as soon as we remembered, we toasted with large goblets of brandy. "I'll cook dinner," he said, and I leaned back and thought of how wonderful it was that men were cooking dinner nowadays, and women were leaning back in armchairs, enjoying it all.

We ate dinner, fish and rice, Mediterranean style. Dark red wine in burgundy goblets. Coffee that stirred the imagination again. Ripe oranges, fruit of the sun. Then we began kissing. He invited me into an inner room, a studio with a skylight, containing a bed, books of poetry, and framed photographs of his parents, who looked like my grandparents. We held onto each other, and I thought how wonderful it was to be sexually liberated from the romantic idea of suffering, to be ready for the next experience so close to a negative one, which would have formerly taken the wind out of me.

Then he broke the spell. "I'm sorry," he said desperately.

I stopped my enjoyment of his body to realize that he was talking about not having an erection. I told him to ignore it, to enjoy the passionate embraces, the sultry kisses, the murmurs, the wonderful exploration of a new body, two bodies, his and mine, for each other. He tried. He really tried. But it was over for him. He had not penetrated me and fucked me, macho-style. Instead, his penis had given in to whatever psychological fears or angers he might have felt about us being together—and stayed limp.

His body was angry. I tried to overcome it by holding him close. We lay there through the night, clasped, entwined. It was very important for me to be held so close, and I whispered that to him as the snowflakes began speckling the skylight, framing the Magritte moon on this black wintery night. It was more important to me than anything else. He did not understand that I did not mind about the penis. I did not mind for several reasons. One was that it never occurred to me that it would be a consistent problem, for we would talk about it and then it would go away. Or it was because of the fact that we were together for the first time. Or, if it continued to be a problem, we would simply ignore it and make love in other ways. It was an emotion-packed night, and I had had this experience before on such occasions. For me, it did not mean Nick was less of a man.

We slept fretfully, the way lovers do on the first night together. The sun awoke me first, and Nick's body was glistening with enchanting rainbows. He was so beautiful. So was I. There is nothing more erotic to me than the sight of two bodies lying side by side, in the sunlight. He finally stirred. We got up. He kissed me. I returned the gesture, and we went out to the kitchen to have breakfast.

We were listening to Maria Callas with our coffee, a favorite mentor for both of us, a woman who had given up everything for her emotions, personally and professionally. I turned to Nick. "Do you want to talk about what happened in the bedroom?" I asked gently.

His eyelashes tightened. "No, not particularly," he said.

"A lot of things happened. We should talk about them," I said, meaning if we were going to go on being lovers.

"No," he said again firmly, with his melancholic darkness curtailing me. "No, I believe those things happen or they don't. There's nothing you can do about it. It's probably because I'm not in love with you."

I flinched under his attack. Was he assuming I was in love with him? So soon? What had happened for me was consideration, affection, holding, need, but he had only focused on the impotence. I waited for him to change his attitude. But he did not.

I had waited with men like this before, thus a short amount of time seemed ages. When I finally left, he did not even say goodbye.

I walked slowly down the tree-lined streets, fighting depression, realizing, as I had so many times before, that here before me was a situation full of opportunities for a deep passion, a deep love, which could not even begin because of a man's need for sexual performance and evaluation. So things hadn't really changed at all, had they?

But I was confused, too. Why was I so understanding in this situation? After all, I always liked a man to perform, didn't I? I was a woman who liked my orgasms, my many orgasms. I began to get angry, but my anger was tied somehow to my feelings of vulnerability to the sensitivity of the situation. *What do you do when a man you like blames you for his sexual failure?* I had no answer.

I thought, if he could only understand that I did not see it as a failure. Compared with the rest of the evening—his concern, his cooking dinner, his warmth—it was only one thing that hadn't worked out. These other things should have been just as important to him. Why was this not so? Was it because, to him, the only thing he had to offer me was a stiff prick? We both had had orgasms in other ways than penetration, so there was sexual enjoyment. I began to think of performance as an undermining element in sexuality in our modern times. When one keeps thinking of how one is doing, one cannot possibly enjoy a sensual feeling (*sensual*, to me, as opposed to *sexual*, means a vulnerability is present). I thought, if men feel they must fuck or they are not men, do women feel the very same about them? Women are becoming more and more open about sex, more sexual, at least that's what all the sex books say. Do they really just want to be fucked, or are other things still important to them?

I began to think of the answer to this puzzle, the puzzle of eroticism of women, the puzzle of what turns them on. What turns me on? I thought, always beginning with myself. What has always been erotic to me is a man with a combination of many traits. Looks, prestige, wealth, power do not count among them. It is always a man who can be vulnerable and generous to me as a human being, affectionate to me as a friend, and sensual to me as a woman.

It seems to me certainly that eroticism must be a blend of fact and fantasy. Unfortunately, in men, eroticism has almost become a scientific thesis; a pair of silicone breasts will manufacture one huge erection, preferably if the breasts are on a woman they do not know and will never see again. Even more stimulating to men are the silicone breasts on two women making love to each other, and the mystique goes on and on. Yet, men can be turned on by these images, as we all know.

But women have always been mystified and frankly bored with this so-called eroticism, simply because of the pat and dull *Cosmo* Cover Girl and *Playboy* fold-out style they have been served up. Yet, women think and talk about sex, just as men do, but *to each other usually*. They talk about the length of a man's penis, they talk about his desirability, the way he speaks, how often he calls, when he doesn't, but they never take his physical parts and separate them from the other parts. Women see sex as a composite thing, the sum of many parts.

To a woman, a large penis is fine, but it has to be attached to a man whose behavior excites her. And when his behavior is one of strong protection it often excites her even more.

This is a popular fantasy. There is an etching above my desk of a delicate lady of noble character holding on for dear life to the chest of a knight in shining armor. He, in turn, is grasping the reins of a thunderous *Equus* horse—white, strong, swift. In the knight's other hand is a long, slim, steel blade drawn from a shield of chivalry. The artist's conception highlights the knight's long hair flying in the wind, with a background of a sky of golden hues contrasting to the horse's silver-white body. Etched all over the knight's armor are tiny rosettes. He does not look fierce, he looks like a sensitive soldier, a poet. My God, I think, how can he defend her in battle?

But the knight epitomizes the fantasy of all women who have entered my rooms. They have all remarked how sensitive and how brave and strong he is. Yet, I feel if he had not been placed upon a horse of such substance and given a weighty steel blade, he would flounder. But every woman looks upon him, knowing he has the soul of the poet, the heart of the lion, the passion of the cannibal, and the strength of the mighty fortress.

If we look at this etching realistically, we see that the horse is the hero, not the knight. If the horse were not so strong and swift, I am certain both the handsome knight and his fair lady would be destroyed by some unlucky dragon.

Hanging parallel on the wall is another etching by the same artist, which is a supreme contrast. It is the portrait of a goddess, strong, sure, defiant. Her hands and feet are like a man's. She has a firm grasp on the globe of the world, which she is standing on, and also on a mirror she is holding, reflecting her own image to herself. Throughout her body are etched beautiful flowers and vines growing, erupting from her blooming flesh. Her eyes are dark, luminescent in honesty, her hair embellished with Botticellian flourishes.

I have worked out a fantasy story between the two etchings. For me, when the timid lady fair realizes realistically that it is the horse and not the knight who is saving her, then she begins to put her feet on the ground and develops into the beautiful, strong, flowery goddess. But unless she is realistic about her fantasy, this will never happen.

It is difficult for women to give up this illusion, for our fathers and mothers have perpetuated this theme, the myth of the white knight on horseback rescuing the damsel in distress, computerizing daughters to feel that they are in distress, educating them to sell their sex for marriage and support for the rest of their lives. But it is a scenario that works, it is a scenario in which men are comfortable, which touches their fantasies, which gives them their erections. Modern women who dream of a time when this scenario can be different must be ready to be enticed into areas heretofore unexplored and which, if they are not aware of them, may lead into areas of complete and depressing desolation.

Why have our parents computerized us to so desolate a dream, an illusion? Perhaps because all fathers are interested in seducing all daughters, if not in actual seduction then in the seduction of the mind, in the control of what later will be the erotic impulse. This is the reason that the romantic idealism which requires male lovers to be male protectors turns so many women on. And at the risk of being accused of being old-fashioned, I am not only talking about the traditional wife's being turned on. I have found this strain of romanticism running through the personality of all the women I interviewed, including prostitutes, lesbians, feminists, and that supreme acting-out group, the women in the sadomasochistic world. Romanticism, male protection, female fragility seem to be the main artery of the female erotic impulse.

In my own case, I always looked for a particular vulnerability, a particular poetry in men, the softness that some women look for in other women. When I realized I was attracted to men who had this sensitivity, coupled with a feeling of responsibility, developed from the urgency of their particular sense of macho, that this is my early memory of my father, a sweet poetic man with a sense of duty, I had found my erotic turn-on. I have discovered also that this type of man is erotic for many other women also—the combination of male and female instincts in the same body in an exhilarating and organic balance.

While I was researching this book and collecting my thoughts, an old woman with streaked white hair kept appearing in my dreams, saying I had become hard-hearted because I was analyzing logically matters of the heart. She warned if I were truly a woman I would not do this. "You will no longer love," she kept admonishing me. I walked away from her in the dream, and came to a bridge over a valley of female souls crying out as if in purgatory. At a break in the bridge, I wondered whether I could make the jump to the other side, which seemed to lead to a mountaintop of clarity. I hesitated only one moment as I thought about the two possibilities of my jump: Either I would reach the other side or I would fall into the lost hell of female souls below me. But I knew that I would jump, because there was no place else to go.

In a recent interview in *The New York Times Magazine*, Ingmar Bergman expanded on this theme: "The women are finally beginning to take over their full burden of responsibility. Of course, they still have so many difficulties that it is impossible to know what will happen. On one side, there is the vocal avant-garde, on the other, a great crowd of women who remain invisible. Yet almost every woman, even in the avant-garde, has some kind of saboteur inside her. I don't know if it's her mother's voice, or something complicated with her physical construction, or what it is. But they all have a bad conscience. They feel that something is wrong and they don't know how to manage it. Even so, something has started which is not to be stopped, though where it will go and what will happen we don't know."

This phenomenon grows. In Truffaut's brilliant film, *The Diary of Adele H.*, the heroine, after describing the character of the man she has given up everything for, says: "Yes, he is a scoundrel. But we are not responsible for who we are passionate with, are we?"

Adele H. (Adele Hugo) has left her sane and famous father (Victor Hugo) and his home to travel to a new world for a man who isn't worth it and who doesn't want her. Of course she gives up her entire life for him. Of course she collapses and gives up her sanity. She is expected to go mad for her great passion.

In her thoughtful analysis of the Truffaut film in the *Village Voice*, Molly Haskell says: "Truffaut understands . . . that such an obsession is not only magnificent but terrible, not only sublime, but selfish and cruel." Ms. Haskell also makes the fascinating statement that the interesting difference is that the male obsession is fixated on the idealized image of a woman, while the woman's is in the emotion itself.

In one of his most successful movies, *Letter from an Unknown Woman*, Max Ophuls has the heroine worshipping her lover from afar since she was a child, bearing his illegitimate child in grim silence, loving him all the time. When she finally marries a gentle and adoring husband, and has everything in the world, she sees her lover again and says: "I cannot answer for my actions. It has always been this way with him." It is the confession that passion is uncontrollable, that it is something that women cannot handle, cannot give up, if they are really in love.

In the feminine mind to define emotion is to kill it, and logic breeds dispassion. If women are logical about their emotional choices, they feel they are not truly passionate women. The concept of womanhood that a *real* woman suffers for love has put women in situations destructive to their lives. Today, women are beginning to realize that suffering is silly. Still, love without suffering seems to them empty. Sex without love, just a luxurious pastime. True eroticism for women comes from the combination of both.

The reason that women cannot give up their suffering is simple. The reason we have held on to this concept of passion is simply *that there is nothing to replace it.*

II

So many women think that everyone else knows more about sex than they do. This makes perfect sense when we recognize that even in these modern times, women still experiment sexually much less frequently than men. The sexual revolution has benefited men, but what has it actually done for women?

Certainly, in the area of science, it has caused many changes. Birth control has relieved the enormous pressure women used to feel, a reason much joy was missing from their erotic relationships. But outside of science, has the new sexual morality enhanced the emotional and erotic nature of women?

Whatever a woman's life choices, tension between the sexes goes on and on. Sexual anger, a primary force in the creation of passion, is often avoided, excused away, and displaced by women in their relationships to men. There are reasons: The forces of women's liberation, while attaining enormous advances in areas of politics, education, and employment, seem to have caused an unfortunate backlash for women who desire to relate to men emotionally and erotically, in a climate which always merges their personal responses to women's lib. When a woman used to be angry, a man may have wanted to soothe her, perhaps as a prelude to sexual ecstasy. Nowadays when a woman is angry, often the male of the species reacts as if this woman is from another planet, the planet of women's rights which is threatening to him. Her anger must be eliminated or he will become impotent.

Yet, sexual anger between the sexes has been an acceptable fact of love up to this point in time. (I do not want to belabor this by citing the wonderfully dialectic films of the Thirties and Forties, the Shakespearean ordeals, George Bernard Shaw, or the most contemporary example, the marriage of Richard Burton and Elizabeth Taylor.)

There is a kind of sabotage of modern women's freedom, because of the concept that loving for most women is a great intense emotion, a passion that includes in it a feeling of suffering. If a woman really loves, she is expected to give up everything. If a man experiences this kind of passion, he is considered a sort of "cuckold." No *real* man lets a woman affect him so, but every *real* woman, of course, must. Obsessional love in women has always moved them to great emotional and erotic depths. Yet many modern women avoid obsessional love because they have been educated to realize the entrapment of it.

Modern women, as women before, both hate and love the object of their desires. Formerly, the beloved man was a strong authoritarian figure and to obey him or disobey him turned women on. Nowadays, modern men are divided into two camps: those who are trying to be understanding of women's changing needs, and those who are not, preferring instead to keep women in the old position of subservience.

But many of our modern changes are only on a reality level. According to the research for this book, on an erotic, passionate level, women are still turned on by the myth of the cave man. Thus, while modern women are fighting for their individual rights as free persons on a conscious level, the majority are often still getting turned on by the fantasy of the strong, dominant man.

This ambivalent and confusing situation has caused much anger in women, anger which is difficult to express directly. Women have handled it the best way they can. Some have become sexual mechanics, imitating men in their nonemotional sexual activity. Some have become lesbians, stating they do not need men but imitating them every chance they get. Some have become "total women," with its necessary courtesan characteristics. All of the women I researched have been trying to deal with this fiery anguish they may feel in the best way they can, and many of the ways they have chosen are covered here.

There is a small percentage of the population which has dramatized the tension between the sexes in the most extreme way possible—a didactic, structured, role-playing scenario with the strong man absolutely in command of the obedient available woman. This concept, covered in the following chapter, is commonly known as sadomasochism, a dramatic acting out of the fantasy of bondage and discipline, which appears to be the real, central dynamic of all erotic relationships, a dynamic which is present in one form or another in every chapter in this book.

THE
SECRET FIRE

One

❀ ❀ ❀

THE EROTICISM OF
MASOCHISM/
DOMINANCE/DEATH

Many people believe that passion has become diluted. So some people have been searching for a way to put pepper back into passion. Since the Sixties hippy culture convinced the world that only love is present in passion (and the enormous influence of these naive children on adults still amazes me), anger, an important element in passion, has been relegated to expensively filled hours of psychotherapy, group therapy, or encounter sessions. Everyone is afraid of anger, of facing their anger directly. It is whispered and hidden by all, especially women who have never been encouraged to be direct in anything.

We know the nagging wife, the manipulative mother, and the high-priced insulting whore have been angry for years. But none of these women admit to their anger directly; it is too expensive. And for good reason: Anger in women is not considered an attractive emotion; an angry woman in America loses her sex appeal almost immediately. Yet the European film stars like the late Anna Magnani, and now Jeanne Moreau and Sophia Loren, women who express their passionate anger in their lives and in their film roles, have been considered sensual and desirable women. European men, while being mightily chauvinistic in many areas, seem to adore and encourage women with spice. Alas, for American men, the vogue is the sweet girl who hides her anger from the world.

An angry woman is an honest woman, and there is much in life for both men and women to be angry about. But the young men and women of the Sixties denied the existence of anger because of their contempt for war (which has more to do with male ego than with anger) and convinced everyone that being angry was unloving, thus unsensual. The tone of the times was love, love, love your enemies, and give flowers to them. Of course the hippies—the "children of paradise"—needed drugs to enforce this illusion, and oddly, the drug sounds, the rock music of the Sixties, contain extremely angry rhythms.

Because anger is such an awesome responsibility for everyone, especially women, we have seen an increase in the existence *of that supreme acting out of indirect anger: the sadomasochistic world.*

Certainly not a modern phenomenon, the S/M world was historically a prerogative of men. We have the Marquis De Sade and the Austrian novelist Leopold von Sacher Masoch to thank for making it known through their writings, and also Gilless de Rias for his infamous activities. These men were exponents of the kidnaping of young girls and boys, using them for sexual thrills and very often killing them. (Gilless was reported to have slaughtered hundreds of youngsters in his debaucheries.)

From this information, we may have thought that no human being was ever a willing victim of the S/M world. However, willing participation of the victim was graphically depicted in the much publicized *Story of O*, supposedly written by a woman. With the publicity of *O*, the sexual role-changes, and so-called consciousness-raising in the S/M world (borrowed from the feminist world), women are now beginning to admit that they are turned on to the slave role, traditionally known in the S/M world as the masochist. One major reason that role has become popular is that most women still do not want to accept responsibility for their lives and enjoy, as always, shifting it to the male. In the S/M relationship, it is the S (sadist), usually male, who has to be inventive and make all the decisions. It is the obedience to the S's orders that gives the M (masochist), traditionally the female, a very sensual feeling commonly referred to as a "rush."

Here, in the words of a masochistic woman, is the way it happens:

The M faces all the obvious dangers; but there are also some subtle, insidious problems. When an M teams up with an S, there is a necessary element and transference of trust. The M is, in effect, putting her life and existence in the hands and control of the S. The M is therefore also giving the S the full responsibility for his or her physical, psychological, and emotional safety. With this transference of responsibility, the M is liberated from the burden of self-responsibility. This freedom can be tempting. Given that the person is a true M, the "pain," "torture," "headfucking," etc., is all irresistible. Coupled with the release of responsibility, it can be attractive and alluring.*

Another masochistic woman, in a conversation with me, explained it this way: "Anger is such a strong emotion. There are times when I personally feel something only because someone is angry at me. If he's not angry at me, he's thinking about other things, and I am not the center of his existence. When he's angry, all he can think about is me. Nothing else is on his mind. That's why his anger turns me on.

"The worst thing someone can do is ignore me. There is an old joke about the classic S: If he refuses to whip you, it is the worst thing he can do to you. That would be real punishment to me. So if he is whipping me, touching me, caressing me, and going through all that effort, then I feel he is turned on. I work very hard to make him angry at me."

Here we see the M's need to be the absolute center of attention. What better way to attract attention than to desire and accept pain, to become a vessel for the S's frustration with the world, and his need to have power because of this frustration? But does he have the real power? Or does she?

The female attitude of not wanting to take responsibility for sexuality and life decisions is consistent throughout this book. But the masochist goes one step further. She completely transfers her trust and responsibility to another person, in an obviously painful and perhaps dangerous situation. "I feel very much at his mercy and am the weak female, and that turns me on. It is overwhelming evidence that I am a woman," one M says. Another: "Women feel

* Published in *Prometheus Newspaper;* No. 5, and S/M newsletter.

they need a strong authority figure, and being whipped gets all the hostility out of women. It relieves their anger toward men and makes them sensual."

When I began researching the S/M world, I came to it with much trepidation, since I am, personally, absolutely against pain of any kind being inflicted upon another human being. Yet, my instinctual feelings were not moral, and I came to like most of the women I interviewed. They were sensitive women who freely discussed their activities and fantasies in an honest way. Their main fear was having direct power over themselves, direct independence. Yet in almost every case, I found the M's fascinated by power and manipulation. And they had one opinion in common: that an M had to be very strong.

One evening, I attended a weekly meeting of a heterosexual S/M club. After the meeting, a man came up to me and disclosed that he experimented with Jewish M women, Nazi-style, and said they were willing guinea pigs. I lost my journalistic cool. *I became directly angry at him.* How naive I was then in the ways of the S/M world! Suddenly I found twenty men waiting in line to speak to me. Because of this encounter, I had become the most desirable woman at the meeting. The reason was simple: I had showed direct anger, something rare in the S/M world.

At present, the feminist and other movements are working to encourage women to take leadership roles. Ironically, these women would be popular in the S/M world where there are many M men looking for S women. I was told that in Manhattan there were only three female S's, and they were so busy they had slave rings of five M men at a time. This amused me no end, for what it meant to me was that role-changing was indeed taking place, even in the S/M world. Nowadays, men wanted to be irresponsible, too. Nobody wants to be an S; it is hard work. Some M's experimented with the S role and told me it was terribly difficult; they did not want to be the creative, inventive, responsible partner. They much preferred being taken care of.

Sadly for the S/M women who want to understand their sexual turn-on, there is only incomplete literature at their disposal. All these women said they could not find a psychotherapist who specializes in this field. They say they are treated as "perverts" by the outside world. I was saddened by this. While I found their activities personally foreign to me, I wished someone could help these women discover what made them tick. In many cases, of course, their turn-ons pointed to an incestuous relationship with their fathers which was more extreme than the norm.

Many women are ashamed of anger, and still turn it inward, against themselves. Some masochistic women interviewed in the S/M world were *ashamed of their anger at not being good enough.* Whether it was the fault of society, or their relationships with their parents, or sibling rivalry, doesn't matter. *Somehow this shame translates into a need to be absolutely enslaved and brutalized in order to feel anything close to the "feminine" emotions, to be "soft and vulnerable."* There seems to be no other way for them to get past their fury and feel something close to passion. Since most M's are not direct, they become secret, hidden creatures of the night, compelled by power plays in their sexual nature, often even turning bisexual if it gives them more power over their partners. But when examined closely, these M's are really the power, not the S's, for the S is the manipulated one: He must do all the work.

S/M is sweeping the land. *Swept Away*, a film touted as political, has a strong S/M theme. Abused by the wealthy female employer, the male servant takes over once they are isolated on an island. *She responds to him not because he is mean to her, but because he brutally forces her to have an emotional response,* something her more sophisticated husband cannot do. But in the end, it is he, the S, who suffers. She leaves him, returning to her self-indulgent life, remembering always wistfully the great love passion which she was *forced* to feel. Since, as I have stated in my introduction, women feel suffering is analogous to passion, *many women cannot be vulnerable to erotic love except in a forced manner; the force method of brutality and enslavement turns them on instead of the more gentle behavior of tenderness and sensitivity.* This is the true attraction for women of the S/M world. More humane relationships leave them cold and do not play into their need for unexpressed anger, *i.e.,* their power plays. For when honest anger is dormant and unexpressed, manipulative power plays become the attraction.

7

Although it is terribly popular in these modern times to think that there are no dangers in the S/M world, that it is simply another form of preferred sexuality, I heartily disagree. My disagreement is not moral; it is simply based on human compassion. Most women in the S/M world have something physically wrong with their bodies. I have seen women's bodies covered with bruises. The women interviewed were always going into or coming out of the hospital for everything from kidney disorders, heart murmurs, to internal female disorders of all kinds.

My negative feelings about the S/M world are based also on something they refuse to talk about but is an undercurrent in all interviews and discussions for this chapter. *It is simply that the most erotic S/M fantasy is the fantasy of death.* According to the *New York Post* (October 1, 1975), this is becoming a popular fantasy. It's rumored that "snuff" films are actually being manufactured. The term "snuff" dates back to the days of Charles Manson and his family, who frequently used the word "snuff" to mean murder. There were rumors then that Manson and his clan had filmed ritual murders committed during the late 1960s.

In the book *Helter Skelter*, written about the Manson trials by district attorney Vincent Bugliosi with Curt Gentry, the sexual pleasures of the Manson-related activities of mass murder and torture are vividly described.

Susan Atkins says of Manson: "Charlie is love, pure love" . . . "it feels good when the knife goes in" . . . "[When the gun went off] he climaxed all over himself."

"It felt so good the first time I stabbed her, and when she screamed at me, it did something to me, sent a rush through me, and I stabbed her again."

Killing itself was something else. "It's like a sexual release. . . . Especially when you see the blood spurting out. It's better than a climax."*

Thus, it is my contention that the sexual orgasm felt by the killing of another was an important reason for the Manson murders. Manson promised his family "the high of all highs"—mass murder of strangers.

* Vincent Bugliosi with Curt Gentry, *Helter Skelter* (New York, W.W. Norton, 1974) pp. 117, 118, 128–29.

But how are we to accept a sexual practice whose ultimate high is someone's death? If we approve of voluntary enslavement, isn't the next step the voluntary right to take human life, in order to be turned on? But is it really voluntary, since the fear of death runs through all of the women who are in the S/M world? Although they try to be meticulously careful about their choices of S's, it is a misplaced trust even in the best of relationships.

The only person to take responsibility for her sexuality is the person herself. But responsibility and direct anger are feared by the masochist and their avoidance can lead to her death, not only the desired psychological death of the ego, but physical death.

If this is what the M wants, perhaps then it is not unfair to think of the S/M sexual practice as *slightly suicidal.*

One of the few M women who admitted that she was turned on by death was Marlene.

Marlene

Thirty-two years old, earning $25,000 as an advertising executive, Marlene has grown a long way from the girl who grew up on a Idaho farm. But her fantasies have remained the same.

"They started when I was a little girl, and they all had to do with medieval crime and punishment. There were lots of processions and pageantry. I fantasized the rituals of these processions as my being brought to a sacrificial altar as the victim, an offering to the gods."

Nowadays, the only way Marlene can have an orgasm is to fantasize death while masturbating. "I have this fantasy of an executioner. I'm not sure whether the executioner is male or female, but I know it's switchable. All I see is a black hood, coming closer and closer, till I am no longer. It really turns me on!"

To prepare for this death orgasm, Marlene has scenes with an S. "All that interests me is the S/M turn-on of bondage and discipline. I have a rubber fetish and everything is the color black. The rubber is very hot and very cold, very protecting and engulfing. I am put in rubber sheets, tied up, and then ice cubes are dropped in, blankets put around me and I am hot and cold alternately for many hours."

"How do you feel about these turn-ons?" I ask Marlene, a slim, poetic young woman with a very, very sad face, who doesn't seem happy about what she is discussing.

"I hate it and him. But I hope someday my hate will turn to love. The S's like to think of themselves as creative geniuses, and the M's, that's me, are basically nonexistence. Whenever there's a scene, the S runs it and I have to go along."

Some of the scenes are of a German concentration camp where Marlene, who is Jewish, is a prisoner and her S is the jailer and the judge. "Before these scenes, we go out to dinner, and everything is normal. Then we go back home and he changes into black boots and black pants tucked into the boots. He wears a wide black belt, and a white ruffled silk shirt. Over this he wears a tight black vest, and a coat, and sometimes he puts on black leather gloves. I wear dungarees and a work shirt. I can never get my act together.

"We smoke a little grass, and he makes eye contact with me and then takes over. The minute he touches me or commands me, I feel like melting. It's the most powerful feeling I have ever felt in my whole life about anything. I don't know how to explain it, but it's also a feeling of terror, complete terror. It's like a dream where you think you're getting killed and you wake up and can't scream, but then you realize it's all right."

To get to this warm feeling, Marlene takes as many as two hundred whip-lashes in a night and has found her pain threshold enormous. The pinnacle of the evening is the killing fantasy where they play with knives or the S strangles her with a rope or with steel collars. Marlene trusts that the S will stop before she is dead. However, one time another man was asked to join. Her S asked Marlene to play at killing this visitor and the S told her he would stop her in time.

"He wanted me to get in touch with my feelings of wanting to kill my father and to act it out. He said I would have to trust him to put the brakes on. But I said no, because it was too dangerous. After all, his fantasy was to murder someone, and if he didn't have to take the rap, I didn't trust that he would stop me."

"How do you feel about murder?" I ask.

A wide smile covers Marlene's face, and she becomes a different person. It is as if I have spoken the most wonderful word in the English language. Marlene's cats, six of them, see her expression and begin to move about the room as if in a ritual dance. Suddenly there is a loud street noise, and Marlene tells me a bomb must have exploded somewhere, smiling all the time. I am astonished that this sensitive woman becomes a wild, happy stranger at the mention of violence, which seems out of place in her chic East Side apartment, with its terrace overlooking a quiet garden. The apartment is dark and bare, the only decorations are strange wooden collages and dark paintings. I wonder whether this is considered S/M chic, because I have visited the same kind of environment in all of my S/M interviews. As I look about the room, wondering about its interior decorating, Marlene calmly tells me of her most treasured wish: the desire to kill her father.

"First of all," she says with a lilt to her voice, "I always felt that I should be punished for something. My father wanted me to be a boy, so he would take me to the public men's room and I would stand by the urinal with all these men around and wonder what I should do. When I was about twelve and started becoming a woman, started to have breasts, started to have my period, I would lock the bathroom door because my father usually came in. It was then that he would beat me every night.

"When he would ask me about school, I wouldn't answer him and then he would take the thick black belt he wore and beat me blue. My mother and sister would just watch. I didn't cry out, but I used to think, *My God, I hope someday he'll murder me so that he can go to jail and everyone will know.*"

Although it seems Marlene baited her father by her brittle answers and baits her S by the same behavior, she does not comprehend that she plays the other side of this game. "They just set it up," she explains when I point out to her that she is the other partner in this brutality. Although as a child her brutal father was really responsible since she was so young, in the adult S/M relationship, she does voluntarily participate. "I feel like I'm somebody who is carrying around a lead weight and I want someone to take care of me. It would be a relief for someone to murder me." Although Marlene has tried suicide, she thinks it's a dreadful idea because it spoils her murder fantasy.

Almost all of Marlene's friends have dropped her because of her S/M activity. "My S is the only human being alive who really knows what's in my head," she states.

When I ask her if she could be an S, she looks sick. "I can't give a personal command. I would feel totally exposed. If I could do that, I would make a mint in business."

Marlene cannot be direct in her anger to anyone, even her father. "I'm a zombie when I'm with him," she says. "I can't even blame him."

Marlene, in fact, takes all the responsibility for her peculiar way of life. "I feel like a creep, a really bizarre human being. I don't want to reveal what turns me on to anyone." She leans over and whispers to me, "Only you and my S know."

As a result of her feelings, Marlene lives most of her life in an antisocial closet, not even socializing with the S/M world, because often she does not like what she sees. "One time a couple took a little child to my apartment and the man jerked off in front of her. I kept thinking the child was consenting, even though I knew she was only seven." She talks about this without any feelings, although she might have identified with the little girl.

"S/M has destroyed my ability to feel anything. I cannot feel any love anymore for anybody. I tell my S I don't feel anything. I tell him he's ugly, that I can't really stand him, that I don't like the way he looks, the way he moves, the way his body smells, stuff like that.

"Then he starts punishing me," she says happily, although she admits she does not have orgasms with him.

Marlene always feared violence on the streets of New York City, where she was sure she would be raped or robbed. "Recently, I had this dream where I saw my father murdered and the three killers, all men, were coming to get me. But then I thought, *That's not true. This is a hoax. I really killed my father and made up the murderers.* When I awoke, my fears were gone. I began sleeping with the terrace door open all night. I'm so happy that I got over my fears."

"Did you?" I ask carefully. She wonders what I am talking

about. "In this city, opening a door to your bedroom on a first-floor landing is a little bit like asking for it. Isn't it?"

She smiles, a glowing smile, the smile of happiness. "Yes, it does seem that way, doesn't it?" she says with great enjoyment.

Marlene's turn-on seems to be entirely mental, since she does not have an orgasmic response to acting out her murder fantasy with her S. She leads a double life, functioning in her profession and enjoying her strange S/M activities in her personal life. I was convinced if Marlene could experience her anger toward her father for his brutal practices when she was a child, or for the world in general, she could free her sexual turn-on from the macabre brutality of desiring to die. But anger is too much of a responsibility for Marlene, who sees suicide as a responsibility, too. She wants her life taken away from her, with no decisions on her part. Thus, perhaps in the future, Marlene will be another newspaper item, if a stranger enters her bedroom by her terrace door and takes her up on her invitation for death.

Marlene is honest about her wish to die. Most women in the S/M world do not consciously admit this wish. Clara became terrified when she became aware that her S had a death fantasy and she was playing right into it.

Clara

Studious, with big, dark glasses hiding beautiful, dark eyes, she looks very pristine as she sits in my living room. Her figure is perfection itself in its tiny, pert proportions. She is very delicately munching on an English muffin, since she rushed here on her lunch hour from the hospital where she works. At thirty, Clara is having her second long-term affair, with Charles, a stockbroker. They see each other every weekend when he chains her and whips her, to use her description, "in a gentle manner." I ask her what this means.

"Well, a lot of people are into heavy pressure on genitals and heavy whipping. That's not my scene. I like cuffs tied together with a chain and some rope. Usually, I am spread-eagled, and my rear parts are exposed, and he plays with me gently. I'm extremely passive in the situation. I love being dominated and not having to persuade Charles to do things. It's very exciting for me. I'm a new body to him, a new mind, and a new person to manipulate. He finds me very attractive."

Charles likes to have oral sex with Clara but doesn't like her to have oral sex with him. "I think he has a weird fear of losing his penis in the woman's mouth or something. It sounds irrational, but that's the way it is. However, I like oral sex because it is the only way I can have an orgasm."

Charles can have orgasms different ways. In one scene that he improvises, the aftereffects were very dangerous and scary to Clara. She speaks of that scene in a low monotone, with no expression in her face at all.

"It was a scene where I was supposed to die," she says quietly. "He had a stranglehold on me. He was saying, 'You are going to die, and before you die, you should come!' It was very exciting. My head was over the edge of the bed, over the frame, hanging upside down, and the side of my face started going numb. I didn't know until later that I started blacking out."

She looks frightened as she continues the tale, and I notice the extreme paleness in her face. "I had the feeling of going under, which is really very exciting. I was being pulled, and saliva started pouring out of my mouth. My face got red. I noticed this because we always have a mirror around. The blood rushed to my head, and I passed out. He was on top of me at the time. Afterward, I was very upset about it. Up to that time, we had never done anything so heavy. We had just normal things, normal whippings and stuff." I chafe at the word "normal" used in regard to whipping and ask Clara why the whole frightening thing was so exciting to her.

"Normally, I feel more in control of myself. Suddenly I was under someone's else control. I realized he could probably kill me if he wanted to and that was exciting, of having your head under such pressure and your whole body trapped. I could hardly breathe, much less do anything.

"You know, anger is such a strong emotion." She continues to speak impassively, looking down at her half-eaten muffin, not wanting to look at my face as she is speaking. "There are times when I feel that's the only emotion I react to. If he's working hard whipping me, strangling me, then he's really interested in me and not thinking of anyone else."

Strained by this image, I ask Clara if there might be another way for her lover to prove he loves her. She shakes her head. "I always hated going through the motions of sex because I felt I was simply performing. Many times I got involved with men only to be accepted, so someone would pay attention to me. I went down on so many guys who had no interest in pleasing me, and I always felt so negative about them afterward. I always felt like I was being ripped off."

Recently, when Charles professed an interest in other women, Clara felt that way again. Grudgingly, she consented to swinging with him rather than having him go off on his own. Oddly, she behaved very differently with her swinging partners. "I'm generally very aggressive with swinging partners. I want to dominate because I don't want to be passive. I sit on a guy's lap, go down on him, then more or less dismiss him. I hate the whole scene, so I don't want to be passive with them because being passive is being vulnerable."

Another fantasy Charles has which Clara performs in is that of making little girls his slaves, with Clara as his ringmaster. Clara understands his desire, because she dreams of making love to her own father. "Charles and I do this fantasy where he's my father and he sends me to a priest. He plays the priest's role, too, and I confess I have been bad with little boys. Then he gets me into his confessional, and I go down on him. After that, he plays my father and I tell him what the priest did and he says what a dirty, dirty priest. Then, as my father, he makes love to me. I love it."

Clara was a very dominant child and manipulated her parents. "My mother was retarded, and I had to be the adult. I used to run around the house with nothing but a towel on, flirting with my father. His response to that was to slap me."

She sees brutality as a way to make love affairs more exciting. "I don't want to be comfortable like an old shoe. To me, a lot of love is stress, proving someone cares about you. Sex right after stress is great: The worse the stress, the better the sex. When everything is going well, it's very dull."

I ask Clara if she expresses her anger. "No," she says almost like a child. "No, I never express my anger. To me, anger is a very frightening thing. If I was angry at someone, I'd want to kill them."

One of the things that Clara is angry about is that she is not important to the world, does not have its attention. "I'm important to Charles, though," she says matter-of-factly.

She cites the classic romance *Wuthering Heights* as her dream of the future. "That was the ultimate romance. I loved it because, even though he was dominated by her in many ways, ultimately he was extremely dominant. He got back at her."

"He certainly did," I agree. "She dies!" I have always been amazed that women get turned on by this concept and often thought they did not realize what it meant. But Clara has given it much thought.

"Yes, she dies, and the reason she dies is that she lets herself die. He did not kill her. I just love the idea of him loving her so much, of loving each other so much, that they would die for each other. I love the idea of giving up everything for your love.

"Even your life. . . ."

Clara, a woman who is not satisfied with her role in life, will do anything to be the center of attention. Looking like an academic librarian, Clara's sexual turn-ons seem foreign to her appearance. Perhaps because Clara looked so dull, she had attracted dull men in the past, and Charles seemed pretty wild as a result of that.

Clara wants so much to be famous and different that she will do anything in that search. Warmth, tenderness, and everyday comfort seem to Clara a dull way to live. As a result, each weekend she joins her S lover in an attempt to make her weekend life mean something. It is unfortunate that Clara cannot change her life to be exciting in a more rewarding way.

The difficulty with the so-called normal S/M practices is that, like everything else in life, one gets used to them and escalating these practices can lead to danger—or death. However, women who are thrilled by this possibility are very popular with men, as witnessed by Nanci's sexual activities.

Nanci

Her Boston apartment is a mess; memorabilia of her father's career covers the walls. Famous actresses dedicating their portraits to their favorite playwright imply a professional relationship tainted with the personal. In one corner stands a tiny altar, shrouded with photographs of him, taken at different times in his life, some still in the silver-chrome frames of the Twenties.

"Some people say I'm competing with his legend," Nanci mumbles as she sips a soda. Tiny and twenty, looking like a French sex kitten, she is dressed in unchic hot pants with black-lace tights underneath, feet straddled in Joan Crawford sequined ankle-strap platforms. Her blouse is an Indian wraparound, the swirling patterns cupping the too-tiny breasts. Her long, reddish locks are casual, and she speaks softly of her favorite kind of sex—sadomasochism—which for her is as much whipping as she can take without fainting.

"I have one continuing fantasy that began when I was twelve years old. It starts with my being kidnaped and thrown into a car. I am taken to a great underground secret society. When I was younger, I was kept a prisoner, with chains, by faceless, nameless males all dressed in leather. Later, as I grew older, I stayed voluntarily and kept other women prisoners. I found out who the leader was and became part of the management." She sips on her straw. "That's how I am in real life, too. I never want the spotlight, but I'm always on the side of power, the second in command."

A cat, formerly invisible, jumps on a lamp, overturns it, then lands on a pile of garbage, where a tremendous wall of empty soda cans falls onto the floor in a clattering mess. Calmly, Nanci removes the straw out of the can she is drinking from, throws the can onto the others, spraying leftover remnants of the mixture about, possibly shaking up the shuddering souls of her elegant parents who used to live in this Victorian room.

"How was it, growing up in a sophisticated environment?"

"Something was always happening. It was either feast or famine. People were always stopping by for drinks. Or calling about suicide at three in the morning. It was a pretty free atmosphere. My parents were very relaxed about sex. When I asked, they gave me simple answers. I was shocked to discover the other kids had to whisper about it.

"The only thing we never spoke about was my father's affairs. He was always 'working' when he wasn't around. There was another taboo, sadomasochism. When I used to provoke the boys in school to beat me up, my mother used to get very upset. At that time, I didn't know I was being sexual."

"What do you mean?"

She sighs, looks at me suspiciously, then decides to trust me with the answer. "I get turned on by pain." The way she says it I know she is still uncomfortable talking about it, although it is 1976, and sexual freedom is "in."

"There was no one to talk to about it. Even the freest people would look at me as if I was sick in the head. My former husband used to spank me, and when he saw I liked it, we started to play S/M with bondage. He used to spread-eagle me, then tie me to the furniture. Then we got scared because the S/M play got heavier and heavier."

Somehow the echoes of two parents living a successful life, amid the avant-garde world of theater and leisure, ring in my ears as she describes her sexual activity. I wonder what they would say.

"I'm amazed at how much pain I can take," Nanci whispers. "Even the next day, there's an afterglow from the bruises on my body." She unwraps her blouse and shows me her bruised shoulders, purple from pain. Then she turns around, and I see the mark of the whip.

"How does pain become pleasure?" I ask quietly, for if someone hurt me I would be totally turned off.

Nanci pauses, wraps her blouse around her again, ponders for an accurate answer. "I don't know how to explain it. First, there is anxiety as the S tells you what he is going to do to you. Once it starts, I feel very calm, and a very rosy, warm feeling envelopes me. Then there's a lot of sex talk, suggesting things. I let the person know what I like and that I can take more. Then I start having spontaneous orgasms from whipping, even without having intercourse.

"My ex-husband liked me to wear garter belts and stockings, and a corset of leather. The whippings got harder and harder, and he began to draw blood with the riding crop. When it started to take more and more pain to reach the same level of pleasure and we began talking about piercing my labia with a ring, I called a halt. I didn't want any permanent mutilation. Suppose five years from then I wasn't turned on by this any longer?"

Although Nanci is a swinger, goes to orgies, is bisexual, and has to have sex every day of her life, it was not until she discovered S/M that she found ecstasy. "I get unconscious after I've been whipped for a while. I actually faint with orgasms. I don't even know where I am. People tell me my face is radiant, and I look serene." She begins smoking fast and furiously as she speaks of this experience. The room fills with smoke quickly, and there are cigarette holes in the rug which must have been expensive and rare in its day.

"Do you always play the masochistic role?"

She smiles widely at this question. "No, recently I took on the S role. It happened with a guy who's usually the boss and has a hard time separating his sex play from his daily role. I put him in bondage so he couldn't get loose and I used clothespins on his nipples, something he had been trying to do with me, but I wouldn't have it."

"What happened?"

"Well, he was being very stoic about it, so it didn't work out. You have to enjoy it, and then it becomes erotic. If you just do it to prove a point, it's nothing. Then I began whipping him and drew blood. I got hysterical then. It's much harder to act out the dominant role because I'm afraid of losing control."

She pauses, sips on her ever-present soda, and says: "As a matter of fact, dominant women are very much in demand." Her hands are shaking as she opens another can of soda from a huge security blanket full of them. "I don't drink," she explains, noting that her father did.

"Is S/M popular with men?"

She glows as she answers. "I can have sex every day, all day, if I want. The phone always rings. I'm a fantasy woman for a lot of men. I don't ask them anything, don't ask them to take me to dinner." She slurps her soda noisily with an afterthought.

"But," she says, "if a man would take care of me so I don't have to support myself, I'd make him the center of my life."

Nanci is one of the few women in the S/M world who says she has orgasms with the S/M interplay, and witnesses claim that her body takes on the pink sexual flush to prove it. (This pink flush is documented by sex therapists as covering a woman's complexion when she has a true orgasm.)

Having known her for several years, I am aware that Nanci spends her days having sex, her nights making contacts, and, somehow, although she is not a prostitute, is financed by the men and women in her life.

Not really attracted to women, she uses them to manipulate the men in her life. She is a manipulator par excellence, and there are always two or three people in her life who are fighting with each other for her attention. She has surpassed all her other sexual activities in S/M, finding the true acting-out world of power plays.

Sometimes women relegate these power plays only to their personal sexual life. Vicki, a career woman, is this kind of woman.

Vicki

Vicki is pretty, vivacious, and blonde. She is seated on a sofa in a green satin robe, which opens as she moves to reveal her breasts, and then again to reveal her vagina with her contrasting dark hair. She seems oblivious to her nakedness, conflicting with the bourgeois portrait that is reflected in her apartment's furnishing. A piano in the corner, bookcases, an ordinary sofa, and chairs —there is not a single unusual touch in the room except for two leather candles. I expected something more exotic because Vicki is telling me about her very, very unusual sexual activity, which dominates her personal life.

"I like my boy friend to put shackles on me and use a leather paddle. I have to say thank you after I get stroked. If I forget to say thank you, I keep getting hit until I do. Then I may have to kiss the paddle or his hand and call him master and show my respect and devotion. While I'm being stroked, he also sexually excites me. He kisses me and fondles me. He plays with my vagina to see if I am getting wet. The more he plays with me, the more excited I get. I can take a large dose of being hit, it doesn't hurt. I like being blindfolded and not knowing where the stroke is coming from. Then I get receptive and very, very sexy. Then I begin worshipping him because he's controlling me.

"I feel very, very vulnerable and very, very soft. In a sense, very helpless and very feminine. I think I'm going back to the tradition where men were strong and women were the weaker sex, fantasies from my childhood of watching movies of women in peril—Flash Gordon and his girlfriend being captured and tortured by the evil doctor. Sinbad the Sailor in his pirate ship, overtaking the English ship and carrying off the ladies and ravishing them."

Vicki is getting very playful now, sitting on the couch in a kittenish, childlike pose, watching my face when I'm not looking at her, and when I direct my attention to her, not being able to look at me straight in the face. So I watch her watch me, then move her eyes furtively to the corner, the piano, the window, the blinds, as she tells me about her sex life.

"It all makes me feel very feminine and protected, like a little girl, but still a woman. I feel like a protected, cherished possession. I feel I want to be taken to the limits. I have a very strong character, and I want to be forced to give that up."

One of the things that her strong character has led her into is a very vital job as a sales manager for a magazine, earning twenty-thousand dollars a year at twenty-nine years old. "I have a very responsible position and have to make a lot of decisions all day long. So when I come home, I want to feel good and confident about being feminine in the very traditional kind of sense—soft, old-fashioned. You know, it takes a lot of pressure, being independent and self-supporting, maintaining an apartment. It's important for me to do that, to have a lot of freedom."

To find her sexual partners, Vicki runs an ad each week in a

California newspaper which reads: "Pretty, voluptuous blonde, intelligent, refined, submissive with fighting spirit needs to be conquered, ravished, and loved by attractive, straight, dominant, white male under forty." Out of this ad, Vicki hopes to find a husband.

"I want a full-time relationship. I want to find someone to fall in love with, to be married to," she states seriously.

As she waits for this husband, Vicki is leading what she calls a decadent and promiscuous life. One night recently she went to a party wearing her bondage jewelry. One young man came up to her and asked her to go out on the landing. He took her up near the roof, pushed her flat on the floor, and attacked her. "At first I resisted and he slapped my face hard. Then he raped me right there. He pulled my pants off and started fucking me hard. I came and came. Then we left the party with a friend of his and went to my house. First, he fucked me again and again, then he gave me to his friend. They tied my hands up, and I was pretty excited. Then he told his friend, 'Slap her around a little, she likes it.' He was right, I really loved it.

"Last night . . ." she closes her robe which up to this time has exhibited her genital area ". . . he called me and I was very, very horny. He said he couldn't come over, and I told him to send another friend. It was great, a stranger coming into my house and fucking me. I really got off."

Usually in the submissive role, Vicki recently improvised with being the dominant person in the sexual relationship. "You know, S women have it easy. They get their apartments cleaned, their housework done, they are totally catered to. I liked that idea, so I tried it. But it was too much like work. I had to keep thinking of things to do to him. After I asked him to kiss my feet and shackled him, I humiliated him a bit, put his underpants in his mouth, and paddled him. But then I said, 'It's carte blanche. You can do anything,' and he didn't want to do that. He wanted me to direct him in everything. I found that too tedious.

"One of the greatest things about being the M is that you only make one decision: Here I am. Do with me what you will. I can sort of sit back and relax, and he handles the rest. I find that it's a very peaceful thing to do. The only thing I've ever refused is when a man wants me to say 'Please, master, let me suck you!' That really irks me! I feel it's very degrading."

Vicki remembers having bondage fantasies between the ages of five and seven and masturbating in the bathtub, something she still does. "I have the faucets running and my feet up on the wall. The stream of water lands on my vagina and clitoris, and I vary the pressure. I strain my muscles and press my legs out open. I can have an orgasm that way." Often Vicki has to do this because she finds that most men are impotent, which frustrates her, a feeling she hates.

"I was frustrated all through my childhood. I had to go through a lot of things to get attention. One thing I love about being submissive is that you're definitely not being ignored. If somebody's going through all this work to tie me up and paddle me and make love to me, obviously he must care a lot. When I was a child, I got a lot of attention by having temper tantrums, getting into trouble. I used that as a manipulative force, manipulating through weakness."

I am impressed that Vicki knows the origin of her behavior and amazed that she is a successful professional woman with her attitudes. "If I was an M in business, I'd be a fucking typist, a nebish," she says bitterly. "I'd be a clerk who just follows orders, instead of the independent self-starter that I am."

She goes over to the wine rack and takes a bottle of California burgundy. She opens it vivaciously, pours two glasses, offers me one, takes hers, and salutes me, causing her robe to fall open again. I ask her if she gets turned on by women, wondering if her robe action is a seductive act. Her face contorts into an ugly expression. "No, I don't like women," she says brashly. "I have no women friends. I find they're very narrow and prejudiced. They all think I'm sick. Men are much more open-minded."

She looks at me impassively, her voice taking on a threatening tone. "You know, it's important to me how you write this interview," she says, watching to see if she is making me uptight.

"It's important to me," she says, now in a very childish, soft voice. "It's important to me that you view me basically as a normal person, that you don't look at me and say, 'This girl is a freak!' "

I found Vicki one of the most obviously manipulative women I have ever interviewed. Yet I felt she was really trying to tell it like it is for her, a fact I admired. Not trusting that I would portray her sensitively, she had to threaten me in the end. It would seem that Vicki had very little faith in her ability to persuade without being manipulative.

Vicki was fascinating too because she separated her S/M life from her hardworking professional life. It was as if she knew she had to be direct and make decisions to get ahead in the world, but hated this in her personal life, for it did not make her feel soft and feminine, the way a woman should be. (This is an important element in the chapter on creative and professional women.)

Vicki and many other women in the S/M world complain bitterly about the lack of potent male S's, something Lucretia is obsessed with.

Lucretia

When I walk into Lucretia's house in San Francisco, I think she is aptly named and wonder whether it is a name she has given herself, because her name matches the long, dark apartment which is a museum to primitive Spain. Dark wood paneling, dark wooden furniture, stark, heavy chairs—the only sign of life is in the children's rooms, which are lovely with light, colorful, and playful things. In all other rooms, there is a somber, oppressive air, especially in Lucretia's bedroom, which is like the altar in a Teutonic cathedral, with a carved headboard and a large ornate mirror serving as a background to the bier of the flat, wooden bed.

Lucretia answers the door dressed in a long, hemplike skirt and Mexican embroidered blouse. She is silver-haired, intense, fierce. Her face is pale and drawn, and her speech falters when I ask her direct questions, for she prefers to talk incessantly about her spirituality and the profundity of her life, although she knows the nature of this interview is about her sexuality.

Previously married for fifteen years, mother of five children, and fortyish, Lucretia now owns an elegant cosmetic house. Frustrated by her sexual activity, she recently ran an ad in an S.F. underground newspaper which read: "Mature, single, sensitive, profound, deep, relating, good-looking woman wants men for bondage and surrender." Fifty men answered the ad. One of them introduced her to The Brotherhood, a loosely formed group of men who like S/M sex and who communicate with each other regarding any new applicant, a practice right out of *The Story of O.*

"The first man was a very well-known writer. He sent me his picture. He was in his early forties and very handsome. On our date, I wore an empire velvet dress and stocked his favorite wine. We made a reservation at a French restaurant, and just before we went to dinner, he asked me to lift my dress and show him what I was wearing underneath. I was wearing a black bikini I had made myself, with silver-embroidered circles. I had cut one circle right at the entrance of my vagina and was wearing dark stockings and garter belt. He said his favorite turn-on was lingerie."

Lucretia pauses to check my expression to see if I am fully impressed. Satisfied, she goes on.

"In the restaurant, we got very, very aroused. I cannot have orgasms except if I am mentally aroused. I can date someone nice and he can fuck me for an hour and a half inside and out and on my head, and I will not lubricate or come. It's almost out of the question. So when we came home, he sat back on the couch, sipping his favorite wine in a glass which was very tall and blue with an iron trim. Very lush. He asked me to go on my knees with my back to him, with my underwear down over one leg, kneeling with my head on the ground and legs very straight, which is a very helpless position, completely exposing the anus and vagina. No face showing, just sexual organs. I was very turned on because I felt I was dripping. Then he told me to put a pillow on the floor and spread my legs and touch myself. He asked me if I felt humiliated. I said, 'No, I feel like a goddess.' "

The writer introduced Lucretia to The Brotherhood of about fifty men. All but one was impotent. This one man excited her tremendously. "He was the only real dominant man I'd ever met. The others just wanted to be dominant. He said I was the most exciting, beautiful, vibrant human being he had ever encountered. He wanted to possess my beauty. He captured the depth of my eroticism. When he hit me, it was very orgasmic.

"One night I was belly-dancing for him, and he asked me to follow the music. Instead, I danced faster. He slapped me, but I was startled to learn that I was turned on in my genitals. Then he leaned me over the desk and upside down. I looked at the water in the Bay through my window as he opened my legs. I was balanced on the weight of the desk.

"Then he chained me from the ceiling. My body was glittering with light. I was swinging like a beautiful ballet dancer. His body was charged with energy. He asked me to spread my legs and penetrated me. He was fucking me without touching me. I was really aroused. He said, 'Come now!' I came endlessly! I just came and came! I felt that his penis was the bridge of life, my point of support. It was very, very beautiful.

"He was six-foot-three, with a strong body, and had eyes like Paul Newman. He was very perceptive about my body, except one time we had an accident and I ended up in a hospital."

She is so nonchalant about this that I have to ask her what happened. "He put a dog collar on me, and I truly understood the relationship between the dog and his master, where there is unquestioning surrender. But, he made a mistake and really hurt me," she states, but refuses to tell me how.

Although Lucretia says she has no sexual fantasies, she does think she lived in Egypt and was and is a goddess, thus she is into "spiritual sex." "I can interact sexually only with people who I touch profoundly, spiritually. The man must own me completely. I surrender completely. I blank out."

One time during a ménage-à-trois, she investigated a woman's vagina. "I felt very spiritual. It was such a mysterious and beautiful place. I have dreams that my vagina is a box of powdered cookies, lush, a place of glittering rainbows. I can have orgasms without it ever being touched."

Although Lucretia indulged in S/M sex for six months, she now feels it's a ritual for security. "I like jumping into an abyss. S/M can often be a means for grooving so you won't have to dig deeply. It prevents intensity. I know when I surrender to a man it's like surrendering to God, or the next life," she says ponderously.

Although Lucretia claims she is at one with her body, she suffers from all sorts of serious psychosomatic illnesses. As a result, when she is to meet a man whom she will have sex with, she spends a long time getting ready. "I have a ritual. I take at least two hours to prepare myself. I do a skin treatment all over my body. I shower and take an oil bath. Do a facial. Wash my hair. Have a woman come in and do my hair and nails. Give myself a total facial with sour cream yogurt. Make up very carefully and lightly. Use a French perfume that an ex-lover in France sends to me.

"I put flowers all over the house. When there isn't a man in the house, there aren't any flowers. When I cook dinner for a man, there is always a different arrangement at the table, each time. My house is fairly imposing, so when I first meet a man, I usually go to his house not mine. I won't tell a man I own a house, playing down my imposing self. I'm a very overwhelming person, so I don't want to threaten men.

"Because," she concludes pragmatically, surprising me, "if I want a good heterosexual fuck, I'm dependent on a cock, aren't I?"

I found Lucretia very hard to interview because she kept wanting to go off into outer space whenever I asked her personal questions. Typical of the drug-induced Sixties consciousness, Lucretia must fantasize about why she wants love. It is not good enough to want a man to be with, she must make it an eternal special consciousness with profound effects all over the stratosphere.

Yet she made an interesting and important point about S/M being an emotionally secure place for its participants. As I researched the S/M world, I was struck that so many women responded the same, as if they were quoting an S/M line of propaganda. I found S/M people really do think they are special and their activity will shock the listener into admiration. But so often, as in the case of Jane, that rarity, an S woman, I found that the women were not sensuously involved and complained bitterly about the impotence of the men. It was as if brutality had taken the place of sensuality, which made me wonder why on earth the S/M world flourished.

27

Jane

Jane's place is a mess. Cat shit is all over the place. The room we are in is filled with chains and whips and strange portraits of satanic faces. Twenty-five-year-old Jane is very, very plump, and she offers me a seat on her messy bed. Fortunately, I look first and see remnants of broken glass and tell her about it.

"Jesus, where did that come from?" she asks, as she sprinkles the glass from the bed onto the floor, while I pity her bare feet. But Jane doesn't seem to mind.

"A friend of mind made a very stark remark to the effect that dominant women are not very feminine, and it got me very upset," she states outright, affirming her S status in the S/M world. "I may be sexually dominant, but I try to be very, very superfeminine, despite my looks." She sighs unhappily. "Everyone always thinks that I'm a bull dyke.

"I don't know why. I enjoy wearing frilly, feminine attire." She points to the spotted ruffles on her dirty housedress. "During S/M scenes, I wear frilly attire all made of leather." This comment baffles me and I ask her to describe what she means. "Well, I wear a corset-type thing and no midriff. You know, feminine?" she urges me to understand.

Jane describes herself as a dominant woman, an S woman, one of the few on the West Coast. "I love to take dominant males home and teach them a few things. I rap to him, and before the evening is finished, as a rule, he is my submissive partner."

"How do you do that?"

"I play to him. I cater to him. When he's really nice and comfortable, really digging what's happening, I pull a scene on him. You know, I get the whip, or the clothes hanger, and start in. I can get any guy. Believe me, I've had terrific success." The S/M world whispers about her success, challenging whether it is true or not, but I sit still and listen to her story.

"Last weekend I went camping. There was this guy who was the most sought-after man at the entire mountain area. Beautiful, six feet tall, bleached-blond hair—his body was gorgeous. When he went skinny-dipping, all the girls were wild. I just ignored him. I had someone bring the wood for my fire, someone else build the fire, someone else bring food to feed me and cook it so I could eat it. I never left my spot. I admit that I enjoyed watching the faces of those pretty girls as they watched this short, fat broad get men to do things for her.

"Well, this guy watched my style all weekend, and finally he came over and ate with me. And we had sexual relations during the night. I got into mild pain with him, and a couple of times he said he was ready to leave and I said go ahead. Well, he wouldn't leave. He said, 'I can't put my finger on it, but you have this power over me, and I can't leave. I've been with a lot of women on this mountain, and none of them would have ever made me feel this way. From now on, I'm going to be bored with normal sex.' "

Jane moves clumsily on the bed and gets a glass splinter in her foot, spending the next five minutes trying to remove it with dirty fingers, amid the bed's massive dirt, and cursing like a bandit. Finally, she leans back, satisfied, telling me of her success with men, all kinds of men.

"I can change my man any time I feel like it. I like to play head games. Let me say that I consider a man's only purpose is to be there for my satisfaction. A man that I dig has to be willing to do anything I want. When I was married, I had my husband so well trained that he did all the cooking, cleaning, sewing, and caring for the house. I was so bored with him, I couldn't take it any longer."

Quite frankly, I wish he was still around because her place is a mess. She knows I'm uncomfortable and says snidely, jumping from men to women, "I'm not much of a woman lover. Even if I was the only woman in the world, I wouldn't miss them because most women to me are catty. I identify with cats—a lot of my traits are similar. I like playing with people like a cat does. You know how a cat will let a mouse run and grab it and bring it back and let it run again and grab it? That's what I do to men!" I shiver at her concepts and wonder whether her manipulation is popular with men, and with what kinds of men.

"My favorite men are truck drivers. My scenes are not heavy pain. Mild pain is a different situation. It's not vicious. With big men, you have to be careful. One time a guy got so turned on, he nearly choked me half to death. I was giving him head, and he had his legs around my neck. He got so turned on that he kept squeezing and squeezing, and I got a little scared."

I ask Jane if she has any sexual fantasies. "I think my favorite sexual fantasy is being the head of my own male harem. With my personal needs, I need a lot of men, as no man can keep up with me. I need at least a harem of approximately seven men."

Interestingly connected to this fantasy is that Jane's first sexual experience was with a group of boys. When she was eighteen, they gang-raped her. "I was dating this guy, and he said we were going to a party. I found out I was the party. The next thing I knew we were in an apartment where four boys were grabbing at me and tearing my clothes off. I couldn't talk or do anything because my arms were each pinned down by a different person. I was used every way possible, literally two guys getting off at the same time. They didn't believe I was a virgin because I used to know all the dirty jokes. It was a very bad experience, and it stayed with me for years afterward." I look for the emotion to match this terrible trauma, but Jane seems to have none. She relates the story as if it is just another fact of her life.

I ask her gently if she enjoys sex, wondering about the effects of the gang-rape.

"As a matter of fact, I've never had an orgasm," she says, her tone softer, startling me. "Because of the rape, I still have hang-ups and can't reach that level.

"But," she grimaces, her full face now filled with pain and sadness, "I tell myself at heart I'm really a nymphomaniac who doesn't want to reach completion."

Jane seems to be a living example of the belief that if tenderness and warmth are not present, then one's capacity for sensuality vanishes. Certainly if sensuality were present, why would she be so consumed with the task of being brutal to men? Also, without orgasmic response at some point, is it really sensuality?

Alas, more and more women in the S/M world confess to a lack of orgasms, attracted to this world of melodramatic brutality because of the drama they undergo. Jackie is another.

Jackie

"I'm a very hard person to get any emotion out of. I will not cry unless I'm made to cry. So when my lover and I are together, he ties me up and makes me feel helpless. Then he stimulates me by caressing me with leather or paddling or whipping me. I'm lucky that I have someone who really cares enough to help me get out my emotions, someone who loves me well enough."

The young woman who is repeating this familiar masochistic rhetoric is Jackie, who, by her own admission, weighs 250 pounds. Five feet tall with charming freckles, she hates other women because they so easily can be slim and pretty. For her, it is almost impossible.

Bordering between a little girl and a full-grown woman, Jackie is having an S/M love affair with a married man. "His wife is all right, but she can't do the things to him that I will. She's no competition. She won't stick a dildo up his ass, and he loves that."

I ask Jackie, who is barely twenty, how long she's liked S/M sex. "Well, I used to dig all those violent television programs, so I guess you could say it started when I was a child. But although I've slept with very few men, this is the first one who dominates me."

Jackie in turn dominates her husband. Although she earns far more than he does, he pays all the bills. When he comes home from his job, he changes into a maid costume and cooks dinner for her. Then he serves the food, washes the dishes, and if he gets sassy, Jackie punishes him very severely.

"I usually spank him. I have a heavy wooden paddle, and he likes leather, too. He likes dildos up his ass, and if you run one up his crack and put Ben-Gay on it afterwards, it won't do any damage. I tell him what a bad girl he is, what a sassy bitch, that it's not proper for him to bad-mouth his betters, that he is the maid and a very low-class person and must do better. Then he's got to agree with me, or I will hit him. Under no circumstances will I let him have the enjoyment of his cock either!" she says with great determination.

I wonder why the severe determination, and ask her about her childhood. She shifts her weight on the chair uncomfortably. "The first time I spread my legs was when my goddamn father got me out of the orphanage. He had put me in at five, and I was fifteen when I got out. One night he got high and took advantage of me and raped me. At first I thought, *He really loves me. I'm getting the attention from him I never had*."

She shows no anger about this occurrence. "That's why I let my married man dominate me. He's older. I like to be hung from the ceiling on a chain and whipped until I plead with him to stop. Then he takes me in his arms, and I'll just snuggle up to him like a little girl or animal who craves attention. Then I blow him. Thank goodness, he doesn't flow a lot because he's so old. I don't particularly like the taste of sperm."

Often her married lover takes her to the S/M Hollywood parties, held bimonthly, where S/M couples go and meet other people for their sexual scenarios, or scenes as they are commonly known. No single men are allowed. Once there, he wants Jackie to perform in his scenario, but she resents performing in front of other people. She does it, though.

"I'll wear this long, flowing, Old-World-style gown with some rabbit fur trim on it, all soft and smooth. And he'll ask me to pick up my dress. I hate it. You know, I'm not exactly skinny, and I don't particularly like strangers seeing all my excess flesh, which I don't think is very pretty. I also have a lot of scars from operations. But he says that I'm needed, that I'm helpful, and that he wants me to do it. So I do."

"Do you love him, Jackie?"

"No. I've attempted to love two or three times, but each time the person threw me out. I don't want candy and flowers from a man. If he won't cook and keep the house clean for me, that's it. I don't like to argue. When I was a kid, I got into a fight with another girl in the orphanage. I nearly strangled her. It scared me in the sense that I suddenly knew what I could do with my hands. I went berserk.

"She cried and cried. If I'm angry enough, I can make just about anybody cry."

Although Jackie was so terribly bitter for her age, she certainly had many father-given reasons for it. Incestuous rape, a gift from brutal fathers to their daughters, which will color the rest of their lives, runs through all of these interviews, but the actual occurrence rather than the fantasy (as in Jackie's case) runs more commonly in the Lesbian/Bisexual Chapter 7. The incidence of incestuous rape has absolutely shocked me. It is something that has no class or race distinction and is more prevalent than I ever imagined.

I was terribly sad for Jackie who abused the husband at home who supported her, and who was abused by her married lover. After I interviewed her, Jackie went to the hospital for a major operation which the doctors thought might be critical. I was so saddened that such a young life with so much harshness and sadness in it might be gone, even before she could learn to enjoy life.

Sometimes S/M activity has nothing to do with the accepted world of S/M. Violence and sadism runs through many women's lives, for instance Charlotte's.

Charlotte

Charlotte, a very beautiful, tall, thirtyish, thin, black woman who lives in St. Louis, is about two hours late for her interview. When she arrives, her face is angry, controlled, and suspicious. I ask her about her erotic activities, and she answers very defensively.

"When I left my husband, he told me that I was dried up, that nobody else would want me. Well, I'm not only working at a great job, but I've been pursued by so many men I can't count them all."

Charlotte cites her sexual aggressiveness in bed as the reason she is so popular. "I've become a bit of a flirt this year. I personally feel sexuality is emotional and biological, but if they cannot be filled together, there's no reason why the biological can't be satisfied. I enjoy sex. I don't wait for a man to fondle me. I will approach him. I will begin to undress him."

"How do they respond?" I ask, because so many women have complained that they cannot be aggressive with men.

"They're sort of surprised. You can feel it. No one has ever refused to let me be aggressive, although one fellow actually said, 'What the hell is going on here?' He stopped in the middle of everything. We were making love, and I was on top. I suddenly put my finger in his anal tract while we were screwing and that blew his mind. So he stopped everything and yelled."

In an animated fashion, Charlotte tells her story as if she is appearing on television. "Men usually tell me how great I am in bed. I'm very free. I just enjoy! I'll indulge in all kinds of sex, but I must call all the shots." Then she tells me about her preferences. "I don't swallow semen, because it's fattening. I don't do anal sex anymore because it destroys the buttock muscles. I have a well-turned-out body, and it is a great turn-on."

Charlotte's lovers have a variety of roles in her life. "One is always there when I need something, like fixing wires and putting up nails." Another takes care of her body. "He gives me baths, helps me undress, bathes me very gently, and then dries me off. Powders me down, talcums me, and perfumes me. Massages me and helps me get dressed. It's really very thrilling."

"My fantasy is to have a man or a woman live totally for me for two months, and I would be everything to them." As she speaks about her life, Charlotte's face drops its animated mask, and her fear shows. She takes off the huge sunglasses she was wearing, and I see behind them the eyes of a frightened little girl who's been very, very hurt.

"One time a lover began slapping me. I went into the kitchen and got a kitchen knife. Then I began slicing him. I cannot tolerate a man throwing another woman in my face, and that's what he kept doing. My father used to beat me methodically. He would say, 'I'll give you seven licks, and if you cry, you get seven more.' He would bend me over the back of the bed and do it. I wouldn't show any emotion at all."

Thus, Charlotte uses sex to manipulate men. "If I need money, then I can borrow and not pay them back. I just have sex with them," she says.

I tell Charlotte I must end the interview because her lateness will cause the next woman to wait. She refuses to leave, examining my rooms while she delays and manipulates for my attention.

She has deliberately come late, using someone else's time. Finally I am firm and she leaves.

Charlotte is a case of a woman who is using S/M tactics in her relationships but doesn't name it. This is the claim of the S/M world: that the entire world is sadomasochistic but the S/M world is simply honest about it. They may have a point, but not one that the world should be proud of.

The S/M world has established a series of scenarios for their sexual interplay. Most often these scenarios are repetitive and boring, for they say nothing about feelings. Also, as documented here, there is very little sexual activity going on. When I asked at an S/M meeting I attended how many people had orgasms, only about ten percent said they did.

A group of S/M women talk about their favorite scenarios commonly used in the S/M heterosexual scene.

Martha

"We dress up in black monks' robes and have sex in parks, doorways, and behind parked cars. Churches are our favorite places, especially confessional boxes. He goes in, and I confess my sins. Then I go down on him."

Mary

"We do it in threes with a junior S. They shackle me, put an old-fashioned whalebone corset on me that pinches in my waist and makes my thighs and breasts huge. They follow me around and keep hitting me. It's terrifically exciting. They suspend me on top of a ladder, then take the ladder away, and watch me squirm. The pressure on my wrists is terrible. I swing myself around and get on top of something and never come down."

Janet

"I tie up my guy with scarves and beat him and humiliate him. He gets into women's clothes in bed, garters and stockings. He loves it when I have my period. He loves the blood spilled all over his face. One night he thought I was smearing blood on him, but it was my vaginal fluid. He came without my even touching him."

Louise

"I have rings in my nipples and labia. I have been branded. I'm Jewish but am a converted Catholic. I want to die like Jesus did at the Crucifixion. I want somebody to crucify me. I check into my S's dungeon every Friday night. Everything is steel and locks. I can only hobble to the bathroom."

Toni

"My S keeps eight women in cages. He binds them and whips them once a day. He has a Ph.D. in criminology and observes them. He feels if they get whipped enough they will get the hostility out of their system because whipping actually relieves their anger against men and the world."

Sally

"My guy is an executive vice-president with a major corporation. He has to have control and power over people all day long. When he comes to me, he wants me to shit and piss on him. It makes him feel vulnerable, since he has to assert himself so often."

The last scenario is the toilet scene, which is commonly put under the label of S/M. Quite honestly, it was too difficult for me to handle. The enjoyment of feces or urine on one's body is beyond my comprehension.

S/M is also beyond my comprehension. I cannot conceive of anything turning me off more than brutality. Yet, I cannot condemn these women. In interviewing them, I was very conscious of their miserable childhoods, the parental brutality, their longing for attention, their desire for manipulation.

Yet, all of us have these elements in our character. I believe it is the existence of unexpressed rage and the guilt about it that leads people to enter the brutal S/M sexual world. When rage is directly experienced, it changes peoples' personalities and life options, but the S/M people keep their rage secretly to themselves, busy manipulating each other for power.

While the S/M world may be correct in saying that all of us are governed by power, what they don't seem to consider is that power can be used for positive support. It does not have to be manipulative, brutal, and negative, as it surely always is in their S/M fantasy world.

For even if S/M does not eliminate physical life, it surely eliminates psychological pride and vulnerability for truly erotic relationships based on tenderness. An erotic activity which can accelerate only to death is morbid and ugly. Sensuality should not be attached to death, for eroticism is a part of life's energy. Only a puritanical attitude attaches eroticism to death.

Perhaps, then, that is what the S/M world is. *Perhaps it is one of the most infamous modern bastions of puritanical sex.*

Two

❁ ❁ ❁

THE EROTICISM OF
CREATIVE AND
PROFESSIONAL WOMEN

For the creative and professional women interviewed for this chapter, sensuality sometimes is the bitterest disappointment of all. Using all her energy for the dream of being effective in a competitive society, a woman may wake up from this dream disenchanted by its rewards. Why do women who successfully forge into the jungle of power and competitiveness frequently fail with men? When women become powerful and direct (something absolutely necessary in the business and creative world), they become less desirable to men. Thus, these women become terribly confused and conflicted. For using the very methods which have obtained for them all the world has to offer, they cannot realize their earliest dream: to have a career and a man, too.

What then must be given up? There is only a finite amount of energy that can be tapped. Thinking that we can be everything imposes *superwoman* anxieties upon us. A consistent, fascinating statement in my interviews of creative women, such as painters, writers, and musicians, was that the act of creativity itself was such a sensual high they felt a diminishing need for sexual activity. Men do not seem to experience creativity in this manner. Masculine art and ardor often go hand in hand. Creative men seem always to have a *sexfrau* about. Most creative women operate differently. Female creative energy seems to come from the sensual center, not from the intellect.

While men who are powerful and direct are the object of female sensuality and desire, women who are powerful and direct are not the object of male desire. When a woman becomes successful, she finds that her male contemporaries are not interested in her sexuality, only her success. Thus, powerful women continually undermine themselves in their drive toward success, convinced that they will lose their sex appeal. Oddly, this is a reason that lesbians fare much better in the corporate game. They have identity problems, but can indulge in their competitiveness with men and also enjoy the fact that a powerful woman is considered very desirable in the lesbian erotic world.

How can a powerful heterosexual woman be vulnerable? Vulnerability is a conscious decision to experience another person in a situation which may cause deep, emotional pain, with the hopes that it will not, and that the experience will deepen. Powerful women fear this kind of vulnerability in erotic situations with men, for the powerful woman knows the world's admiration has come to her *in the denial of this emotional vulnerability, not because of it.*

Dr. Rollo May writes in *Love and Will*, using the ancient Greek myths as source:

> Eros is the child of Ares as well as Aphrodite.* . . . Love is inseparably connected with aggression. . . . This brings us to the very heart of what has also gone wrong in our day: eros has lost passion, and has become insipid, childish, banal . . . eros, even then, loses interest in sex.**

Thus, if dynamic women pursue their eroticism with the same survival and assertive tactics as they pursue their worldly destiny, then perhaps something will change in their erotic love lives. If they realize that they are very, very angry and very, very anxious about men, then perhaps they will be able to do something about it.

* Ares is the god of war and aggression, and Aphrodite is the goddess of love and beauty.
** Rollo May, *Love and Will* (New York: W.W. Norton, 1969), p. 95.

True eroticism is connected with aggression and is expressed nonviolently. This struggle has always been known as passion. When the passionate element is missing from sex, the result is impotent, anonymous sexuality which really doesn't interest anyone. With this brand of sexuality, it is no wonder that dynamic people prefer the corporate struggle of power and wealth: It is much more exciting.

This first interview, Nancy, is an example of a woman who prefers a competitive, exciting job to eroticism with a man.

Nancy

In a high-rise, terraced apartment house near Sunset Strip in Hollywood, Nancy invites me into her apartment for a drink. The apartment is decorated in old English style, unusual for sunny California. Lots of royal blue and white porcelain and very sentimental family portraits surround the room, which surprises me for Nancy is the essence of hippiness. It has taken me a dozen phone calls to finally settle a date, and even now I find four people conferring with her about problems on the film she is producing. Nancy is a very busy woman and at thirty is a full partner in a film production company.

Her appearance startles me. She is short and dumpy, and her face looks like she has just come out of a steambath. But on the phone her voice is silk itself, soft-sell promo. I watch her use this voice as she soothes the ruffled feelings of one person, manipulating the others into agreeing, escorting them to the door, kissing them on the lips, bisexual, chic style.

Then she pours herself a long tulip glassful of thirty-year-old Scotch and sits down. Before I can say a word, the phone rings. It is someone who wants to walk off the set. Nancy cajoles, seduces, flatters him, and tells him he is the only real man on the set. After this conversation is over, she turns to me and sweetly asks me what I would like to know about her sex life.

"You know, women's lib has hurt businesswomen," she begins

bluntly. "I find it very difficult to operate and function now because the men think you're a high-powered, pushy kind of lady. You know, this business functions twenty-four hours a day, it never stops."

Nancy tells me that if she goes to bed with a man just to get off she feels very, very guilty. "A male executive can fuck around with clients and the help, and everyone thinks he's a superstud, but a woman executive can't. The men always think she's weak in business if she does that.

"When I like a guy, I set up a situation. I believe that ladies should set things up." She surprises me with her old-fashioned rhetoric.

One situation she set up recently was inviting a business associate to dinner. "I did lobsters and steamed clams—something you don't get out here. The minute dinner was finished, he stretched himself on the couch like he had been here all his life. I turned off so fast. I threw him out. I said, 'Whatever your plans are, I'm not ready for that.'"

Confused, I ask her what she set up the situation for.

"He was married, and there is no way a man is going to touch me emotionally if he's married. I've known too many girlfriends who have gone through that married-man agony," she explains, though I am still confused.

The phone rings again, and it is an actor who needs dope. Nancy opens one of her three mammoth address books with paper slips hanging from it and gives him the number of a connection. She talks to him about his problems with his old lady, his newest movie, and the fact that her door is always open to him. There is a subtle message that Nancy can be all things to him, and I wonder why she is trying to convince me that she doesn't fuck around, because her reputation in Hollywood, where she is known as a "real cunt," is absolutely contrary to this.

When she tells me that she was brought up to be a "nice girl," I ask her what that means to her. "I asked my mother once to tell me when a nice girl stops and a woman begins, and my mother didn't know the answer. She married four times and never found Mr. Right.

"When I meet a man who's a real man, I don't think about how

41

he humps, how he fucks, how he sucks. I think of his ambience. If he walks into a room and speaks and people listen, then you know he's not going to jerk you off in business." She slugs down her drink.

"If you're a woman, you're torn—man, you're torn—constantly. If you meet a man like that and he wants your job, you say, 'Hey now, I'm not going to get involved with him.' I just don't have any physical relations or desires with any of my partners or clients, because in this business if you're a woman, you have to step back and let them see your business sense. I don't want to convince them sexually."

When Nancy meets a man, she likes to fantasize about how his skin feels, not how big his cock is, because that really doesn't matter. Kissing she finds is one of the eight wonders of the world. 'I can kiss somebody and if he kisses like a dead rat, there's no way in the world he's going to turn me on. I lose my hard-on," she says, surprising me with her male idiom. "I have orgasms, but they're not like the ones I've read about. There aren't any bells ringing and things going off. It's just like cold cream," she says calmly.

Nancy is frightened to death of penetration. "I can't stand to be pumped to death. I just can't handle it."

She refills her glass and begins to make notes about all the calls she must make. She wonders aloud why the phone hasn't rung in the last half-hour we have spent together and then it begins to ring again, and I spend the entire next hour listening to Nancy's call-girl routine. Finally it's over.

"Jesus! This business is exciting. When we make a movie, man, it's like a giant orgy! People who are putting something together from the first word to the last touch—it's like fucking. It's great!"

After these kinds of days on the set, Nancy comes home by herself. "When you come home from a hard day, you throw your purse on the couch and sit down and think, *What will I eat now?* You don't have time to shop, so you order bread, cheese, hot dogs, bacon and eggs, just in case you're ever home. So you make a grilled cheese sandwich, and you only made it because it was fattening, and you eat half of it only because you're guilty.

"Then you sit down and put on the television, even though you've been on the set all day listening to noise. Then you say,

'Shit, what am I doing in this business? I really hate it! How in the world am I ever going to meet anybody outside of this business who will make any sense? You'll hate him anyway because he's never going to understand your life,' like . . ." she motions to the phone ". . . like these phone calls. He'll never understand your life being taken up so much by them. So you say to yourself, *Well, either I'm going to be very, very successful and really love the rest of my life, or I should give it up!*"

One time Nancy gave it up for two months to be married. "I was so bored. It was awful!" she says sadly.

Sometimes a professional woman becomes sensual only when she is away from her theater of operations. Irene is a case in point.

Irene

At thirty-eight years of age, Irene has not only put herself through graduate school and raised three children alone, but also has a thriving psychotherapeutic practice in Cleveland, Ohio.

At a recent therapy convention on the island of Jamaica, Irene became sexually involved with a colleague. "He was a lovely person, very dynamic, very interesting, and I liked him very much. We had very *nice* sex together."

Her voice becomes lower as she speaks about the sensuality of her lover, and I ask her what she means by "nice" sex, which sounds as if it bores her.

"Well," she says, smiling, her blue eyes snapping, "it was the kind of sex that one expects. The kind where you go to bed and the man kisses you. Then he moves down to your breasts and you know exactly what's going to happen. You're programmed. You kiss, then he goes between your legs, and then he thrusts maybe fifteen minutes and ejaculates and goes 'Ahhhahhh, how wonderful it all was!' relaxes for a while, then gets it up again, and you probably go down on him. Then he puts it in again, and it's finished.

"So," she says unhappily, "it's routine."

Even though Irene thinks this kind of sex is routine, she does have orgasms. But she is not thrilled by the whole aura. "It's the kind of sex I found in marriage, routine sex," she repeats. "It's now with somebody new. Only the faces change, the penis remains the same." At this moment I am so depressed I am about to cry, for the kind of sex Irene has described is probably thought of by other women as most adequate. I ask if she ever has an enjoyable sexual experience.

"It's not the kind of thing where I go craving for something. I can't do much about it because I don't really have the time and energy to hunt for a man. My practice and my children leave me exhausted. But . . ." she pauses provocatively ". . . sometimes it can happen. It happened in Jamaica."

Irene then goes on to tell me that the eighteen-year-old son of Jamaican acquaintances kept sending her mash notes which she ignored because she was old enough to be his mother. "He was very, very persistent," she explains. "I was almost nasty and rude, but one night I came home about midnight after having dinner and sex with my colleague, and this young, naive native boy was waiting for me in the lobby of the hotel."

Irene is very tall, and at this moment she gets up from the couch and walks around the apartment with her very, very high heels, pulling up her jeans which are elastic-tight over her body, waving her long, blond hair, looking as sexy as a cat in heat. A kind of happy smile has taken over her expression as she tells of her experience, something which I find happens to many women when they are relating stories of sexual pleasure. It's as if all the sadness and tragedy leave their lives at these moments.

She continues her story after walking about the room, as if her excess energy must be worked out physically. I wonder how comfortable she is in a shrink's chair, for she looks more to me like a glamorous horsewoman competing with Lady Godiva.

"He asked me where I had been and said he was waiting for me. Then he grabbed me, picked me up, and carried me into my hotel room. I was very excited by the whole thing. I was thinking, *My God, I'm being raped at this late point in my life.* He didn't tear my clothes off, but pulled open my blouse and the buttons snapped. I enjoyed it thoroughly. It was the element of surprise for me. I really hadn't intended to go to bed with him at all."

This began an idyllic, sensuous experience which lasted throughout the convention's ten days. Irene began coming home earlier from her dates with her colleague. From 10 P.M. to 6 A.M., she saw her young lover. Even though she was fully twenty years older than he was, he was very experienced in the art of making love.

"He loved to kiss and spent a long time kissing, putting his tongue inside the ridge of my mouth, exciting the hell out of me. You know, other men never kiss. They have a cookbook recipe for sex. This young man told me how much he wanted me and how he had waited for me. I was thoroughly surprised at his expertise. I thought he was going to shove it in and come very quickly, as any other eighteen-year-old might do. But instead," she says passionately, "he was the best lover I have ever had.

"It was because he responded in all ways. He took his time kissing and caressing, we talked a lot in between. He talked about my body and how beautiful it was. I told him he was beautiful, too, which he was. He was built like a black Adonis. He seemed genuinely interested in me and my body. He was jealous of the other man I was seeing.

"I began to have orgasms that I had never had before. It was a total surprise for me. After all, I've had a lot of experience, had been married a long time, and have had about two hundred lovers since. Also, I know the technical part of sex, but never did I feel this way."

I asked her what about her young lover impressed her the most. "He has mastered one thing that the majority of men don't even know about, and that is the element of surprise. It existed from the very beginning when he picked me up and carried me to my bedroom." Then a look comes over her face of such absolute pleasure that I wait in envy for her next statement. "Also, the other thing was he had the ability to maintain a constant erection." Her face breaks into a wide smile, and suddenly tiny freckles appear on her cheeks, like tiny glitters that have burst through from her erotic soul.

"You know, there is a theory around that a small penis is just as good as a large one. This is really not true. A big sexy man with a big penis is better than one with a small penis any time.

"It was very, very surprising to me for a man to have an erection from ten at night to six in the morning and have maybe seven or eight orgasms and not any lag in between," says the therapist, who probably advises her male patients that this is not desirable or probable. "He also pleasured me a great deal in between by making love to my legs and my feet in a very sensuous way. I haven't learned anything new sexually for years, and, somehow, I found myself learning from this eighteen-year-old.

"He wasn't fumbling or floppy like most men. He knew how to hold my body with a firmness and a security." I wondered whether Irene's patients know about her pessimism regarding most men.

"There's a difference between rape and dominance, and this young man was very, very dominant in the bedroom. I'm usually the one who is dominant, and it was a pleasure to have someone telling me what to do in bed. And they were all the right things, too."

"Is there anything you didn't do with him?" I ask, holding my breath.

"Yes, anal sex. That's because homosexuals, who have a great deal of rectal intercourse, cannot hold their feces as they age, and I don't want that to happen to me."

Recovering from that information, I ask: "What about after you left, how did you feel about everything?"

"I was very, very happy that I had the experience. Of course he said he was in love with me."

Returning to Cleveland, Irene resumed her "regular" sexual life. "Most men don't know what to do. You know, I'm a professional therapist, and in my private life I don't want to give instructions. I can forgive and tolerate some clumsiness, but generally men are so totally clumsy, I just don't enjoy it. It spoils the magic of the moment. And then, when you say something is lacking, they can't say anything in return, they just withdraw sexually. I don't want my bed to be my office. You know, I spend my entire day being the dominant, decision-making therapist. When I have sex, I want to be a woman!"

Irene is a classic case of a woman who comes in contact professionally with needy men, but does not want them as lovers.

Thus, what is more erotic than a young, native Caribbean with a twenty-four-hour lust. The only sad part of the story is that it is not part of her everyday life, impossible with its professional and motherhood demands. Many professional women seek eroticism on their vacations, away from their decision-making lives. I think Irene enjoyed herself and I wish her many more happy vacations.

Sometimes the vacation does happen right at home. Often it takes women years of marriage and children before they attain success. Once there, they look to younger men (as Irene did on vacation). Helen is an example of a woman on this kind of erotic search.

Helen

At forty years old, successful in her own marketing research business in Boston, mother of teen-age sons, Helen has lived with a twenty-seven-year-old dancer for the last two years.

"When I met him, I never thought he'd be interested in me," she says candidly, "but he was very warm and direct and immediately moved in." Living with her, Mark paid for his out-of-pocket expenses, but Helen carried the burden of the household. "He wasn't in a position to pay for the household I was used to," she remarks fairly.

Making love twice a day, Helen found her young lover was very, very intense. "He usually initiated sex with affection. When he came home from a performance, I usually blew him because he was so tied up. He would unwind after that, and we would make love. We made love for hours because he had such good control. We did everything but anal sex."

Her lover told Helen—pert, tiny, and slim—how very beautiful she was. "I wasn't too concerned with the age difference because I have friends all ages. I loved the way Mark was built, like a boxer, huge cock, beautiful legs. I was fascinated by his cock. He was very well hung. He whispered to me constantly that I had a sensual body. We would stand in front of the mirror and admire ourselves. We had very few problems. I loved him because he was so emotional and most of my friends are well-known intellectuals."

Problems occurred when Mark was in the company of these famous brains; he felt they were so much smarter than he was. Also Helen's teen-aged sons disliked him, and Helen was torn between her needs as a woman and her needs as a mother.

Then Mark's own career began to blossom, partly due to Helen's financial investment. When she became his business partner, she saw less and less of him because he spent more and more time on the road. As she tells me this part of the story, her former reserve is broken with bursts of emotional tears, completely surprising me. A product of English Protestant parents, Helen has never learned to express herself emotionally, a fact that has made her successful both in her career and in intellectual circles. Thus, Mark must have meant a lot to her because she is breaking one of her parents' rules: She is crying over spilled milk.

"He began telling me that every time we quarreled he had no place to go because he had given up his apartment. Finally he borrowed money from me because he said he needed some new equipment. Instead, he rented an apartment." When she found out about this, she could not shake the feeling of having been ripped off.

There is a strange, fearful look in her eyes as Helen tells this part of her story. "I still sleep with him, but now I feel very aware of protecting myself against him, which I never felt before. In sex now, I don't have the feeling of completeness, of sharing myself emotionally.

"It reminds me of my husband. I was married very young, and he took complete advantage of me." Without vulnerability, Helen's and Mark's sexual activity then becomes just "fucking."

When she began complaining, as she certainly would have done earlier if a business colleague had taken advantage of her, Mark couldn't believe it. Since she had been so easygoing about supporting him for two years, he just had no concept of her power and directness. "He thought I was easy so I was an easy mark. I had treated him very well and resented this. You know, I had hidden my strength from him, the advantages of my experience, because I thought it would frighten him if I pulled that kind of clout. So he was totally flattened when he saw me be firm about money."

"Why did it take you so long?" I ask. If Helen had been this inefficient in business, she would not be a success.

"I feel I am failing as a woman when I say no to a man who needs me. I like the feeling that I'm able to do things for a man, to suck him off, put his sexual needs before my own. Then I can control my negative feelings about me. My mother taught me not to burden other people with my emotions, so I felt I should never be angry at Mark, no matter what he did."

Helen is a clear example of a woman who does not use her mind and logic in her emotional relationships. She suffers from common female schizophrenia: the intellect directed toward business, the emotions toward the ambivalence between maternalism and eroticism. If Helen had used her good sense with Mark, she would not have been such an easy mark.

In Helen's case, age had much to do with the balance of power. But often this can happen in the same age group, as it did with Jean.

Jean

She is a stunning black woman, patterned after the chic, African-princess look, with her very, very frizzy hair and African silver jewelry, which complements her simple denim skirt and soft jersey blouse. Long stockings and high heels complete her soft and demure costume. But her attitudes toward me conflict with her appearance, because she is very, very distrustful, and I ask her why.

"Black women don't trust white women," she says, and I wonder why she has agreed to be interviewed.

"My husband was white," she says in a deadly tone of voice as if she is very ashamed of this. "I didn't have any sexual experience before him. I was a virgin. After we married, I suffered from vaginismus [a tightening of the vagina during penetration], so we got divorced."

She talks matter-of-factly, as if to deny her beautiful, sensuous appearance and our surroundings. We are sitting in her small Chicago apartment, completely furnished with African sculpture and art. It is as if Jean has denied the need for furniture—a simple bed and bureau make do—and wishes to exist on another continent. I ask her how her vaginismus developed.

"I was very afraid of penetration. My vagina would just close up, and my husband would complain that he couldn't enter me. The first time he finally got inside of me, it was so painful I screamed. The doctors told me there was nothing physically wrong with me. I guess I thought his penis was powerful, and in my mind, it was a weapon."

Although Jean suffered with her husband, she was open to masturbation, which she did by rubbing her legs together or rubbing her pelvic area against the sheet. Her husband also succeeded in masturbating her just by rubbing his penis against her. She could reach orgasm that way, usually on top of him.

After her divorce, Jean began climbing in her computer programming profession, now earning $20,000 per annum. Functioning well in a career, she began to give her social attention to black cultural functions, living in a black community, seeing only black people. At a party, she fell in love with a black man.

"I waited and waited for him to call. I knew if I took the initiative, he would turn off. When we finally got together and made love, I came down with a vaginal infection. He was very, very understanding about this, but afterward he constantly lost his erection during foreplay. That was okay with me, because I felt if a woman is too uninhibited the first time a couple has sex, she threatens the man."

Dating Tom for six months, Jean became involved in his life and his problems. "I'd lend him money when he was broke. I didn't mind, because I loved him."

But because their sex life wasn't pleasurable, she went out and bought a vibrator. As she tells me this, I look for anger in her expression and find none. Instead, it seems as if Jean is simply stating the facts of life that everyone knows: that men simply cannot fulfill women.

Tom was upset because Jean used a vibrator. When she used it, she would fantasize about a woman lying on a beach and a man kissing and fondling her. The man was always strong, athletic, popular, smart, and black.

I ask her if her fantasies are always about black men.

"I'm not going to tell you," she answers smartly, as if it would be disloyal. I ask her to explain her attitude. "Black women these days are not going to admit that they have sexual relationships with white men," she says adamantly. I tell her that she is incorrect, for most of the black women interviewed in this book do talk of multiracial relationships. She is angry at my statement.

To change the focus, I ask her about the most erotic experience she has ever had. "One night I told this married man I work with about my sexual problems. He was a beautiful black man, with a well-endowed behind and big beautiful thighs. He really turned me on."

I look at Jean and am surprised that she is absolutely radiantly, sensually beautiful at the mention of this man. Her eyes are flashing, she is rubbing her legs up and down against her skirt in a fondling manner, wearing a warm, charming smile.

"I was very, very nervous. First, we danced nude together. Then we started kissing and petting. He went down on me. In a few minutes, I was able to have an orgasm. Later, I had multiple orgasms. He said, 'Look, you don't have any problems.' I felt so good about the fact that we had intercourse. At the same time, he rubbed my clitoris, and I continued to have orgasms. We had sex so many, many times that night, and it was great." The relationship went on for several months, and Jean said it was the one time she had met an American black man who was assertive. "Most assertive men I have dated are African men. They really know how to pursue."

Thirty-year-old Jean's Prince Charming is a black man, about the same age, who is a couple of inches taller than she is, with a good body—attractive, educated, and successful. She is absolutely certain she would be happy with him.

Meanwhile, her consistent fantasy is: "I wish I was a prostitute," she says, startling me. I see her as a very powerful woman.

"One of my conflicts with men is that I don't like to wait, that I can't ask, can't initiate sex. So I envy the power and mobility of the prostitute. I like the idea of being attractive to men and having as many sexual experiences as I may want."

Jean has allowed herself to be angry at the white world but not at her black lovers. Feeling disloyal at her wish to change these men, Jean fantasizes that a prostitute would have a better time sexually, completely ignoring the fact that prostitutes simply perform at sex, and do not feel any pleasure. Using her analytical powers to get ahead in her career, Jean seems to be very conflicted about how to be a successful, erotic woman in our society.

Often marriages break up when the wife becomes more successful than the husband. Harriet began having trouble with her husband at this point in her life.

Harriet

When twenty-eight-year-old Harriet got a terrific illustration job at a leading magazine in San Francisco, her seven-year marriage to a fellow illustrator began to deteriorate.

"I would come home from the office and feel an obligation to go to bed with George, especially if we weren't getting along. I was in complete control of the times we did, the rhythms, when it didn't happen, and when it did. I would think guiltily if we're married we should have sex. The thought that maybe I wouldn't want to was too terrifying for me."

Harriet, in the throes of a divorce, looks too thin and fragile, and although it is two o'clock in the afternoon, is drinking much too much. She looks completely disillusioned, although her career and an exciting life are before her.

She explains what the dissolution of her marriage really meant. "I want to be perfect. I want to be the professional woman who has both marriage and career. It was funny, our emotional problems never affected my orgasms. I always had them. But I didn't ever want to kiss George. I began being very passive in bed. I would expect him to do everything, to caress me, where at the beginning of our marriage I would direct him a lot sexually. But now I had to make so many decisions in the office, I just wanted to come home, lie back, and be satisfied without reciprocating. And I felt guilty about this, all of the time."

Wives have been understanding about this for eternity, but husbands are conflicted about indulging professional wives.

Harriet has turned her attention to feminism as a result of her marriage failure. "Men think I'm too strong, too aggressive. I feel I have to downplay my strength, even though I don't think I should. I feel men won't like me. I won't be lovable. Men have never admitted to this, but they stop being sexually interested and don't explain why." Her voice gets all crackly now, and it is the voice of an old woman. "My husband doesn't like to confront raw emotion. He doesn't like loud voices. He'd rather sidestep problems."

She drags on her cigarette, the last of a pack she has already gone through, already preparing for the next pack, taking the cellophane off, crackling it in her hands, looking about for a place to throw it in the neat, clean, and efficient apartment which has no personal touch except for a window filled with plants—a very sterile existence.

"I work hard all day long, and I want a man who can take care of himself emotionally, a man who is strong enough and secure enough so I can come at him with passion, anger, and affection, and he won't fall apart. I don't want to spend my life caring about how fearful he feels, wondering how we're getting on."

Harriet seems to have absolutely no concept of the dynamics of a relationship and the dynamics of her emotional power plays. "When I trust a person, I become very unleashed. I expect my man to initiate what's going on with me, without my having to tell him. If I share my passion, he should appreciate it." Harriet echoes the female romanticism of generations. "I don't think men are trustworthy or sensitive. I think a man will simply say no he doesn't want you, if he doesn't."

"Why do you think a man will be so brutal?" I ask, having run into this curious thinking among feminists before. Although I know that men are different emotionally, I still believe they are capable of loyalty and consideration and wonder why they are often lumped into a big crowd of monsters with no hearts and feelings.

"I don't feel as if I exist unless a man says 'I want you.' I'm embarrassed about my feelings and won't let my colleagues or friends know that I feel this way, because it makes me feel weak, vulnerable, hypocritical, and humiliated."

I tell Harriet that most heterosexual feminists, and many lesbian feminists, feel this intense need for male approval, a need they fight against, because they understand how unrealistic it is. Thus, many women come to feminism because of this extreme need. But I often wonder, *Why not attack the need, instead of the men?*

"Aren't you setting up a situation where you are expecting unrealistic heroism on the part of your lovers? Getting into bed with you means he must be a god, not a man."

She turns into a snide little girl at my remark. "I think I'm worth all the trouble," she insists, "because I'm special."

"Everyone is special to someone. When wanting to be special stops you from looking at yourself clearly, it is then illusory," I say quietly, hoping she will hear me.

"I am special," she repeats, like a little girl wanting more ice cream. "If I'm not special, then I don't have the right to demand so much from them."

Harriet is a case where the desire for power and ambition for a career has made her completely unaware of the human condition. A baby in the Machiavellian power play, Harriet thinks by ordering men to do such and such, they will do it. Why on earth should they? What does she have to offer them except a lot of rhetoric about unfulfillment? And worse, she can't accept her anger. Instead of admitting she is absolutely angry, she tries power plays. Naturally men, and everyone else, are going to back away from her. No one wants to be vulnerable to someone who says one thing and does another.

This is what political feminism can do to women. It can give them a platform on which to voice their dissatisfaction instead of looking at themselves, working for their growth, accepting their responsibilities, and understanding the dynamics of their changing roles.

Only if women become responsible, honest creatures does feminism have even the faintest chance of working. All people, even sexist men and women, will admire feminist women who take responsibility for their own lives and don't just talk about it.

I was amazed at the way Harriet geared her appearance. Trying to look as much like a little match girl as possible, she thought she fooled people regarding her ambitions. I came away from this interview shaking my head negatively, something I do not experience often. But I have always had trouble with hypocritical behavior.

Sometimes traditional hypocritical behavior works better for a woman. The age-old custom of making a man feel he is first in a woman's life, whoever the woman is, however successful she is, is something that Lilliana believes in.

Lilliana

Although a renowned actress of the theater, beautiful Lilliana takes only her career as a woman as the most important thing in her life. "I was weaned by a Brazilian mother. Since I was a little girl, my mama always told me I would be walking in the shadow of a man, that he will mean everything to me. I've always done this. Whatever my man wants sexually, I give him. I'm a firm believer in the sex act, and if a female will give of herself, the male will give in return."

This astonishing philosophy, uttered by someone who is successful in the hard-nosed marketplace of the Broadway theater, seems entirely natural in this setting of plush lavender walls, white couches, golden-spun accessories. We are sitting in the morning room overlooking a garden with fig trees which do not bloom and a lovely Renaissance statue emitting water in the center of flowery fountain splendor. Inside, the apartment is large, each room dedicated to a different country. Africa, India, Italy, France call the minute you step into the doorway. Only the morning break-fast room is dedicated to another continent, the continent of the psychic.

"I'm a Pisces, so everything is purple," she says simply when I remark about the wonderful and unusual decor.

Lilliana herself is a typical Piscean woman, with her long purple lounging gown, dark eyes and long hair, slender limbs, though voluptuous body. I ask her about her erotic love life.

"My last gentleman was, without a doubt, one of the greatest human men that I have ever encountered sexually," she says in a breathless tone of voice. "He is built like an Adonis, gives like an Adonis, he is an Adonis. When he would arrive, I would prepare my apartment for him. I would have my lavender sheets, my special grapes, my special wine, my special herbs. I'd give him a Roman bath, which is the essence of candle and music, and use the special witchcraft herbs which I always concoct myself. I would prepare my own body to please him. I would be waxed from head to toe—leg wax, arm wax, lip wax, face wax, hair wax. Everything had to be feminine and smooth. I would prepare my body with lotions, too—creams and powders. If I had sufficient warning, I would soak in oils, then wine, then milk. Then I would choose an exciting lavender outfit. It would depend on the day. He had a favorite, a Roman gown, very beautiful and very old."

She daintily sips from an elegant cup as she goes on with her tale. "My clothes are either Roman or Egyptian. I believe that I was Cleopatra's handmaiden in another life. I must have washed her feet, rubbed her body down, must have worked over her as she prepared for her man, her Antony," she says with complete conviction.

"Thus, there's never an electric light burning, always candles. The garden is filled with candles and torches, too. Real grapes hang from the fig trees. When he walks through my doorway, he leaves the outside world, the world of business, of his family, where he is very successful, leaves it behind, and he and I are on a little desert all by ourselves. When he steps over the threshold, whether I strip him of his clothes right off his back, or if I am in a different softer mood, I get down on my knees to him. Whatever mood transpires, it is beautiful."

Lilliana looks astonishingly happy as she tells me of her way of loving a man. "I don't believe in keeping fantasies to myself. I bring my fantasies to bed. When it comes to the old sack, I want to feel it and taste it and smell it and touch it and lick it for real. I bring my fantasies down from the clouds into my purple sheets. I pour Strega all over his body and lick it off. It burns, but it is sweet. He puts strawberries up my vagina and eats them one by one, giving me a bath of love. He puts an unlit candle inside of me and moves it around. Then we go outside and make love in the garden. The torches are burning and are very, very low. The moon is out, and it is very strange. It is only the two of us and our night of eroticism." She continues, "I feel every touch of him and every touch of me. Every touch is an electric shock."

I am spellbound by the beauty of her descriptions and think of her lover as a very lucky man. I ask about their relationship and its dynamics, surprised to find her mood change dramatically from sensuality to sadness.

"It is very, very difficult," she sighs sadly. "After four and one half years, he has left me, only a month ago. It's very difficult for me, because I am a one-man woman. I am in love, but I must divide myself now. I am a very sexual human being, and when he is not here, I have to make do with someone else. I had to walk many months to find my man. He is my superior, my god, my masculine self, my male, my epitome, and whatever he wants, it is.

"But I was not his Mrs. His wife threatened him about me. He said, 'I don't want you to get involved in court cases, in a scandal.' But I said to him, 'I know you're coming back to me.' "

At thirty-five, Lilliana has never married, though she has had many opportunities. She explains that her career was time-consuming, but that it has never been the most important thing to her. The most important thing to her has always been her man.

"When I was very, very young, my daddy had a mistress. At the races, this young lady was sitting in the box with us. I didn't understand her purpose there. My mama wasn't there. The girl was a lovely person, but I would go home and say, 'Mama, there was a lovely lady sitting with daddy.' I always remember my mama never said a word. When I grew older, she told me that the woman has to understand the man's need for a mistress, and if she is a smart woman, she will give him all the leeway because someday he will return to her. She is *his* woman.

"I've always gone along with my mama's belief, but I am ashamed that I am the mistress in this situation." Her lovely deep, dark eyes fill with tears. "I have a great respect for his wife, for she is his woman, his real woman. She loves this man as much as I do. She is the respectable part of him, something I will never be. Even though I have had access to this same gorgeous man, I bear her no malice, and I would hope she would bear me none."

Her fairness doctrine uttered, her face now turns from an expression of sad understanding to one of lively fire. "On the other hand, I'm also part cat," she says, astonishing me, "and I know if I love my man and another woman is there, I'll claw her to death." She smiles sinisterly as she says this, giving me a chill. "I've always admired those elegant women who live in their suave grays, never getting too upset about anything, but I . . ." she pauses, dramatically putting a lavender lace handkerchief to her brow ". . . I have always been a creature of extremes."

This dramatic extreme personality is one of the reasons Lilliana is so successful on stage, the kind of creative success which would be an enormous fulfillment to most women, but Lilliana insists this is not so. "My career has only been to fulfill my desires to make a success of my life for him. If my man called me to his side, I would leave everything. If my man called me, I would be there.

"I believe in the twosome of things. Everything has always been done in twos, the cats of the jungle are like that. When the male lion roars, *the jungle trembles*, but when the female lion roars, *nature trembles*. It's because of the feminine thing within us that we are very soft, that we are here to give. It is true in cat land and it is true in female land. I would be very proud to be a Mrs. one day. When he comes home, I would be ready for him in every respect, emotionally, physically, sexually, because I firmly believe the competition of our world today is keen. There is such a number of marvelous women. If a woman is smart, she greets her man with every possible weapon."

Her butler announces it is time to get ready to go to the theater, but she ignores him. I sense her maid is inside preparing her clothes, her chauffeur is outside, ready to drive the shiny Rolls, everything is ready for her every wish, her every desire.

"I earn excellent money, but I'm not married, and it still bothers me. I don't know why I have not married, because I have had several excellent opportunities. I've never had an engagement ring on my finger, which is a deep hurt in my life. I say to myself I am a failure, it is my fault because I am not enough woman." The butler moves her chair as she prepares to rise.

"Sometimes I think to myself maybe I won't get married. If only the word 'husband' did not exist," she moans. "It would be a lonely life for I would feel that I have failed." She raises her arms like a ballet dancer in motion, an elegant good-bye, as she leaves to prepare her toilette, to enter the world outside, the world of drama, the world of theater, the world of the public that adulates her.

Any man who enters Lilliana's very special world would have to be sensitive and successful to enjoy her romantic dreams. I found Lilliana very special, from another era, the era of the courtesan, of the dramatic woman. I wondered how the special atmosphere of her erotic world would wear on a man, whether the special herbs, wines, the sensuality could be enjoyed on a daily basis.

Lilliana was fortunate to have a career that tapped her special dramatic talents. Hopefully, she will add to her life's enjoyment, too, with the discovery of *her* man, to which she devotes so much thought and care.

Professional women often use their careers to express much of their frustrated sensuality. Joan is one of these women.

Joan

I have often pondered why some writers choose sexual matters to research, to analyze. One answer, vulgarized by a cigar-smoking relative of mine, was, as he said to me quite calmly one day, "Those writers who write about sex have the most awful sexual problems. The rest of the people are not like that." I was shocked at the time by this bawdy interpretation of reevaluations in our personal sexual lives.

Thus, when I met Joan, a well-known writer about sex, whose prose is so filled with imagination and pain, but who always promises a sexual nirvana, I was interested to learn how she came by this optimism. I was astonished to find that she was controlled by romanticism and illusion, those same enduring emotions that make it so hard for most women to fight losing their vulnerability, which is the most precious element of love.

Joan admitted quite frankly that she is completely romantic, although she is twentyish and into drugs and free sex.

"What about the new sexual freedom?" I asked.

"It's full of shit, at least for me. The only time I really have orgasms is when I feel that I love a man desperately and really need him. Then I lose myself, lose my identity, and want to be such a part of him that I lose control and come all over the place."

We are sitting in Joan's West Seventies studio, which reminds me of the famous Bogart film *Casablanca* with its white wicker furniture, palms, ferns, and cats. It is like a photographer's concept of what a bordello might be. Joan is a tall, thin, willowy brunette, wearing a white, silken sarilike outfit, one earring through her left nostril, Woodstock-style. I ask her what these men she falls in love with are like.

"They usually have very big penises and very full erections. They drive very hard, and I have spasm after spasm, and then it's all over." I am amazed that she told me what they are like physically, instead of what a thirtyish, romantic woman would do, which is to tell me what they are personally.

I ask her if she enjoys her sex life.

"I always suffer so. I've gone to therapy to learn how not to suffer. I'm now making it with a man who has a half-erect penis, and I have orgasms, but they aren't the ones of pure pleasure. I guess I'm still old-fashioned and romantic about sex." She offers me some pot, puts on some hard rock, and sits back in a wicker rocking chair. I can't imagine why she is still old-fashioned with her taste for the Sixties rock. So I ask her what her fantasies are like.

"They aren't romantic," she says brightly, as if to help the cause of my research as only a fellow writer can understand. "I'm generally getting fucked by a series of men I don't know in a public place like a stone altar or bier. Some guy fucks me, and the others watch and get off on it. But I challenge them all, because none of them can make me come."

"Sounds pretty sacrificial to me," I remark, amazed at the symbolism of her fantasies.

"I know," she agrees sadly, knowing what I mean. "I'm very masochistic. I can't even masturbate, because there's no one to touch and hold me afterward. I feel very, very vulnerable when I don't have a lover. Very lonely, with a sense of loss. I need a person to affirm my sexuality and my specialness.

"My current lover and I are bored with each other. Last night, he asked me if I wanted to make it with another woman. The last time I tried that the man left me for that woman and I was hysterical. But I was writing a book on sex at the time so I really didn't miss him that much."

I ask Joan what happens to her when she writes about sex.

"When I write about sex, my sex drive goes into a dive. I get so tired of analyzing and writing about sex, it takes all the spontaneity out of it. But my fantasies continue. When I get on the subway, I always fantasize that the car is going to get stuck in the middle of the tunnel for three days, and we fuck our way out."

"Subways are sexy," I agree. "What else makes you feel sexy?"

"Being half-undressed. I like to have my skirt on and my blouse off, with my breasts hanging out. Or I like being naked but wearing all my jewelry. Sometimes I go out on the street without panties, and it makes me feel really great. The men on the street know I'm turned on; they hassle me and hassle me. Other times, I can wear a low blouse and wiggle my hips around and not give a shit, and nobody will bother me."

"Has your sexual research changed your own personal sexual life?"

She drags on her marijuana cigarette, and her voice is lower now. "Yes," she answers. "I began to get the courage to ask men for sex. You know, I've been shocked at the turndowns and realized for the first time how vulnerable men are constantly with women. I've had twenty lovers, but the two I asked turned me down.

"But real sex for me, good sex, is losing control and giving myself over to the other person. Then I don't exist anymore.

"I've got to change that, and I don't know how," she admits sadly.

Joan is an example of the twentyish woman from the Sixties culture who knows where it's at, has accepted the drug and music culture as a normal part of her life, but is still suffering from the strains of old-fashioned romanticism, which does not find a fulfilling expression in the promiscuity of the men in her age group. I have found many women in their twenties caught between the media blitz and the rock-culture propaganda, and the desires of their own hearts. It's as if they are in worse shape than older women. For in older women's romanticism, at least, there were male partners to share it, and their culture and their music reaffirmed it. Thus, they were not so alone. It was only as they matured and realized that romanticism did not work for them that they could begin to usurp its hold on their sensual erotic desires.

Ellen is an example of a romantic older woman who has changed her style.

Ellen

After being widowed at fifty, Ellen, the mother of married children, working as a fashion consultant in a Kansas City store, was on the job when an engineer on the set put a spotlight on her. "It was very dramatic," she says gleefully. "The models were on one side, and he was looking at me. Then he came over and touched me. It was like going to the dentist when I was ten years old. I loved his being close to me."

Buxom, looking like every bride's mother, Ellen talks of the relationship that has developed since this meeting five years ago. "He's my idea of a man. He's complete authority. I'm turned on by his sturdy, broad shoulders, the hair on his chest. He stands for maleness."

After five years in the sack with him, Ellen complained to her lover a month ago that she hated the awful boxer shorts he wore. "He has narrow hips, and I love to see them. So we went out and bought two pairs of jockey shorts just for me.

"I like his penis very much, but sometimes I don't look at it for months. One night recently I noticed his penis through his jockeys and asked, 'Is that just you or are you particularly erect?' He answered, 'No, that's just me,' and I said, 'That's very nice.' He acted surprised at my remark. I guess he was pleased, because he made love to me immediately."

Ellen likes the way he makes love. "He starts with my breasts, then I turn my back to him, and he puts his hand down my vagina. It lubricates, which never happened during my long marriage. It's like when I was a little girl and used to put toilet paper down there because it was such a nice feeling. I didn't dare touch myself."

Ellen is very happy with her career and her lover, but she wants very much to be a couple. But since she refuses her lover's offer of marriage, I ask her how she is going to accomplish that. "I feel like an old maid, incomplete. But I wish he would stop nagging me about marriage. He's always challenging me, accusing me, making me feel guilty because I don't want to marry him. He says it means I don't love him."

While she has taken a somewhat modern stand on marriage, sex to Ellen is still dangerous business. "I feel if you have sex too much, the intensity will evaporate. Maybe if we had sex four or five times a week, it would be bad for him." She adds with all seriousness, "There's a certain loss of protein, which he needs, when a man comes too often."

Ellen, certainly a product of a romantic age, would never have dared not to marry a man who wanted her had she not lived through a marriage, had grown-up children, and had a functioning, well-paying career. She still carries on the propaganda that too much sex will hurt, but even with that attitude she is enjoying sex as much as she can.

A much younger woman who is suffering from romanticism and allows it to destroy her sexual experiences is Minerva.

Minerva

She is terribly tiny, the fragility of her bone structure almost dangerous, as if a sudden whiff or fast action would break her into a shattering mingling of pieces. When she speaks, she talks in small, breathless shifts of vocal cords and looks at me appealingly as she speaks of her desperation where men are concerned.

"For the past two years, I have been having sexual intercourse with many, many men. I find this is the way men are, so they won't become emotionally involved. Because I always become emotionally involved when I'm sexually attracted, in order to justify what I am doing, I decided to embark on this experiment. So I did date a lot of men who said they weren't ready for relationships. But I am now very, very disillusioned, because screwing around is not for me."

A partner in a Hartford law firm where aggressive performance must underlie her fragile appearance, Minerva finds that she is frustrated by the fact that men must initiate. "Once I wanted to get to know a man, so I called him up. We spent some time with each other, but he honestly admitted to me that because I had initiated the relationship, he couldn't get very interested or taken with me. I was shocked. Since then, I haven't initiated, even though I know it is foolish not to make an attempt, but I was a liberated female once and you see what it got me. We are not at that stage yet."

Minerva feels that men and women are at a different place in time. "Very few men seem to be at the same stage of self-awareness and self-honesty that most women are. One of my main objections about the men I date is that they don't become friends first. It happens that they come on instantly. Of course I'm very flirtatious," she admits, slightly embarrassed about it all. "I need approval, so I used to be very compliant. They would arouse my compassion, so out of pity or feeling I would give in. If they gave me money, as they often did when I was a law student, I would also give in. I always felt I had to pay them back with giving them sex."

Minerva seems to like everything possible that could happen sexually. "I like my eyes licked. I like being caressed a lot. I like oral sex. I like the moment of penetration. Most positions make me instantly reach an orgasm, and I have continuous orgasms. One night a lover and I counted and I had reached twenty-six. They are very tense and high-pitched, and I get very sensitive. In fact, I can't be touched afterward or I pass out. What I like most is to reach an orgasm by cunnilingus and then be penetrated immediately afterward, because it's all throbby and enlarged, and it's just delicious. When I have that combination, I'm totally satisfied. But I know if I have one climax after the other, some men are frightened and think that I can't be satisfied."

A professional life and her psychological difficulties seem to weigh deeply on Minerva's ability to create an erotic life she can count on. "I like to have regular sex, because then I don't rush into relationships and crave involvements with insecure people. I need daily intercourse, but I don't know where to meet men who want that, too. I went to a singles' bar once and hated it. No one paid attention to me until I was ready to leave, and then I was bombarded. It was much too noisy and vulgar, a flesh market. On the whole, I find men are terribly frightened of women, and women are too eager these days for any kind of man."

Since she has difficulty having regular sex with a man, Minerva masturbates two or three times a day, regularly. "I prefer the circular motion, concentration on the clitoris. My fantasies are about threesomes all the time. Two men and me. But I never have realized them because I have not been able to get the right men to do it."

Minerva seems uncomfortable in the interview and holds herself tightly with her fragile arms. She seems very anxious to know what I am thinking and asks me all the time. I tell her I am listening to what she is saying, interested, and have not thought about it in an analytical way. She then starts to analyze herself and I ask her not to. Minerva seems angry at my request and pouts.

"Have you ever acted out your fantasy of threesomes?"

"Once a man I loved asked me to make love to another woman and him," she answers with quiet anger. "It was pleasant. Then he brought another girl in. He said they were old friends, but I think they were hookers. I stood for that. When he brought in a third girl, I got up and put my clothes on. He was treating me like a goddamn whore."

One of the reasons Minerva feels she has to do what her man asks of her is that she suffers from the harem-girl fantasy. With her very long hair and her tiny body, she could indeed pose for one of the sheik's dancing maidens. I see that she also uses kohl around her eyes, an interesting contrast to her business glasses. I ask her about where and why the harem-girl fantasy started.

"My mother hated my father and all men. So my father was out of the house a lot. He would take me to meet his girlfriends. My mother used to nag him about his capacity. I seem to take after him. When I began to like sex, I became almost insatiable. I can go on and on. Men have been frightened by my capacity. When I don't get enough of sex, I withdraw and sulk, arouse pity, start crying, hold it in."

To make up for her dissatisfaction in sex, she writes many love letters and poems to men. Most men do not respond. "I don't know why," she says. "I give him everything so he won't need anyone else. He will be all mine. I am seeking to have all men desire me. But when I go to a man's apartment, I know I'm just there to be screwed."

Minerva seems to be an excellent example of the sham of the "helpless woman." If she argued in law courts the same way she acted with men, she'd never win a case. For Minerva, being sensual and feminine means giving the feeling that she is helpless. Many women have Minerva's fear of being too sexual, though it is inconsistent with what men say they want. Perhaps Minerva, in looking for a total relationship, thinks she can get it by being the best lay in town. Minerva shows men her vulnerability only in sex and then wishes to possess them. She did not mention ever communicating in any other way.

If Minerva realized that finding a man to love completely is as difficult a trial-and-error program as anything else, and that she should relate to men from her strengths rather than her weakness, perhaps she would have more opportunity to be more successful in getting what she wants. One try at initiating that didn't work out turned her off completely. I do not know why strong women relate to men only out of their weakness. Vulnerability is certainly a combination of both.

However, the next woman, Natasha, living a very different life, confirms Minerva's fears.

Natasha

The sculptor's studio in San Francisco is stunning with its coal-black walls, ornate chandeliers with gaudy crystals forming art-deco designs. Incense pipes in from a homemade water-pressure box, invented by the woman of the house. Paintings and sculpture, decorated with peacock feathers, turbans of silks, Moroccan jewelry stand atop black rock pedestals. Dark-blue silk curtains blow softly as they would in a harem.

It is a fantasy world, dream time, and the sensuous, imaginative creator of this scene is Natasha, a Polish Catholic from the Bronx, who changed her sturdy black pigtails to a multicolored afro, her Catholic school uniform of blue and white for a ruby-red silken robe, decorated with golden designs. Wearing her own jewelry—long, decorous necklaces and earrings, finger and toe rings, a large belt—she paddles around her dream in bare feet. On her head she temporarily models a fabulous crown, decorated with tiny Coke bottles and Botticelli angels, trying to decide which of her giant sculptures will wear it for her forthcoming one-woman show.

"My sexuality is the same energy I paint with, that I make sculptures with, that I write poetry with, that I fuck with. It comes from the same place," she replies in answer to my query about her erotic life.

"I'm too much for one man," she says sadly, putting the crown on a wild sculpture of a piratelike male figure with a huge penis ornately decorated in gold leaf. "In fact, I'll never forget one night when I was really getting into it and this guy stops me and says furiously, 'Please control yourself.' I was really wounded. But after a few minutes, I began screaming and yelling. How dare he? It was really cruel."

She pauses, takes the crown from the pirate's head, and stands in the center of the studio, holding it pensively. "There are men out there who just don't care very much about women and what they do to them," she says sadly. "So my vagina is a very closed area, it's mine. I don't like to let a lot of people in there because I feel very vulnerable about it. It's very dangerous out there if you're sexual."

"In what ways?" I ask.

"Well, when I meet men, I come on strong. My body just exudes when I feel sexual. My legs start to melt, and my eyes get all misty. I get glowy, and they can see it. It's sexual energy, and when it's picked up right, it's incredible. But sometimes it's picked up on a much lower level, and the man doesn't understand the rhythm.

"Then I get into scenes where, as he's thrusting, I'm counting the strokes. I find myself going one, two, three, because I'm so bored. And I fake orgasms, although I hope I never do that again. I really find very few men are suitable sexual partners for me."

"What kind of men are suitable for you?"

"The imaginative ones. One time I put this scuba-diving equipment on, and my lover put on the mask and fins, and we had sex for hours with that stuff on. Another lover invited me to a Halloween party. I put on boots, a coat, and jewelry. I rubbed baby oil all over my naked body. I was all shiny and had little golden chains on my stomach. When I arrived at the door, I took him into the kitchen and opened up my coat. Well, he was so turned on that he went into the other room and announced that the party was over. We fucked for two days after that."

She is still trying the bejeweled crown on her masterpieces, trying it on an eye, a penis, laughing to herself with the humor of a self-possessed believer in the absurd. I settle down on the embroidered quilt covering the couch and imagine what it must be like to live in this wonderfully acted-out version of sexual fantasies. She sees that I am enjoying myself and offers me: "Coke, pot, cider, or tea?

"You know a lot of men don't understand the nature of a creative woman," she says, as she gives me an imitation eighteenth-century goblet, filled with cider running cool. "If I let myself, I'd fuck my whole life away. But I don't because I need and use that energy for my work. When I work, I get sexually high. In fact, one time I was so high I was stoned and took five clean paintbrushes, got under that quilt, and masturbated with them. OOOooooh, it was great! Now I use them all the time. Especially the really fine ones. They're just like the most sensitive tongue I have ever felt."

"Do creative men understand you?"

She shrugs angrily. "No, they feel it's a woman's responsibility to give herself because it's her job as a woman. When I work, it's just like fucking. I work in a passion until I'm exhausted. My last lover was a rock musician and he'd say, 'Don't do that. Work for two hours, play for two hours. You're going to burn yourself out, working like that.' He was worried because I would refuse sex at those times because I was exhausted.

"With most creative men, they want you to pay attention to them all the time. This guy wouldn't let me sleep in the morning. I had to get up and watch him make phone calls, watch him at the piano, go out on his business lunches. I was part of his signature. He didn't understand that I needed my own time and space for my own work."

"What is the most erotic experience you've ever had?" I ask, having visions of cocaine-induced ménages of avant-garde freaks.

She giggles, takes up a paintbrush, and begins waving it like an orchestra conductor. "It was with a butcher," she says, laughing. "He had the biggest butcher shop in Sausalito, and he was a pig in a lot of ways, but he was so sexually fulfilling.

"One time, he asked me to go to Hawaii with him, and I said no. So I got a ticket for the same plane. He was in first class, I was in coach. I sent him a Beefeater martini, his drink, with a note saying I had noticed him and he was the man of my dreams. He came pounding down the cabin to tourist class and grabbed me. When we got to Hawaii, we made love four times a day. We'd go out to the beach, then come back and cover each other with Vaseline and slide around in bed for hours."

She gulps her cider. "I'd take a butcher over a painter any day," she says.

Natasha, like Minerva, is disenchanted with her contemporary males, but, like Irene, she is creative enough to enjoy sensuality with someone who may not really fit into her life. With the dynamic women of the creative and professional world, this seems to be true. Because sensuality up to this time has always been acted upon from female weakness, rather than female strength, strong dynamic women are a threat to men in our society. Men have to compete in their daily survival and do not wish to compete with women. I have no remedy for this situation except to say to professional and creative women that they should take stock in the fact that they have made their own lives exciting and do not look for a man to do it. They must accept the fact that probably their creative and professional desires come from this disappointment of romance (if Freud's sublimation theory is correct).

For these brave women who make their way into a man's world to act like men is absurd. But they are bound to be more assertive, more knowledgeable than their housewife sisters. This is a genuine underlying fear of women who repulse feminism. They are afraid that if they become functioning, self-serving, exciting citizens, why will they need a man?

They will need a man for eroticism, unless they are lesbians. But they must rethink the myth of the male hero, the desire for a strong man, the age-old romantic idea that a man must be everything to everyone. They hate it when men expect women to be everything to them. Then why, if dynamic women are stronger than their lovers, can't they enjoy it and not let it destroy the eroticism of their relationship?

Relationships must of necessity be out of balance. The writer Carson McCullers, in her brilliant thesis on love in *The Ballad of the Sad Café*, says: "First of all, love is a joint experience between two persons—but the fact that it is a joint experience does not mean that it is a similar experience to the two people involved." * This is only the beginning of the most compassionate and complete theory of love written in the modern world.

Erotic love is not equal; to make it so is to destroy its very foundation. One partner is always more passionate than another. Thus, it seems to me that women who are successful in the world

* Carson McCullers, *The Ballad of the Sad Café* (Boston, Houghton Mifflin, 1951), p. 26.

must reconsider the kinds of men whom they can love and stop confusing eroticism with power. There is no room for power plays if vulnerability toward another is to succeed at what it hopes to succeed at: the deepening of the erotic love for another.

Three

❀ ❀ ❀

THE EROTICISM OF
MARRIAGE

There is never a more dramatic point in a young woman's life than when she leaps onto the marriage bed. Often, she has been emotionally educated that a strong and successful husband is *absolutely* necessary for her emotional security and happiness.

To examine whether this is a workable concept, a class distinction is important. In the lower classes, marriage is often the only path for a woman's emotional and financial security. Uneducated because of poverty, a woman can improve her life through marriage to a man of the working class. For this woman, her emotional security comes from the fact that she has established a home with its inherent benefits for herself, her husband, and her children. If this woman feels any dissatisfaction with her life, she is often resigned to it. (I found only one blue-collar wife who was not resigned to marriage. She is in this chapter.)

Dissatisfaction in marriage among the rich has never seemed to be a problem. The rich have chic and dramatic ways to enhance the sensuality of their lives—a cruise to the South Seas with a new lover, a mistress of younger years provided for an aging husband. I do not mean to imply that all marriages of the upper classes are filled with such dalliance, I only suggest that in the absence of erotic fulfillment, there are many acceptable ways to avoid boredom when one has money.

It is with the middle class that the phenomenon of marriage seems to be most provoking, because the modern middle-class wife is better educated now than ever before. Yet, I was astonished to learn that there still seem to be many of the same frustrations as in yesteryear. The only important change is that some wives are reacting to dissatisfaction differently.

I'm sure that there are happy, erotic marriages. When I was recruiting for this chapter, I wanted the women stably and happily married. I wanted a fair sampling, committed to marriage. I strove to find successful marriages. However, I found that women interpreted this to mean that they had accepted their marriages as permanent fixtures, and felt loyal and affectionate to their husbands. Most women admitted that, erotically, their marriages left much to be desired.

I found a consistently important fact: The women usually expect their husbands to be big, strong men and constant lovers. When pressures of life and business change these husbands' priorities, the wives, bitterly disappointed, begin to turn off marital sex in defiance of this neglect.

Whereas wives of other eras simply became nonsexual in these circumstances, modern wives are taking other paths. Indulgence in fantasy while masturbating is common. Often, these fantasies are turned into reality when lovers, anonymous or otherwise, can be discreetly enjoyed. This middle-class practice has been documented by Linda Wolfe in her book *Playing Around* as happening in close to forty percent of the married population.

Even when dissatisfaction does not cause a wife to stray in reality, she may often stray in fantasy. In a recent experiment published in the *Journal of Consulting and Clinical Psychology*, in a sampling of suburban housewives, sixty-five percent fantasized about an "imaginary lover" while making love to their husbands, and fantasized that this lover was a dominant man who forced these wives to be excited into "submission" to him.

This common need for wives to view their men as strong and dominant is interesting. Living with a man, day-to-day, proves to many a wife that he is not the fantasy man of her dreams, who will court her every night into a romantic sensuality, forcing her into erotic submission. Thus, wives often fantasize that an anonymous, strong stranger will turn them into wanton and lustful whores, something their husbands may never approve of. Women, often suspecting their unlimited capacity for orgasms and sex, fear exploring erotic places with a husband who might ask a wife who has suddenly made love in a new way: "Where did you learn that?"

Most modern husbands, of course, would be absolutely delighted, for many modern marriages are aiming to be erotic. But the traditional marriage, built out of a sense of affection, duty, and responsibility, is still the norm. Alternative life-styles of communal and open marriage have not been in existence long enough to observe whether they can work indefinitely. Because marriage often is the giving up of personal freedom, sometimes its participants do not flourish well in the self-indulgent gardens of deep eroticism.

A majority of modern men and women are trying to explore different expressions of the marital experience. While this is happening, the most startling information revealed in this chapter is that unhappy wives are taking steps to fulfill themselves in fantasy, and often in reality.

There are several stages of this behavior. Lynn, a young bride, is at Stage One, where she dares not make her fantasy a reality.

Lynn

She is right out of *Modern Bride*—small, fragile, with long blonde hair and innocent eyes. She must have looked wonderful in her white wedding gown. The apartment is all new, modern furniture. Lynn is wearing a low, tight sweater with sequins on it and tight jeans. She is Cassandra, Seventies-style.

"Something changed after we married," she says sadly, drinking a Tab. "Something different happened. Before marriage, we had no place to be alone because we were living separately with our families to save money. We'd make love whenever we could. It was quick, but it was exciting. It was great.

"I was worried that I wasn't having the kind of orgasm I'd read about. But Bob said not to worry, it would happen when we had a place of our own. But it hasn't. He's working around the clock at the hospital, I have to get up for my job, and everything seems to be rush, rush, rush.

"You know, guys come on with me all the time. There's a black guy down the hall who always says that I need loving. I just pretend I don't understand his mutterings. But I do understand. I come home and masturbate every time I see him. I think about him, not Bob, and then afterward, I feel so guilty."

"Guilty just about thoughts?"

"Yes. Because someday I'm afraid I'll get hung up and do it with him. What would Bob think? How could I face him?"

"Do you tell Bob you have sexual fantasies?"

"He'd die. I know he would. He'd be so hurt. I couldn't do that." The universal remark of the universal woman. *Her* fantasies would destroy *him.*

"But he has fantasies all the time, about movie stars, girls in magazines, doesn't he? Would you leave him because of them?"

"Of course not." She pauses. "All I know is that when I come back from seeing that guy, I'm hot all over. I usually take the phone off the hook and take a real hot bath. Then I stand in front of the mirror and pretend he's there, pretend my hand is his hand, pretend he has this big black cock. Then, too, I bought this." She goes over to one of her bureau drawers, opens it, and takes out a large Kotex box. Digging into it, she takes out a smaller box. When she opens it, I see a large plastic dildo. "It's incredible. It feels like what I've always dreamed the real thing is." The dildo is black, like the man in her fantasy.

"Good hiding place?" I question.

"Oh, yes. Bob would never go into my bureau drawer. He respects my privacy."

Lynn is a young bride, talking before the true responsibilities of marriage and children have entered her life. Yet, she is keeping her erotic fantasy separate from her husband, almost as she would from a parent, as if it were something to be ashamed of. It is interesting that Lynn's story, what I call "Stage One" of the marriage experience, runs through the other interviews.

With the next interview, Alice, the marriage has developed into Stage Two, the executive wife:

Alice

"I met my husband when he graduated college as an engineer. He's worked very long and hard to get where he is," Alice says, playing with the long blue ribbon in her curly blonde hair. *Alice-Blue-Gown* and *Alice in Wonderland* images come to mind as I sit opposite this tall, thin, thirty-year-old woman who is dressed like a high-school student in a T-shirt and jeans. Her apartment in this suburb of Detroit is furnished in the *House Beautiful* style for an executive, with its plastic look. A large parking lot in the rear boasts Detroit's own autos almost like national pride.

Alice is playing rock music loudly and makes gestures to the music as she speaks to me.

"How's your sex life?" I ask, above the roar.

She moves her glass of iced tea to the music's timing, nervously answering the question. "When I first met my husband, I started sleeping with him almost immediately. It was a good, nice, normal relationship. He was grabbing me everywhere. We rented motel rooms for an hour just to have sex.

"Then we got married, and we began having sex less and less. It wasn't as exciting somehow. Before we got married, I never had any trouble coming to a climax. But after, I just never came anymore."

"What happened?"

She scoops the lemon wedge from the glass, munches on it, tearing it hostilely to tiny little pieces, putting tiny bits in her mouth, munching some more, all the while flitting her false eyelashes at me in Santana rock time. She is a study in conflict, her bleached-blonde locks and her cosmetically made-up face jarring the casualness of her dress. "Well, my husband is very, very wrapped up in his career," she says sourly. "His family were Polish immigrants, and his father was a mechanic who wanted his sons to get ahead. So my husband is a very, very hard worker, very conscientious, and just doesn't think about sex as much as I do."

"Do you think about it a lot?"

"All the time. I had very boring jobs after I left school to get married. So I had a lot of time to think, and I thought about sex all the time, masturbated all the time. I started to flirt with other men. As a matter of fact, we went on vacation, and I fell in love with the ski instructor."

"Did your husband know?"

"No!" She hangs her head in shame, then says defensively, tears in her blue eyes, "We have a pleasant life. My husband really fulfills all of my security needs, and he never makes me jealous. I went through a whole childhood of being insecure, and my husband is the only person who gives me a feeling that I'm okay."

"If you care for him so much, why can't you make love to him?" I ask softly.

"I feel I can't make a fool of myself. I want to say and do things that are physically totally free, loose, uninhibited, screw anything, no holes barred, but I feel I could never do that with my husband."

"Why not?"

Now she looks totally vulnerable, with hurt in her eyes, a sad hurt, an old hurt. "One time when we were still dating, my folks weren't home, so I came to the door in a little shortie nightgown with holes at the nipples and at the vagina which I had cut out. My husband laughed at me. I was really upset, and he tried to say it was cute. But I guess since then I've always been turned off about being sexy with him."

"Can you be sexy with other men?"

She sighs, as if dreading the subject. "I knew you'd ask that question," she says defensively. There is a silence while she decides whether to tell me or not. I remind her that the interview is anonymous and she relaxes a bit. 'Well, I began driving to coffee shops at the university every afternoon where I met young students. And things began to happen.

"One would phone me every morning after my husband left for work. He'd ask me, 'What are you wearing?' and I'd say, 'A T-shirt and undies.' He'd ask if I was warm or cold, if my body was warm. Then he'd say, 'Take off your panties,' and I'd do it. He'd say, "I wish I were there. If I were there, I'd just put my finger in your cunt. How's your cunt?' I'd tell him it was warm and wet. Then he'd tell me to touch my nipples and tell him how they felt. Then he'd tell me to start masturbating and I'd mastur-bate myself to climax." At this very moment, the rock record goes into a long wail, and I wonder at its timing. Alice looks terribly, terribly ashamed of what she has just told me.

"The student excited you, didn't he?"

"I liked hearing his voice describing things. I like verbal peo-ple. My husband is not one of them."

"Did you have an affair with this student?"

She gets up from her chair, does two steps to the music, bumps and grinds as she avoids my question, and I wait doggedly for her return. "No, not him, but one of his friends," she finally answers.

"Why not him?"

"Because he knows my husband and I know his wife and I just couldn't do it behind their backs."

"What about his friend?" I ask, always fascinated by the moral-ity codes of sexual partnering.

The phone rings, interrupting the interview. Alice, answering it, takes on the gestures of a child, her voice becomes sickeningly sweet, and I wonder whether it is her telephone lover. In a min-ute, though, I realize it is her husband because she is lying to the caller, telling him she is having lunch with a neighbor and is very bored. When she returns, she explains that her husband would get very upset if he knew she was telling personal stuff to a stranger.

"How about the young man? What happened with him?" I persist.

"Well, he lived alone. When my husband left in the morning, I would drive to his place. I'd say hello, and he'd hop on me, and a second later we were undressed and in bed. We would fuck for hours, until he had to go to class. I became totally involved with his cock. I had never really liked penises much before, but I gave him blow jobs constantly. I could go on for hours. With my hus-band, that really never turned me on.

"I told this young kid that I wanted more sex and I thought about sex with him all the time. He said that was fine with him. He turned me on, and we just fucked and fucked for eight months. I would sit on his head and he would eat me. My husband and I rarely had oral sex, and I didn't know how great it was."

"Why didn't you have oral sex?"

"I always thought: How could anyone possibly want to lick and kiss my cunt? To me, it was just a smelly piece of fish. When I first met my husband, he wanted to touch my cunt, and I told him I'd rather he'd fuck me than touch that dirty thing."

"Did you feel that way about his penis?"

"No, because his penis was clean, but my cunt had all those secretions. As a matter of fact, I would make my husband brush his teeth before going to sleep if we had oral sex."

"Did you tell your husband about the affair?"

She looks defeated, old, and tired suddenly. "Yes," she says guiltily. "He said, 'I don't want to know about it. I just want you to promise it won't happen again.' Then he said, 'Don't you think I fantasize? Don't you think I want to do all kinds of different things, want to experiment?' I told him I really didn't know if he did or not. Since then, our sex life has been completely different."

"How different?"

"Well, when we first got married, I used to ask him what gave him pleasure. He would say that spoiled it for him if we talked about it. He would say that talking was just like using a cookbook. But now, he told me that the most sensitive part of his penis was right under the rim. So I kiss him, I suck him there, and I can see he loves it."

She draws a sharp breath as she speaks of turning her husband on. "I never told him that I wanted to be sucked. He would always suck my breasts but not my vagina, so I told him to suck me and I loved it. He does it all the time now. I do it to him, but I don't swallow the semen because I saw a prostitute on television who said she couldn't lose weight because each ejaculation was two hundred calories."

I laugh at this caloric information. But she doesn't join me—her tone is ultraserious. "We go to porno films now. We went to see *The Devil in Miss Jones* and went home and fucked for four hours that afternoon. We were both extremely excited by watching the woman masturbate.

"Generally, I want a lot of sex, so we have sex every night now," she says proudly. "He'll touch my breasts, then my cunt. I'll kiss his chest, stomach, cock, balls, legs. Then his ass. He's very into asses and I'm not, but sometimes I get into the mood. Then I

79

suck him and he becomes hard, turns me around, and I go down on him. But I'll never throw my cunt in his face, even though he always wants that. Then we'll switch positions, and I masturbate and take my juices and rub them on my face, and he sucks them off. Then I have a climax when he enters me. And that's it for me. The second time around is never as exciting."

She feels the interview is over because it has a happy ending, and when I ask her the next question, I see her getting very, very angry. "Has your husband been faithful to you?"

Startled, as if I have said something totally unrealistic, her voice gets very nasty, and she starts to twitch. "He said it would be very easy for him to go out and grab a piece of ass if he wanted to, but he didn't because of me. I couldn't stand it if he did."

"Why do you think you could do it and then couldn't understand it if he did?" I am almost always totally amazed at the fascism involved in adultery.

She is annoyed at me and ends her conversation with me rudely. "Because there are two different sides to me. Part of me is the executive wife"—she waves her hands around, motioning to the sterile apartment—"and part of me is a hippie. I am not the woman you are talking to all the time. It is very easy for me to slip from one role into another." She begins ushering me toward the door.

"Which one is the most sexual?"

"This one," she says defiantly, opening the door. "The other one, the executive wife, is just putting on a show. *It's like being a puppet, being someone's wife.*"

I step through the doorway, and she slams the door after me.

This interview was interesting for many, many reasons. For one thing, upon the admission of her extramarital activity, Alice did get closer to her husband and his sexuality. Thus, their sexual life seems to be more enjoyable for both of them. But, unfortunately, Alice does not give her husband the very thing he has tried to give her: understanding of his sexual fantasies and needs. This is a rare instance of reversal of roles, for it is usually the woman who is the understanding one, trying to accept her husband's sexual fantasies and needs.

It is always amusing to me when I interview married people (and the male side of this is discussed in Chapter 8) how, when they admit their "adulterous" activities, they never even consider that their partner might be equally driven. Except in open marriages, where frank discussions of this kind are encouraged, marriage seems to exist in a totalitarian state ruled by a fantasy of always being faithful.

Of course, Alice was very lucky because her husband decided to be understanding rather than give in to his jealousy. Amy, in her second marriage, is not so lucky.

Amy

She is wearing a turtle-neck sweater under a smashing tweed suit, accessorized by handcrafted boots and bag. Her skin is tawny, giving the impression of an Egyptian queen. She is tall, thin, conservative, and is married to one of the busiest black movie producers. Although they have lived in their beach house for over a year, it is furnished sparsely, with no personal items in evidence except for plaques bearing his name for various awards he has won in the industry.

The furniture is brown, the drapes are brown, the rug and the picture frames are brown. As I enjoy the elegance of Amy's appearance, I wonder at the drabness of her surroundings.

"I'm a fairly conservative person," she says of herself. "During the day, I'm prim and proper. I like to be alone a lot, like to meditate. One of the reasons I like living with my husband is he makes no demands upon me. He comes home, stretches out with the paper, and leaves me to myself. Until, of course, we get into bed," she smiles mischievously. Then she describes what she calls the wanton part of her personality. "We have sex all the time. I don't particularly like oral sex, but I like to be on top. My husband is very, very good, and the only time our sex has fallen off is when he's had business pressures. He's so very sweet and old-fashioned about women and what their roles are. But perhaps he's clever, because he often lets me play the part of the aggressor in bed and at other times."

She giggles as she changes her personality from a chic, tailored woman to the delightful courtesan. "I embarrass him. If we're at a party, I'll say, 'Come on to the bathroom with me for a few minutes,' and he'll blush and say, 'No, Amy, you're going to embarrass me.' But if he comes, I just invite him to sit down on the john and say, 'Drop your pants down.' He thinks I'm just a wanton hussy, and I love that. In fact," she goes on in her courtesan mood, "I hate the fact that husbands don't come home for lunch or whenever the mood hits them. That's why I stay home, hoping he'll come home. And . . . my husband doesn't want me to work."

She points to a photograph of a very handsome, vital-looking man in his early fifties. "But I have to protect myself. I've got a pension fund I collect money from when I'm fifty-five. After all, he's so much older than I am and doesn't want me to work. What am I supposed to do later in life?"

Amy's gorgeous green eyes are reminiscent of Cleopatra, and I imagine her in those clothes in another setting. Thus, I ask her about her fantasies, wondering about the drabness of her environment, the tailoring of her dress.

"I constantly think of making love to men I don't know. I keep feeling sensuous in elevators and wonder what would happen if I did it. I look at a man's body and wonder how it would be to sleep with him, but I can't do anything about it," she says bitterly.

"Why not?" After all, we were in Hollywood, U.S.A.

"Because my husband said if he found out he'd kill me," she says matter-of-factly. "He's been married before and says that I'm his last chance for marital happiness and he loves me very, very much. So he said he would murder me if I was adulterous."

I can see that she absolutely believes he would. "Do you think he's unfaithful?"

Her eyes look suddenly concerned. "I don't know. You know, there are the usual wife suspicions. Like when women call here. But in his business . . . well, I've never really asked him."

She changes her mood and takes a cigarette, lights it, flips an imaginary ash, puts the cigarette down in the ashtray, putting out the flame. She is disgusted with herself for giving in to a momentary need for tobacco. "I'm happy with him because I get a lot of emotional support from him. I'm kind of a neurotic bitch, and my husband is too wishy-washy sometimes. Like, he never expresses his preference for things.

"I'm very opinionated and very bossy and aggressive. But I can't get him to talk about certain things, like how it feels to be inside me. I know he gets very far inside, and I really want to ask a man how it feels to be inside and what happens to him in there. But," she adds, "I can only talk to my girlfriends about that kind of intimacy."

"But he really turns me on," she says happily. "It's his hairy chest and his buttocks. They're so firm, and his little pants fit him so well. I really love the way those slacks fit him. I like the fact that I'm special in his life, but I tell him I'd rather not be a wife. I'd rather be his mistress, because wives are so dull. I want to be the kind of exciting sexy person that men slip around and see and so forth. But he's so old-fashioned, it's hard for him to express his feelings. And I bitch to him—I'm not a nice, sweet, boring wife. It's the kiss of death to be sweet and nice."

"Do you tell him about your fantasies?"

She shakes her head with wifely concern. "No, I feel I'm being charitable, because if his head can't take it, why inflict that kind of hurt on him?"

"Will you forget them, or are you going to do anything about them?"

"Well," she smiles, showing her beautiful white teeth, perfectly formed. "I go to the Caribbean a lot. I love the men down there. Their bodies are so beautiful—swarthy, very dark, firm, and lean. Last winter a strange man kissed me in an elevator just as he got out and said, 'You're so beautiful.' When he went out of the elevator and the doors shut, I thought, *My God, that's one of the most exciting highlights of my life.*

"You know, a new, strange person can really fill your fantasy. He doesn't know that you are a bitch and mean and that you have cramps and how you look in the morning. But," she concludes, a sad note in her voice, "when you get to be thirty and say—Well, listen that's ten years from forty and instead of being little and cute, you're going to be awfully old and cute, and you wonder, *Gee, is there anything out there that I've missed sexually?*"

Amy seems a practical, sensible woman who really loves her husband and ignores his possessiveness, playing with it rather than making it an issue. I was struck by her demands for a pension fund. Like the old courtesans of earlier times, Amy seemed to be saying, "Okay, if I give up everything for you, you'll have to take care of me." Naturally, as his wife she will inherit his estate, but she prefers that he give her a pension fund, almost as an employer would. I liked Amy and her fantasies and wondered if there were any circumstances in which she would act them out and/or tell her husband. But I doubted it, because she seemed absolutely certain that he would resort to violence, though perhaps she needed to feel that way, to use that lever to hold her eroticism in check.

A major ingredient in marriage for women seems to be making their husbands almost a censor of their particular erotic fantasies and needs. Often, when a woman has had children and is unsatisfied with her sex life with her husband, the fact of being a mother somehow gives her permission to branch out. This is true of Mary.

Mary

Now thirty, and married since she was nineteen, Mary is the mother of two children. Mary has used affairs and fantasy to get through her days. "My husband is not an affectionate person. I like sexual foreplay a lot. With him, it's, 'Well, the basketball game is over, let's go upstairs and screw.' Or, 'There's nothing on television tonight, let's go upstairs and screw.' While I'm a cuddler when I like people, John never touches me until he penetrates."

Small, dark, petite, with wide birdlike eyes, Mary is not uncomfortable about complaining. "When I was a bride, we'd get undressed and screw, but I always felt like a whore. There was no prelude, no affection afterward. This went on until I had the kids. After that, everything changed. Because I changed it."

I look about the cliché white-frame house on a country lane in Connecticut, to which men in dark, conservative suits give most of their energy and thoughts to maintain. It really is a house devoted to marital fantasy, and has everything—a pool in summer, ice skating in winter—and is decorated gaily with cherry gingham curtains and hardy furniture. I get very depressed that the idyllic setting in Mary's case does not seem to have any validity. Or does it? Is this what marriage is all about?

"How did you change things?" I ask, although I suspect her answer will be the same as most of the married women I have interviewed.

"Well, one night we went out with the neighbors on the right." She gestures to another perfect, Connecticut, white-frame house, higher and narrower. "Johnny, my husband, got very tired and so did my neighbor's wife. I said I wanted to go get ice cream, so Sam volunteered to take me.

"I had felt attracted to Sam ever since he moved next door. I thought, *I'll bet he's terrific in bed.* He was so handsome and had so much money. So when we went for ice cream, we sat in his car and talked. Then we were embracing and kissing. We must have stayed out way past midnight. When I got home, Johnny was fast asleep.

"Of course, I immediately fantasized double divorces and remarriages. But that didn't happen." She pauses, reflecting seriously. "What did happen is that he had lots of money so I would go into the city twice a week, and we would meet in the Waldorf for lunch in a private suite." She sighs happily. "It was wonderful."

Then, giggling with pleasure as she remembers what went on, she continues, "We raced to take off our clothes and jumped into bed. We were playful and stroked each other. We ranged from kidding around to holding on to each other for dear life. We touched, had oral sex, kissed all over, shared everything. I really felt turned on for the first time. I discovered there was a whole other way sex could be."

She pauses in the interview as her children return from school. They too fitted the marriage fantasy—a beautiful, blonde girl and a dark-haired boy, appropriately hungry, raiding the refrigerator, regarding me with curiosity, then running up to their bedrooms to watch something or other on television. *My God, the television commercials are right!* I think. *This is a happy family.*

"Sam was only the first one," she continues, handing me a cup of hot water for which we share a Lipton's tea bag. "After Sam, I realized that it was a fantasy to think that affairs would lead to re-marriage. So I stopped thinking that. Then I met this younger man, and we had a thing. As a matter of fact," she says in a motherly tone, "we became good friends. He just got married, and we managed to keep close, which is nice."

When Mary isn't having an affair, she indulges in sexual fantasies. "I ride the train and close my eyes, and if anyone on the train is attractive, I think about sleeping with him. I make it real with faces, and voices, and words. Or if I'm having lunch alone and see someone, I wonder what it would be like to be alone in a room with him. I visualize passionate kissing and kissing all over and bodies and stroking.

"I try to get a mental picture," she giggles. "When Johnny asks me what I'm thinking, I tell him I'm thinking about the kids."

Mary's fantasies are becoming more and more real, more often. "Last month, I met this guy, and we had a quick snack, and I realized I wanted to make it with him. I said to myself, *Fuck it, I'm going to sleep with him and I'm going to tell him.* So we had terrific eye contact, and I said, 'Wouldn't it be terrific if we could go to bed together?' and we did."

"You sound proud of yourself, Mary."

She smiles and seems to grow several inches taller as she straightens up in her armchair. "I sure am. You know that movie with Barbra Streisand and Robert Redford where she was the ugly duckling who got Redford. That's me. I had always been fat and unattractive as a child. Now I'm getting my share. I'm crazy about it. When I discovered I was a woman and it's nice to have a great body, it was wonderful.

"It started when I began to diet. And when I began to masturbate, all in the same year. I was twenty-seven years old and my husband was still cranky if his dinner wasn't on the table. So every day after the kids went to school, I would go up and masturbate in my bedroom. It was great to realize that I didn't need him. Then I could tell him, 'Fuck you, buddy, you can cook, too, you know.' "

Mary is getting prettier and prettier and gayer and gayer as she talks to me. She begins to blush. Can it be sexual, just from talking about it?

"I'm really turned on now," she says happily. "The other day I went to a lunch given by the teachers at the kids' school. One teacher sat beside me. He said, 'You know that orange pants outfit that you wear sometimes? When you walk down the hall, everybody turns around and looks at you.' I told him I wasn't aware of that. He said, 'When you pass, everybody looks at your ass.' I loved it. He really turned me on then. Then he said he liked my ass, and that other people liked my ass, too. We were sitting in a restaurant, and he asked, 'Are those eyelashes yours?' I said they were mine. He said, 'Your eyes look so nice by candlelight.' That's nice. That's really nice.

"People like that touch me. They send out messages, like they want to come over and put their arms about me. I love to have my hair played with, and he reached out and touched my hair. Then I could have been his slave forever.

"Sometimes I'm not really quite sure how I look. If I'm walking down the street or standing in those incredibly crowded elevators and I see people looking at me, I sometimes look back at them and wonder what they see."

Mary was courageous, after having had an unhappy childhood, to reach out and form affectionate and sexual friendships which could give her a security about being a woman which marriage, her husband, and her children have not been able to give her. I guess Europeans call Mary sensible, for she is not upsetting the apple cart, is keeping her husband and children happy, and is still getting what she wants sexually. Sometimes I think we Americans are much too romantic when we feel that men and women should live openly and freely with their sexual needs and preferences.

Something quite humorous to note, incidentally, is the occurrence of elevators as a turn-on in these married women's erotic fantasies. I wonder whether it is symbolic. I wonder whether the elevator symbolizes the claustrophobic atmosphere of marriage, with the elevator doors symbolizing escape. Of course, an elevator does travel up and down, and marriage does that, too.

The modern view of fantasy claims fantasy is experienced even in happy marriages. In this marital chapter, it seems that the use of fantasy coincides more with Freud's view that frustration with their lives and their marital partners leads these women to openly fantasize. The only deviation from Freud's theory is that these women seem to be doing something to act out their fantasies, whatever they may be, with the only concern being that the husband should not know about it. This intriguing, romantic, rendezvous idea, once a possession of the chic upper class, seems to have no class distinction now, probably due to the great media blitz on sexual change. Even in the blue-collar class, always the last bastion of fidelity because of religious and material reasons, sexual rendezvous have made their frontier landings. Marie is a case in point.

Marie

As we drive down the street in the limousine hired for the wedding, we stop suddenly. I know I have to leave the car. My husband helps me out. My gown is of white eyelet. A long veil, with wax forget-me-nots, covers my dark, curly hair. I am wearing nothing underneath my gown, and the soft pink tone of my flesh and my nipples shows through. As I step from the limo, my gown tears right up the front. I realize my vagina is showing. I try to cover it with my hands, but it is too large.

Three black boys are standing on the corner, watching me. I run down the street. One of them grabs my veil in an attempt to capture me. But I run on, away from them. I come to a subway station and run down the stairs, losing a fragile satin slipper as I hurry. There is no one on duty, and I duck under the turnstile, hoping I can catch the train waiting there. I get to the doors too late; they slam in my face. When I turn around, I notice all of the other passengers have left. The black boys are guarding each entrance, mugging the commuters as they leave the station.

I want to escape, but there is nowhere to go. I want to jump onto the tracks, but I'm afraid of death. The boys are coming down the stairs now. I stand there, trembling, my hands still attempting to hide my vagina, and failing. One boy grabs me and tears my dress even more. I fall on the cold stone subway platform. He puts his fat black lips on my vagina and begins eating me with relish. Another boy puts his dirty hands on my breasts, playing with the nipples. I am shocked to see that my nipples are standing erect. They turn me on my side so the third boy can get behind me. He pulls up my wedding train and puts his large penis in my rectum. He begins sodomizing me.

I am trembling with fear. Suddenly I begin trembling with another feeling—a hot excitement. I am losing my head. I am losing my consciousness. I begin to beg them for more. They laugh at me. One boy's tongue is in my cunt, squeezing, probing. I think it will meet the other boy's cock in my rectum. I begin screaming. "Shut her up!" the leader commands. The third boy then takes his penis and puts it in my mouth, forcing me to become silent.

I feel them come almost together. The leader's come is all over my legs. The others' are in my throat and rectum. Their screams are lost as the express trains roar by. They are coming in every part of me. And I love it. I love it. I love it.

The white house seems to shake in its very foundations as Marie, the woman of the house, tells me of her frequent fantasy. The house is in a quiet, segregated neighborhood in Queens. Marie, mother of two children, is talking to me in a low, proper voice. As she speaks, she pours espresso coffee into her golden demitasse cups. The house is decorated in Renaissance Italian, with gilded mirrors and golden baroque angels lining the wall. I sit on a couch of orange brocade, covered with a thick plastic, which conveys to me the feeling that I will be perennially hot and sticky, even though the air-conditioner is hovering near and blowing its mighty wind in my direction.

I do not feel at ease in suburbia since we live very different lives. Marie and I met accidentally at a women's conference on sexuality. She was repairing her eye makeup in the women's toilets. When I entered, she looked at me with a suspicious manner which

I recognized—at women's conferences there are always a lot of lesbians in the ladies' toilets, making out. After she relaxed, I realized that she was in tears. I asked her what was the matter. "Everything," she said.

Later, in a coffee shop, she told me she had been married for fifteen years and was thinking of leaving her husband and was scared to death at the prospect. I asked her what was wrong.

"Sex," she said bitterly.

My head involuntarily shook in agreement for it all sounded very familiar. When I told her I was writing a book on sex, marital and otherwise, she agreed to an anonymous interview.

After I settle back and taste the coffee, I plunge right in.

"What's going on?"

"Jack thinks I'm crazy," she says sadly.

I had heard this from women many times before. "Let's talk about it."

"We have a terrific life in many ways. He's making more as a salesman than we ever dreamed. We own this house. The children go to a private, religious school. I have two fur coats. We have two cars. We both like our friends and love to party. Only, since the kids are busy at school all day, I've been sort of bored."

"Why don't you get a job?" I ask in my best feminist manner.

"I've thought about it, but it scares me. If I get a job, I'll really leave Jack, for sure. You know, we had a terrific fight about my going to the conference. He doesn't want me to do anything outside of our little circle."

"What happens in bed?" I get straight to the point.

"It's—well—all he wants me to do is suck his cock. He just lies there, touching himself. I hear his breathing grow wilder and wilder. I try to touch myself while he's doing that, you know, to get hot. But he caught me and called me a whore. Well, if I am, I'm his whore. I wear all these expensive, silky things because he likes it, and I want to turn him on. He really excites me. I love his body. Love his ass," she giggles.

I am surprised at her language for she is still sitting properly on her plastic-covered chair, legs crossed. Marie is wearing a very proper, floral-print dress which hangs below her knees. An attractive woman, her dark hair is neatly kept, her nails are short and clean and do not reflect the housework she must do. But I sense her anger.

"So then he turns to me and says, 'Want it, baby?' So I turn over and put my mouth on him, and when he comes, he says, 'That'll make you beautiful, baby.' I used to ask him to touch me, but it got too difficult. He'd ask me, 'Like that? Like that?' all the time. Jesus, he wouldn't even let me enjoy what was happening. So now I just lie back and have that fantasy."

"The one with the black boys?"

"Yes, that one," she says bitterly. "I invented it from one of those fantasy magazines," she explains.

"Why that one?"

Her voice gets very low. "I'm not proud of this, but I hate blacks." I wait. "I'm not proud of other things, too," she finally adds.

"What do you mean?"

She sighs. Her hands now gesture as she speaks. "Well, from time to time, I drive into the city. There is a restaurant I found about three years ago where a lot of interesting people lunch. If I arrive there at about two-thirty P.M., there is always some well-dressed guy who doesn't want to go back to the office."

"What do you mean?" I ask, puzzled.

"Well, the first time I did it, I was kind of scared. But the guy was well dressed, he showed me his credit cards, and told me where he lived, and that he was married. He had a key to somebody's ritzy apartment on Lexington Avenue. I told him I didn't want to know what his problems were. That day, it was the best sex I ever had."

"Why?"

"I thought about that. It's because he had no hold over me, no power. I won't ever have to see him again. He doesn't know my real name or address. I never have to cook his supper," she laughs to herself, her lips firm, "never!"

"What was it like?"

"It was terrific. He was well built, like my husband. But he let me do anything I wanted. I sucked it, till it was so sore. By the time he left for Connecticut, it was all red. I hope his wife didn't see it," she giggles. "I was pretty sore, too."

"Why can't you do it with Jack? The same way, I mean?"

"You can't tell your husband what you want sexually. He'll ask you where you got those ideas. He'll think you're a whore."

"But that's so dangerous, going to bed with strangers. One might be a strangler, a rapist, or something," I caution.

"As long as he doesn't kill me, everything else is okay," she says, quietly giggling to herself.

It is unfortunate that Marie must pick up strangers for matinee sex, but in her cultural setting she would be considered a "whore" if she had an extramarital affair. I felt badly that the passion that Marie wanted to explore with her husband had to be fantasized and acted out in such a schizoid manner. For Marie, a woman who is afraid to leave her husband, only another marriage proposal would help her make her escape. And by keeping her extramarital affairs so separate from her real life, I doubt she will have any chance at a second proposal from one of the men she enjoys on her matinees.

An interesting contrast to Marie's story is the story of Nancy, a black woman of the same age group, in her second marriage.

Nancy

In a twelve-room house outside of Atlanta, everything looks like Christmas. The antiques and wood paneling blend with a couch of an orangey color. The mirrors on the wall reflect large candle chandeliers. Around a pearl-top table in this romantic setting, Nancy and I have a cup of coffee.

Working as a nurse, Nancy, who is fortyish, is married for the second time and has four daughters. The combined earnings of the family is middle-class average, and one of the ways they spend it is on good food.

"I put a little sex in the pot, so my cooking usually turns people on," Nancy says, laughing.

A sweet smile takes over her sensuous face, and I remark that she looks twenty years younger. "It's my enthusiasm. I give my food a little different kind of spice and make people wonder how come it tastes that way."

Although there are many, many rooms in their house, Nancy feels she doesn't have enough privacy, so her husband and she only have sex on Sunday mornings. "You know, I grew up in Mississippi with a large family—seven girls and three boys. We were always exploring each other and wondering what things were for. I used to dance with my older brother and his penis would get hard, but nothing ever happened."

Her attitude about this seems easygoing. She describes the practice of her husband and children walking around naked and thinking nothing of it. "We never bother to hide anything. One time my kids saw my sleeping husband with his penis erect, and they started beating it with a towel."

In the short period between her first and second marriage, Nancy discovered that she didn't like oral sex. "I had my first experience with a much older man. He asked me to have a relationship with him and took his penis out. Then he took my head and pushed me down on it. I just wriggled, and that left a very bad taste in my mouth.

"In fact, I didn't want to get married again because it was either participate in oral sex or become an outcast."

However, Nancy has gotten over her distaste. She exudes charm as she tells about a man named Adam she's dying to do all kinds of sex with.

Her eyes get very deep and fill with passion as she speaks. "God, he sends me off. In fact, when I'm making love to Donald, my husband, I think of Adam. I had sex with Adam already. In fact, whenever I think of Adam, I just get warm. In fact, right now." She gets up from her chair, goes over to the stove, turns on the gas flame, and says a bit shamelessly, "I feel warm right here, just talking about him. He really turns me on."

Nancy and Donald have a very casual attitude about monogamy. "I know Donald has other women, but I don't ask questions," she says candidly. "Because I know he likes me and will stay married to me. But he has hurt me in the past and, you see, Adam never has."

"How did your husband hurt you?"

"He becomes cold sometimes. I give him all I have, love him madly, and he still turns cold. I can't keep changing and changing, so I got to the point where I killed off my sensuous feelings. Now I'm warm to him on Sunday mornings, and we like each other, but I can't forget the hurts."

When I ask her what the most erotic experience of her life was, Nancy proceeds to tell me a tale of violence. "When I went to talk to my first husband about our divorce, he said we're going to have sex. I refused, and he picked me up, put me on the bed, took an ice pick, and put it right between my breasts. I lay there, petrified. Finally a sound at the door took his attention away, and I jumped out of the second-story window. I just ran. I even stopped traffic. Then I collapsed."

Nancy tells this story sadly, her tone grim. But there is no anger in her voice, as if she has no right to express it. She confirms the fact that she feels she has no right to vent her fury. "I can't even get angry with my husband. Sometimes I think I didn't marry the right person. He doesn't really turn me on."

Recently, attending a meeting in another city, Nancy was turned on. "I was reading this sex book on the train, *The Sensuous Woman*, and this young man said he'd love to see me after I finished the book because he'd been reading it, too. So I told him where I would be staying.

"That night, he called. We had drinks and food, and he got into bed with me. He was very gentle and touched my clitoris and really sent me off. I braced myself, was on my knees in a position that really stimulated me. I was stroking his head, caressing his penis." She gasps with pleasure as she tells me of this. "I had never caressed a penis before, but the book told me how to do it. I would touch the rim of his penis with my mouth, and he was utterly excited about it. I pushed my buttocks up to him and could touch his balls." She clasps her hands in prayer as she describes the orgasm with this stranger, which she has never duplicated since. "I don't know . . . it felt so *lucrative* inside. I just kept going and going."

As I smile at her use of the word "lucrative," she wipes the perspiration from her forehead. "I wish I could get Adam to do that," she says, and I am startled to find she is talking about her lover, not her husband. "I go up to his office all the time and chase him around the desk, but he's so slow when I catch up to him. A couple of weeks ago I just touched him and could feel this tickling sensation all over my body. What I really want to do is just get inside of him.

"I'd really like to go wild with him," she says ruefully.

Nancy's sensitivity to her husband's callousness is not unusual. In the day-to-day living situation, there are many moments of hurt as well as tenderness. It is common too that once someone has been hurt, the defenses never come down again. Nancy could pursue Adam because the slate was clean, but she couldn't attempt to deepen her relationship with her husband. Her attitude toward marriage was one of extreme casualness. She didn't put too much into it and didn't want too much out of it.

Hearing all these tales of illicit marital affairs, I wondered if it would be different to have extramarital affairs with persons in the so-called life-style of the Open Marriage. Here is one example of this kind of marriage.

Doris

Doris is a voluptuous woman, a goddess in beads and denims. She has a shy quality which is at odds with her statuesque presence. When she begins to speak in a meek, low voice containing the slight southern accent of New Orleans where she lives, one is surprised that she is talking about prostitution rather than what foods her children like.

"I've been married to Harold since I was nineteen," she begins, glowing at her mention of her husband. "That was six years ago. This year, I met a madam at a party and really got turned on to her and worked for her during the day while Harold took care of the children. I loved it.

"The madam and I were about the same size, and when I'd arrive in my jeans, she'd take me to the closet and let me pick out anything to wear. But the job didn't last long because the madam told me I took too long when I gave a guy a blow job," she giggles. "Most of those guys never had a blow job like that because nobody had ever taken the time to play with their cocks.

"Also, one of the last guys I blew was a policeman," she confides, "and that really freaked me out." She speaks with a mixture of fear and boldness which is constant in her entire manner.

"How did your husband feel about your working as a prostitute?"

Her eyes glitter as she answers. "Well, the madam used to let me wear this gorgeous white fur coat home, and I felt like a million dollars. I was also very horny, and I would throw the money all over the bed and say to Harold, 'Well, look at this.' And he'd be there with a grin on his face, and then we'd ball and ball. That's how I got the idea of going into business for myself." She laughs as she opens a bottle of orange soda, in a lusty manner.

"My first customer was a Sicilian truck driver who was very, very short, but very, very strong. He was impotent. So we talked about it, and I gave him a massage. The next thing you know, he had an erection. We got into fucking, and it lasted quite a while. When we finished, we were lying there laughing about how that happened, and he got another hard-on. So we fucked two times. I told him he was fantastic."

"Did he turn you on?"

"Working with my customers can be very satisfying sexually, but it leaves me at a peak. I go home really turned on, and really wanting to fuck Harold. He likes to hear what I've been doing. I turn him on. Last week was great! In one day I fucked seven times, four of those times with my husband, and the other three with customers.

"I masturbate a lot, too, especially before I go to sleep. If I wake up during the night, it always puts me back to sleep. I never used to masturbate in front of Harold or my customers, but I do now. It turns some of them on. I don't have orgasms with penetration . . . never have. My orgasms are from finger-fucking."

Doris then explains her favorite kind of finger-fucking. "A gynecologist showed me a way men can do it to me. The man puts his fingers in behind the clitoris and he spreads them out. You can't do it yourself. Anyway, the man opens his fingers and rubs really fast inside the vagina, pressing up against the pubic bone. There are two little bulbs that come down on either side of the small lips from the clitoris, and he can only get to them from the inside. Oh, that's a fantastic orgasm. That's what I consider my vaginal orgasm. I always dream that I'm going to find a certain size penis that can fit into that place."

"What kind is that?"

"I like men big, strong, tall, and young. I like men with hairy chests, big shoulders, strong-looking arms. My husband is like that. The cock makes a difference to me. And a man's cleanliness. If he's clean about himself, if he wipes his ass, that's good. Nobody is going to blow anybody who's dirty, I tell my customers. Most times most men are clean.

"I'm married to a guy with a big cock, and I get off better with a guy with a smaller cock. I don't like to fuck men who are seeing other women, because I'm really afraid of getting a disease. So I make my customers only fuck their wives, besides me."

"What about your open marriage?" I query.

"I'm kind of jealous of Harold's women, especially the smart ones. He's very bright, and we don't talk about a lot of things because I just don't know about them. I was afraid for a whole year he would leave me because he was making it with a Ph.D. I need a man. Men are the only way I'm going to make it in life."

"Does your open marriage include group sex?"

"Not really, but one time I got bombed at a party and balled four different people in front of Harold. And I watched him fucking, too, but I couldn't wait to get back home because I didn't want to get a disease and pass it on."

"How would you like to change your life?"

"I don't want men pushing me around. I pay my own way so that I don't have to owe anyone. You've got to take the authority, take the control. That's the ball game."

"Has your sex life changed?"

"Yes. When I met Harold, I didn't like to fuck with the lights on. I didn't like my body very much. Now, I'm happy with it. Harold introduced me to oral sex. Before, I had always thought my vagina was dirty, so I wouldn't touch myself or let anyone else. Now, I've gotten in touch with mirrors. I look at myself, watch myself masturbate, taste my secretion. I like playing like a little girl."

She looks like a little girl as she speaks, although her body is very much a woman's.

"Do you have any sexual fantasies?" I ask her.

"There was a woman I met, who is sort of a famous person. I was really turned on by her, but I was very shy. I wanted her to make the first move. I wanted her to attack me," she tells me.

Doris seems to be in touch with her emotional feelings, but I do think that she feels insecure about her husband's needs. Since she cannot stimulate him intellectually, she is determined to stimulate him so much sexually that he will never leave her. In most open relationships, one partner accepts the other partner's need for outside sexuality—usually it's the woman accepting the man's—because of fear of losing the partner. The woman's attitude is that it's better to share in this than to have him go off and do it alone, without her knowledge.

Often when marriages break up, the husband and wife still continue to see each other. Separated now, they have other lovers. This is true in Scarlett's case.

Scarlett

Her name is Scarlett, her mother's gesture to the beautiful belle of southern literary history in *Gone with the Wind*. But she is an older, harder, cynical, 1976-style Scarlett living in California. Short, her figure once lithe and fragile, an A-line dress tries to hide the unnecessary flesh of middle years. At thirty-five, Scarlett wears too much makeup, bouffants her red head of hair like a manikin on parade, and looks at me with large eyes filled with tears that seem to have begun at birth. But as she fights her sad feelings, the tears turn out to be funny, tender, ironic.

"Since I've been separated, my husband and I really get on," she says quietly. "We were married for ten years, and now he comes over often and I know it's going to be a bed-down and none of the flack in between. The first time it happened I cried all day because I realized he was not getting up to go to work, that he was leaving to go back to his own life. It felt so awful, we both started crying."

Separated for the past year—Scarlett's husband left her for another woman—she immediately found another man and began making love to him and faking orgasms. "You can take the girl out of Tennessee, but you can't take Tennessee out of the girl," she explains about the fact that she fakes sexual pleasure. "You know, when I met my husband I had been working in Las Vegas. He loomed up fresh with his tweed jacket and his pipe, like an oasis in the desert, among the queers and the perverts and the weirdo actors. But I was wrong, because he wasn't any more dependable and stable than they were."

Now she feels everything will be different: She doesn't have to change anything, for men come out of the woodwork for her. "You know, if a woman's outwardly pretty, beautifully made up, smells good, dresses well, she can get any man. I have a great gimmick, the southern accent. It's always a great icebreaker. The first thing that happens is the man asks you what part of the South you're from and you blink your eyelashes and open your eyes wide. If he has nice shoulders and a broad back, he's got it made."

She talks of herself as a "product." "I always thought of myself as a product that had to continue improving. When the product shows too much wear and tear, I have to do something about it." At present, she thinks the "product" could use more bust and is getting pouchy under the eyes. "You know you have to sell the product," she says flippantly.

Scarlett has very definite ideas about what men are and what women are. A woman should stand still and wait for men to approach her. A man should pick up the phone. When he doesn't, she says, "What's wrong with him, why doesn't he get off his duff?"

Recently, Scarlett met a movie producer who went absolutely bananas over her. Strangely, she put him off. "He pretended he wanted to help me and was coming on very strong. I told him I was in love with someone else."

Puzzled, I ask her why.

"I've always been a bitch and a fool in a lot of ways," she says grudgingly. "My husband used to call me a castrating southern shrew, and I guess he's right. I guess I would have liked nothing better than to be a little Scarlett O'Hara clinging vine, sitting on my veranda, having a mint julep, and letting a great big strong man take care of everything. But because I want to be a career woman, everything in life has forced me into an alien role, forced me to be strong, forced me to take over, forced me to put up with a husband who couldn't pay the bills, forced me to take lovers who don't give me pleasure."

"You must be furious!" I remark, watching her smoke cigarette after cigarette, her mouth twitching, ruddy red with lipstick.

"Of course I'm furious," she agrees violently. "When have you met a man who's strong these days?"

"But can't you love a man who's weaker than you are?"

She looks at me like I'm mad. "I can love someone weaker than me if it's puppies and children. But I don't want to be mother earth. I don't want to love weak, ineffectual men, but I'm so strong I attract the weak ones. You know, every man always says to me, 'I think you are the strongest, toughest woman I have ever met.' And they end up sitting in my lap." She pauses, angrily smoking. "Maybe if I swoon, the strong ones will come out and help me."

"What do you mean by strong?" I ask, confused by her ambivalent statements, still wondering why she put off the movie producer.

"A strong man is decisive, energetic. I don't think he's frightened by a woman with a good mind. Every cotton-picking time I'm attracted to what I think is a strong man, within three months every one of them is just sitting in my lap, crying."

Scarlett seems very angry at men, at the hold they have over her, thus she keeps from them (and herself) her sexual pleasure, her sexual orgasm, even after she was legally free to enjoy them. When she met a man who could help in her career, she strangely rejected him. The kind of ambivalent attitude of women being courted by men and the search for strong men is very common nowadays. It's as if strong aggressive women feel "cheated" if they love less aggressive men. Thus, many women are sending double messages out to men in these modern times.

Some married women can separate their career needs for strength and aggressiveness from their private lives. Jennifer is a case in point.

Jennifer

"I've been monogamous for the last four years because Tommy and I are very, very happy, sexually and otherwise," Jennifer says gaily. A Camelot bed with white curtains dominates the apartment where Jennifer and Tommy lead a very, very private life, although both are part of Hollywood's film world and Tommy is very, very famous.

"We make love about five times a week," she says, "and that's enough. In the past, sex has always been an escape trip for me. With my ex, we used to fuck six times a day because that's the only time he could be loving and tender. Before Tommy, men were hostile to me. They always wanted to fuck me, but there was always anger behind it. I've been very envious of less attractive women because I felt men treated them better."

It is impossible to explain to Jennifer the impression she makes, for one is sure one's imagination has taken over. Tall, resembling an Aztec goddess, Jennifer is the perfection of a primitive sensual beauty, the beauty of her namesake, Jennifer Jones, in *Duel in the Sun*, only with this Jennifer it is a natural, primitive beauty for she is an American Cherokee Indian.

"Tommy was always different. Maybe it was because he was a friend for five years before we made it. Being with a man who loves you does a lot. I went to acting school, and now I'm very aggressive and ambitious about my career. I never thought I had a chance before."

The apartment is handsome and looks paid for. I have known Jenni for half a dozen years before her marriage to Tommy during which time she was always scrambling for money, working as a waitress, a car hop, movie usherette. Even in the worst of circumstances, her children were always well fed and cared for, something that always had impressed me. I asked her how it felt to be supported in good style.

"I feel great about it. It's the first time in my life someone has helped me out. We've been all over the world. In Paris, I bought special underwear, a G-string, and a white marabou boa. I love to tease Tommy. I wear a simple dress, and when we're alone in an elevator, I pull my skirt up and say, 'Look what I have to show you!' "

She shows me several kinds of luxurious satin and silken underwear which must look wonderful on her body, which has a long, sensuous line one would assume would have been invented by an artist on canvas. However, Jenni is also very natural and modest about herself, but with quite an imagination.

"Are you satisfied sexually with Tommy?"

"Well, I've had orgasms every way. I have a lot of fantasies, though," she says guiltily. "I have this constant fantasy about an older Italian man, like a Godfather. He's in good physical shape and treats me like a little girl. I really love it. I sit on his lap, and kissing him is so incredible I get very excited. I come just from kissing. For some reason, in the fantasy we have to wait until the next day to make love, so we have this entire day and night of this intense excitement. And the next day, we make love and it's wonderful."

Her primitive, sensual beauty now has a girlishness to it, something I have only seen before when Jenni has been sad. It is adorable and a little bit startling, and I think if a camera could catch it, she would become an immediate star.

"I have this other fantasy," she continues, "about sleeping with two or three men at the same time. One is fucking me in the ass, and I'm sucking the other off. That's one of my favorites," she giggles like a little girl having consumed too many sweets.

"Does Tommy know about them?"

"I don't tell Tommy about them because he's very jealous. Sometimes when I'm with him, I wish I were invisible. When I walk on the street, men make such a fuss. I love to wear shorts and won't because of the attention I get. The reverse happens when I go to parties with Tommy. I am invisible. Everyone pays attention to him because he is a star and they ignore me. So when that happens, I fantasize a lot. I fantasize on the subway, in taxicabs, even in the middle of conversations. People know something unusual is happening because I can see from their expression that they're getting turned on."

Jenni looks unhappy when she explains how her life with Tommy has changed within the last year. "I'm afraid to make friends now because people just use me to get to him. I hate it. You know, I've always wanted people to love me for me. I used to screw men I didn't like to get them to like me. It was hard for me to say no."

"Do you say no? Are you faithful to Tommy?"

"Well, generally I am," she says guiltily. "Only one time he came home from a film location and said he had been unfaithful. I hadn't. So the next time he went away, I had three affairs just for me," she chuckles with glee. "I loved every moment of each one. But I haven't told him, because I love him. I want him to feel secure, I don't want him to be frightened." She pauses. "But I think I'm too dependent on him, especially sexually."

The phone rings, as it has been doing for the hour I've been there, and instead of ignoring it, she answers it. I can see from her attitude that it is someone who wants something from her, to get something from her now-famous husband, and a shadow of sadness shows on her face. Finally, she returns, and I ask her what excites her the most.

"You know, I feel him while he's inside of me. I like to feel his penis going in and out, and I get very excited. But," she hesitates, "I feel embarrassed telling you this." She walks around the room a bit anxiously, and I wonder what is embarrassing her since we are such old friends. Finally she decides to go on. "Tommy can make me come with his fingers, but mine don't work," she whispers, startling me. "If I touch myself, I can't feel anything.

"I'd like to learn, though, so we're going to buy me a vibrator. Because when I'm having one of my sexual fantasies, I'd really like to come."

I was startled by Jennifer's admission of not masturbating successfully, perhaps because I knew how sexually active she had been in her life. But Jennifer had always made love to men because she wanted them to like her, so she could never ask them for sexual pleasure. I was very happy that now, although she could not share her fantasies and her extramarital activities with Tommy (as he could with her), at least they were attacking her masturbation problem together. But I was amazed to learn that even in the "wildest" set of the Hollywood film world, the woman was still lying to the man about her entire sexuality to protect his macho.

Most of the women in this marital chapter have done something about their need for sexual activity outside of their marriages. But I think the majority of American women do not act upon this desire. Here is one poignant interview which I am sure is typical of the fiftyish married woman in our society.

Ruth

In a large city in Ohio, a tall, fiftyish woman who could easily qualify for an American commercial about mom's apple pie sits across from me in a noisy bar decorated with neon liquor signs. On the previous Sunday when she had astonished me by agreeing to an interview, I had expected the choice of a Howard Johnson's look-a-like as a meeting place. Instead, we are at Bob's Roadside Oasis, where even a sophisticated city slicker like myself would never willingly choose to be.

Two men in plaid shirts and dungarees are playing pool in the back room as Ruth orders stingers in the early afternoon. *Why do I feel so decadent?* I chide myself, realizing that I am still suffering from the moral turpitudes of childhood, feeling particularly surprised at the whole occasion because Ruth is the local Protestant minister's wife of thirty years.

"Sex with my husband is rather infrequent, about once a month. Certain kinds of hugs mean he wants sex. If he presses hard against me and starts rubbing my back, I know he wants it."

"Do you like his approach?" I ask, amazed that she has gotten right to the point of the interview so quickly.

"I dislike it because he's not direct."

"What about you being direct? After all, you've been married for a long time."

Ruth sips her stinger, looking at me warily. There are tears in her eyes as she speaks. "My mother always made me feel that to flirt with men was awful. It was always the man's job to woo me. She was lucky. My dad was always crazy about her, always ran after her.

"I grew up thinking women who were after sex were women who wore sexy clothes and that I should look clean and decent and pleasant and nice, but I should not look sexy because then other men, besides my husband, would want me."

She finishes her stinger in one gulp. I slowly push mine over to her side of the table and she begins sipping it without question. "We never ever spoke about sex. My mother would say, 'Did you wash down *there?*' I didn't even know what to call it until six months ago. I called it an *it.*"

"What happened six months ago?"

"I took a course in psychology at the college, and we got into descriptions of sexual organs. I learned about things for the first time in my life.

"I knew my sexual organs were *there* and I peed from *there.* I knew my husband would put his penis in *there* and that babies came out *there* and that I got feelings from *there*, but there were big empty gaps."

"Did you ever masturbate?" I ask, startled by this information.

"Started about three months ago. Had my first orgasm and was scared stiff. I read about how to do it in one of those sex books."

"Did you ever tell your husband you didn't have orgasms?"

"He doesn't want to talk about sex. We talk about everything else but that. He gets very uptight when I try."

"Have you thought about other men?"

She gulps down her stinger, checking her wristwatch, becoming very apprehensive suddenly. Quietly, I signal for two more stingers, sensing that Ruth must need more alcohol before she will continue to talk. When she does continue, she talks in a soft whisper as if worried she will be overheard.

"There was this young bachelor in my psychology class. Every time he touched my arm accidentally, I would burn for hours afterward. But I was afraid I might give off signals, that he might know I wanted him."

"Couldn't you have had a discreet affair?"

Ruth looks at me angrily and stops drinking. "I'd get badly hurt. I love my husband. Anyhow, the love affairs I see generally distract people from everything else in their lives. They bore all their friends endlessly with what she said and he said and what is he doing to me and what am I doing to him and what our relationship is and blah blah blah. I hate the word 'relationship' because I hear it all the time."

"What do you want, Ruth?"

"I want to become sexually attractive and screw my husband every night, every way. I don't care if that makes us animals," she says with great bitterness.

"Do you think you can get him to do that?"

"Only when we've been drinking. Then we play all sorts of games with each other. We turn on the TV and turn off the lights. And we get undressed and roll around on the couch."

"That sounds nice. What else happens?"

"Oh, the usual," she answers angrily. Then angrier still, "Do you know I've never even handled his penis?"

"What's the fear of becoming sexual, Ruth?"

"I'm afraid that if I become sexual that I'm going to lose all my feelings, my real feelings. I hate men because they can get sex wherever they want. But if I want to be a lady, the lady my mother wanted me to be . . ." She pauses, telling me she has to go, then continues. "Being a woman is like being a Jew in Germany— what can you do about it? But when I think about all those years and all those orgasms I missed, I get very, very angry."

She leaves quickly, leaving me to listen to the harsh sounds of country western music, vulnerable to the blinking red neon lights, remembering the sadness in her face, and wondering if she drinks stingers in the afternoon every day, because they are really very bad for her.

Ruth's interview left me depressed and very disheartened. When I began interviewing for this marital chapter, I was glad to hear so many women say they were happily married. What with the current antimarriage blitz, I had thought this could not be so.

But eagerly interviewing in depth, I found out that marriage really doesn't seem a very satisfactory way to live an exciting and sexual life. I also discovered that the roles of mother and of sexual woman were in conflict.

Ruth was particularly depressing because she had spent so much of her life not being sexual, and when finally, in her fifties, she began to discover sexual excitement, she was too prim and proper to act upon her feelings. I wish Ruth had had the guts to have a mad impetuous affair with her young student. That, somehow, would have made up for the afternoon stingers and the harsh, uncompromising attitude of her religious husband.

Four

❃ ❃ ❃

THE EROTICISM OF
EXHIBITIONISM

Sex has become a sport in America, not a communication. Like other sports, the youngest and healthiest athletes are considered winners. But athletes train to destroy their vulnerability, and so do sexual performers. The ability to perform sexual intercourse without being turned on is admired, publicized, and paid for. The performer is concerned with doing a good job, pleasing the customer, rather than enjoying herself. Rather than feelings, the performer thinks of efficiency on the job: How quickly can a prostitute make her customer come? How often can an entertainer cause erections in a male audience that will pay dearly for this privilege? In its most exhibitionistic plane, the industry of sexual performance has become a multibillion-dollar enterprise and affects all aspects of entertainment from pornography to serious films, from prostitution to sex therapy. Its status in the media also colors the private lives of men and women, where faked orgasm has been the most common female performance.

At present, we have the "real" orgasms of the masturbatory sex-therapy classes to turn to, for our sexual culture seems to be more engrossed in turning women and men into sexual computers—one ounce of this and one dose of that makes for one great, real orgasm. And after that, so what?

Rollo May's *Love and Will* gives a practical definition of eros. "Eros seeks union with the other person in delight and passion . . . dimensions of experience which broaden and deepen the being of both persons. . . . It is this urge for union with the partner that is the occasion for human tenderness. For eros—not sex as such—is the source of tenderness."

What is sex without that tenderness, that *feeling*? Simply an act of performance which one must excel in. This performance symptom, traditionally confined to the areas of male sexuality, is now swelling into the female, especially females who assume themselves to be liberated by the birth-control pill from the "wages of the sin of lust." But what happens when freedom from sin evolves to computerized performance? Is there any enjoyment at all?

Dr. Martin Williams, sex therapist with the Berkeley Sex Therapy Group, has some interesting things to say about performance as a symptom of sexual problems: ". . . someone who is not suffering from Performance is always capable of being honest about the degree of pleasure he is experiencing . . . the non-Performer might have occasion to utter the following: 'It just stopped feeling good.' To the furtive mind of the Performer this statement sounds like insanity—the Performer would replace it with 'That feels great.'

"Performers . . . simply . . . try not to notice how good or bad it feels. . . . It is true that Masters and Johnson have, with the help of their choreography, managed to turn people on, but it is also true that they have turned non-Performers into mere Performers. In fact, Masters-and-Johnson-oriented therapists might not even be able to conceive of a Performance symptom. They measure success *only* in terms of Performance; erections, vaginal lubrication, orgasms, and delayed orgasms are the measure of improvement."

Another performance measurement is the pink sexual flush (mentioned in Chapter One) that overcomes the complexion of the orgasmic woman. Some men experience this flush, but it is generally the erection which is the barometer of the male turn-on.

One cannot blame sex therapists for they are simply following what the culture seems to revere: efficiency in sexual orgasm. Sex therapy has followed societal demands and attitudes. As a result, in this competitive society no one likes to admit that they are not turned on, cannot have orgasms, do not like sex. To admit that one's sexual appetite is far from this "norm" is considered asexual or uninteresting. So women fake orgasms. (Somehow the pink complexion of the sexual flush has not been popularized, thus men are not aware of its existence in the orgasmic woman.) And men would fake erections, too, if they could. They would never be interested in the genuine kind.

The business of sexual performance, of course, is historically ancient and is manifested most dramatically in the business of selling sex through prostitution. However, it is not only the prostitute who is in this business, as we will see in this chapter. Performance sex is the center of all kinds of exhibitionistic sex: Go-go dancing, sexual surrogate work, acting, etc., has crept into private lives. Only when interviewing these sexual performers in depth does one find often an admission of absolutely no sensual feelings, no vulnerability, no enjoyment. The women who are in the business of selling sex have no time for feelings but just simply perform. Unfortunately, there is a large segment of the male population whose only form of sexual pleasure comes from this type of performance sex.

Because of this, sexual therapy has become big business. An important employee in the sexual-therapy business geared to single males is the sexual surrogate. A sexual surrogate is a woman who acts as a sexual partner to a male client who is being treated for a sexual problem by sex therapists. One of the most successful sexual surrogates in California is a woman whom I have named Sandra.

Sandra

"The only disadvantage of my work is that it takes me away from my music. One day I treated eleven patients, and at the end of the day I felt as fresh as if I played a concert."

I am sitting in Sandra's baroque living room. Two grand pianos, a Persian rug, paintings, and crystal stemware give me a distorted feeling of double vision. Outside, the bright sunlight of San Diego glows, yet this apartment should be on New York's Fifty-seventh Street. Sandra, red-headed, soft-spoken, is posing on a chaise longue, her little dog, Tiki, barking at me. Sandra's eyes are bright blue and, as she speaks, convey a look of innocence. Between monologues, she plays chords on her cello to remind me she has a dual career. Every morning she studies music with her teacher (she plays professionally), and every evening she is a sexual surrogate, fucking any man who meets her hourly fee and who is properly recommended. She claims she has never had a failure.

"A man is very simple to help. First, you relax him. I sometimes put him into a warm bath and give him a drink, juice usually. Then I turn off the phones, put on some very low music. Classical music doesn't work; it's too stimulating.

"The apartment has to be very, very warm, very quiet, and very secure. Then I give him a porno magazine, a vibrator, and tell him to go into the bedroom. I leave him in there for about twenty minutes. Then I join him, sit in a chair, naked, posing in different ways. Then I get closer and closer to him until I am on the bed. Pretty soon I masturbate him with my own hand. I can do it for over an hour and not get tired, because I practice. Then just before he comes, I put it in me. Then I start putting it in more and more often, each time he's here. And it always works."

So I hear. Every sex therapist and patient I talk to tells me that Sandra is the best sexual surrogate available. I ask her why.

"Well, I give my clients homework. I tell them to go to see sex movies. I make a tape for them, reminding them of my favorite fantasies and of theirs. I tell them about their diets, tell them to stop drinking and stop eating cake. I say to them: 'The secret lies within you. I'm not a mind reader, but you and I are going to find out what turns you on.' If they start talking to me about their wives or problems, I tell them to see a psychotherapist."

"Why do they need to come to you for this, Sandra? Why can't they do this with their wives or girlfriends?" The fact that they do need Sandra means that she sees five or six clients a day, charging fifty dollars per client.

The dog is nibbling at one of Sandra's breasts, and she shakes him off her lap impatiently. Her nails and fingers are very long and slim. She poses as she answers my question, as if on display. "Well, I tell them always: 'Look, I'm not looking for an erection today. I'm not looking for a nineteen-year-old superstud. In fact, I will ignore it if you get hard, so forget it.' Then they have a terrific time. I think their wives expect a lot more from them. Of course," she adds, "I have a really nice figure, and I dress up for whatever they want. I tease them. 'What do you want to see?' I might say. I have this dress with the back panel cut out, and I turn around, and they always want to mount me doggie fashion. You know, they love me. When I play at a concert, the entire audience is filled with my clients."

"What makes your work different from prostitution?"

"My intelligence!" she snaps harshly. "One client was ready to commit suicide. I saved his life. I cured him after three visits."

"Do you care about your clients?"

"A lot of them fall in love with me, but I never kiss them because I think kissing is a very intimate thing," she answers, amusing me at how she changed my query to satisfy her vanity.

"What is your personal life like?"

She giggles. "I have a man for everything. I date famous actors. My phone is always ringing. I have lots of beautiful clothes, and I love to get dolled up and go out."

"What about your sex life?"

Suddenly at the other end of the room, near the doorway, a red light flashes and a buzzer goes off. "That's my next client," Sandra says. "Do you have any other questions?"

"What about your sex life?" I insist.

She flinches as if I have struck a blow. Then she answers in a hurried whisper. "I don't have the need for a romantic lover because I spend so much time entertaining men. And I have so much studying to do, so much reading. . . ."

"Do you have orgasms?"

She sighs. "I've done my share of faking them. I can only have them orally or manually. I've had women lovers, and they play with my nipples for three hours, and I don't feel a thing. But I tell them it's thrilling.

"You know, because I've been fucking all day long, who wants to fuck some more? In fact, I'm not sure I like sex that much."

Sandra, extraordinarily honest and humorous about her activities, is an interesting example of a sexual performer. She knows her business. While she is helping her male clients forget about getting an erection, forget about performing, she is performing all the time. It seems to be impossible for her to cut herself off in her own personal life. Sandra, like many other women in this chapter, can perform at sex *simply because she is not vulnerable*. If she were, she would flounder in her job.

Vulnerability in marriage can also be lost with extra sexual activity. I have always wondered if couples who are into orgies, swinging, ménages, are intimate with all these partners. I suspect they cut off at a certain point, and after that, it's just performance. When I met Liz, a film actress, I was interested to discover what the dynamics of her "swinging" marriage were all about.

Liz

Tall, slim, with long sinewy legs, twenty-eight-year-old Liz pouts her sensuous lips as she tells me the first tale of fantasy-acting-out that turned her on.

"A friend of mine and her boyfriend go out to Plum Beach. She lies in the front seat of the car, totally exposed. It's usually early evening, and it gets very misty. During the evening, men walk up and down the beach, and any one of them who cares to can partake of her sexually. Her boyfriend sits over on a bench and oversees the situation so she won't get into any physical danger. She says she loves it because it is anonymous sex."

"Have you ever done it?" I ask Liz, who has been to orgies, swinging parties, is bisexual, and has been happily married to Alfred for ten years.

"No, but I wanted to. It really turned me on. I'm so bored with large groups, small groups, couples, threesomes, sex in orgylike situations."

"Then why do you still do it?"

"Because every once in a while a scene happens that really turns me on. Like the other night, Alfred and I went to a party in a very, very plush setting, a penthouse at the top of a high-rise building. It was just like a movie. We walked into the room, and everything was thickly padded with gorgeous white carpet. There were about two dozen nude bodies all over the place. Everyone was screwing and talking or whatever. I got undressed in a second, and immediately four men started to play with me, and it was very, very nice."

We are sitting in SoHo, in New York City, in Liz's studio, which is part of a large loft apartment where she lives with her husband. The walls are painted red, decorated with a dozen or so black leather accessories, hanging symmetrically. Hats, garter belts, a black bra, and panties are among them. Liz is wearing a black-lace, see-through blouse, a tight satin skirt, and a large black hat. Her upturned nose and her wide, brown eyes dominate her face. She is wearing small golden earrings and has many golden rings on her long, slim fingers. Black leather belt and high-heeled shoes complete this costume, which she calls "her business outfit," apparently oblivious to the fact that the rosy red nipples of her breasts are visible. I wonder what kind of business she is into.

"I was a fine-arts major in college. Now two times a week I'm a go-go dancer while I study acting and wait for film jobs."

"Does your job involve sex?"

"On the contrary, it's nonsexual. You work a half-hour on stage and a half-hour off, talking to the customers, and it's the tips you're after. The girls who get the most tips are the ones who have a joking personality, making the customers the butt of the jokes. You meet an awful lot of prestigious people. Last week I had a long talk with a banker who was here to solve the city's financial problems."

I had visions of Liz in her G-string, pasties, and long black gloves, talking seriously to the banker in his dark, conservative suit.

"You're really into clothes, aren't you?" I motion to her wall of paraphernalia.

Liz giggles. "I love costumes. Sometimes I wear white-lace underwear and play the blushing bride with Alfred. Other times, I wear a black satin corset and boots, and play the lady with the whip. The other night he played the lead, holding me on the back of my neck, and he put his two fingers in my mouth and I had an orgasm. It was the first time that happened and since then, my mouth has been totally different."

"How did you get into this free sexual life? Did you have a strict upbringing?"

"Very. I was a virgin when I married Alfred. But I knew something was wrong with me physically. So after two years, we began swinging, and when I saw how other women responded sexually, I knew I had a block about pleasure. Now it's great. Sometimes we just sit around and talk, and about every twenty seconds, I'll have a vaginal rush. If I put my hand down there, I find it's really moving. I can put my head into certain fantasies and get really super rushes."

"What kind of fantasies?"

"Well, I have a favorite called 'The Cage.' It takes place in a low-lit private club where all the men who attend are black. In the center of the club is a golden cage about three feet by three feet with wide bars. It is the only illuminated thing in the place. Every night it's a different person's responsibility to bring a nude white woman to the cage, blindfolded.

"She's put in the cage and can do whatever she wishes, sit or stand. If she sits, her feet hang through, and she's accessible to everyone. During the course of the evening, there'll be big black hands all over her. If she wants to, she can turn and give someone a blow job. She's a captive, but she's in control because if she wishes, she can stand up in the cage and no one can reach her. Usually, in the course of the evening she's handled by about fifteen men—thirty hands on her. When you have a lot of hands on you, it really feels incredible."

"Have you ever acted out your fantasies?"

"I have. But sometimes they can't be acted out because they need a budget. I have another favorite where a girl is brought to a room where everyone is costumed. She's tied down to a Plexiglas form in doggie position, with a large mirror in front of her, so she can see what's happening behind her. There is a center of light on her and the background falls into darkness, so you don't know where it ends.

"Costumed pages bring her a chalice of oil. Everyone is following the directions of a very tall woman in white clothes. No one speaks. It's as if everything is prerehearsed. Suddenly, she looks up and this woman has put on a white leather costume and has two white afghans beside her. Then behind her is another woman in white leather and two other afghans. And another. Still others. There is a long line of women and dogs which fade into the shadows, and the girl cannot see where they end.

"The women start getting the dogs excited. Meanwhile, the page boys begin to immerse the girl's torso in oil. The dogs begin to mount her, one after the other. When it is over, she is released."

"Are you the girl in the fantasies?"

"I think I'm both the girl and the woman."

"Which fantasies do you act out?"

"Well, I'm very lucky. You see, Alfred is very open. One time we went to a party, smashed. It was a strange party, and there seemed to be a dearth of women there. When I walked in, I was immediately surrounded by many men.

"We started to move together, like a swarm of bees, toward the back of the apartment, to the huge bathroom. Several of these men were touching me, my clothes were being ripped off, while one was inserting his penis. It was an absolute gas. Alfred was in the shower stall, masturbating. Then, it was over."

"And your husband wasn't jealous?"

"No!"

"And he really enjoyed it?"

"Yes."

Have I found what sounds like a perfectly free sexual marriage? But wait . . . "Is there anything that's forbidden to you?"

She stops for a moment, thinks seriously, and bites into one of the ripe peaches displayed on the coffee table. "Yes," she says, her teeth all orangey with peach flesh.

"What is that?"

"It's a no-no if I get involved emotionally."

"What do you mean?"

"It just doesn't work out. I met a superintelligent, witty man last month and became totally engrossed and consumed with him."

"And . . ."

"And . . . Alfred didn't like it! He said it harms our relationship!"

Liz, then, is allowed to fuck anyone she wishes, but must keep her feelings out of her activity. Thus, her extramarital activities are simply performance, nothing else. Here, too, note the vivid fantasies of the creative woman. Both fantasies do contain an element of humiliation in her choice of environment. Perhaps that is why

Liz allows her husband to direct her sexual activity in and outside of their marriage.

Exhibitionistic sex creeps into everyone's life. Often, the woman is only the player in this theatrical piece and the man usually enjoys the drama. This is true in the case of Celine, who has an interesting story to tell.

Celine

She is petite, tiny, with shiny hair, resembling a lady fair of King Arthur's Court. Twenty-five, a typist for an advertising agency, she has had a steady love affair with a man who is fifty, for a half-dozen years. Most of the time they spend together is on weekends where they fuck in museums, churches, streets, stairwells, and in elevators.

"We'll usually get into an elevator where he takes his dick out and I stand in front of him. He puts it between my legs. We can't fuck, though, because I'm too short," she says sorrowfully, crocheting a pillow cover for her couch. Her face could compete with any portrait of an Italian Florentine saint or any portrait of a midwestern lady seated on her porch after dinner is over. Her blue eyes are clear, her mouth serene as she tells of her exhibitionistic fondness for sexual escapades.

"Usually women enter the elevator and assume I'm not with him and he's just doing that. They smile or they turn away and giggle. But one old lady waited until the elevator stopped, got out and turned around and said to Ben, 'You leave that sweet little girl alone!' We both broke up."

On a Saturday afternoon they went to the Brooklyn Museum. "I wore a skirt and thigh-high stockings, and he was feeling me up in dark corners. Then we walked into this large room of abstract art, and no people. We stood inside the doorway where we could watch the entrance, and I started to blow him. He was really getting into it. All of a sudden he stiffened up and said, 'Oh, shit.' I got up. Sitting way down at the other end of the room was a guard on a bench, watching us. We got ourselves together and ran out of the museum, down the stairs. Jesus, I was afraid we'd get arrested."

One of the reasons Celine feels that the police would interfere is because no one would believe she wanted to do those things to Ben. "I'm afraid the cops wouldn't believe we were together," she says, her innocent eyes blinking. I could sympathize with the police because if Celine were in a group of a dozen women she would not be the one I would pick out as fond of exhibitionistic sex. I would rather choose her as the quiet, rigid librarian (excuse this prejudice please) who has a sexual problem. But I may not be far from wrong.

"Why do you like to do these things?" I ask.

"It's a forbidden thing. You know, something you're not supposed to do. We have some favorite churches. There's one on Park and Sixty-fourth Street. We usually hide in an alcove or in a confessional pew if it's a Catholic church. He wears a long cloak so that if we get discovered he can cover himself. We play he's the priest and I'm the sinner in the confessional and I have to go in and go down on him. He loves that.

"Another place we like is stairwells. Around Gramercy Park there are a lot of good ones. There's an empty lot on Twenty-eighth Street where we made it nude. And, yes, I love Broome Street, it's great in the dark, all business and warehouses. People walk right by us and can't imagine what we are doing."

Usually Celine and Ben do their thing about three o'clock in the morning. On a special celebration of Celine's birthday, she had a a wonderful time. "We had dinner at Monk's Court and then we went to Lincoln Plaza, and nobody was there, so we fucked. There's a quiet walk that leads to a garden that's very lovely. We fucked and fucked, and it was a great birthday celebration."

When I ask Celine if she has orgasms from these encounters, she shakes her head adamantly. "I can't have orgasms," she admits sadly. "We do these things because Ben gets a lot of fun out of it. I don't have to put much effort into it, and it makes him happy."

Another thing that makes Ben happy is having other girls. I am amazed that Celine doesn't seem annoyed about this, and ask her why. "Our relationship is very monogamous, but he's married and a swinger and he sees other women. I know he loves me, though, because if a woman was threatening to me, he'd give her up for me."

Some of the things they do together at home are acting the little-girl-and-daddy fantasy. "I put on a little-girl dress and knee socks. He'll pretend he's just seen me in the street, and he takes out his dick and asks me if I know what this is. He has this fantasy of having a cab ready and swiping a little girl on the street and taking her someplace and fucking her, and then taking her back unharmed to where he found her. So I play that little girl. He asks me if I'm bad and what do I want.

"Sometimes he shows his slides of women with their backsides out and then I play that kind of woman." I look over to a nurse's uniform on a hanger with the breasts and rear sections cut out. "That's for our doctor and nurse scene," she says quietly.

One day Ben was angry at Celine and forced her to wear a huge dildo all day long. They biked together in Central Park, went out to a French restaurant to dinner, all the time Celine uncomfortably hiding this apparatus. Yet, Celine will obey Ben because she feels he really loves her.

"He's the only person who really knows what I'm all about. He can take one look at me and know what's wrong. Sometimes I'm really shitty to him, and he just grins and bears it. You know, he's old, and if he dies I'll never fall in love with anyone again. I couldn't do it. I'd become a hermit."

Celine holds up her crocheting, and I see it's in honor of the bicentennial with its red-white-and-blue motif. I stare at the words, "Home, Sweet Home," as she pulls the crocheted cover onto a bare pillow. Plopping it in the center of her bed, which is also trimmed with the patriotic colors, I wonder what makes this young girl so insecure, so accepting, so undemanding.

"I'm a pessimist," she says almost hearing my silent query. "Life is a game. I'm the type who will probably stay with the same job, the same man, because I'll never try to change. I don't want to take the risk, the hassle, because I'm sure I'm going to lose."

She looks at me a bit defensively.

"Why do you think you can't have orgasms?" I ask.

She stares at me, now defiant. "I don't like sex. That's why! I want sex two days a month. Ben wants it every night. That's why I do all those things. That's why I don't mind it if he has other women. It takes the pressure off me. Because when I'm not in the mood, it's duty, duty, duty.

"I feel guilty about it. This American culture tells me everybody fucks, and if I don't like to do it, something is wrong with me. I've only made love to two men in my entire life," she says angrily.

I look at the nurse's outfit which she wears to friends' parties and I think of her public image. I can't believe nothing turns her on, so I ask her again.

"Oh, yes," she says casually. "I like my feet touched, but . . ." She lowers her voice and begins to stammer. ". . . I can't get Ben to do that."

Thus Celine spends most of her time with Ben acting out his exhibitionistic needs and his paternalistic fantasies, but claims she is not getting any pleasure out of it. Her feet, apparently an erotic zone for her, remain cold and isolated because Ben will not give her the only pleasure she asks for. No wonder, with this idea of what sexual pleasure is, Celine wants to become a hermit in the future, as a control over her needs and feelings.

Real control of women has always seemed to me the most dramatic in the prostitute/pimp relationship. Although I have interviewed many prostitutes, none of them would talk about their pimps until I ran into Dolly.

Dolly

A fair woman with dark curly hair, Dolly sits at the corner of a squeaky mattress in an Eighth Avenue hotel room, slugging from the bottle of gin I have brought her. Dolly's fee for the interview was money, drugs, or gin, in that order. When I explain that none of the women in this book have been paid for their interviews, that they offered their time in the interest of helping other women, she smirks.

"Help other women? That's how I got into this in the first place."

I ask her what she means.

"Pimps use older women as control points with younger women, to pull them in. They're called 'bottom women,' and the older women give the pimp's stable some kind of stability. The older women teach the younger women all the tricks."

From the open window, I hear women's voices tell passersby what they can get for fifteen dollars. "Two girls, forty dollars, mister, no cheaper," one harsh voice says. Outside the hotel room door, I hear footsteps coming and going, a lot of action in this sexual nirvana of male fantasy: the brothel with its star, the prostitute, the aggressive woman who grabs his cock, the woman who does not want a relationship with him. But she has a relationship with her pimp. I wonder what it's like.

"When a woman turns tricks, she's taught that she should be cold, be bitchy, be indifferent, and men will love it. And they do," Dolly says. "And the pimp uses the same attitude with his women.

"You see, a pimp is very involved with his macho. Screwing your pimp is almost like being with a trick, it's so structured. First he kisses you, then he fucks you, and that's it. He never gets into foreplay. He never gets into oral sex. He's not concerned whether you've had an orgasm or not. *Pimps are the worst lays in the world.*"

Dolly takes another swig of the gin, laughing heartily to herself. Plump, soft, young, but hard around the eyes, she seems to be the picture of the classic prostitute whose hard life has somehow not affected her sense of humor. I ask Dolly why prostitutes stay with their pimps if they are such bad lovers.

"In my fifteen years on the street, I've always had a pimp," she says. "And you won't believe the reason. You see, I think down in the deepest part of me I really believe I'm supposed to be with only one person sexually. So when I have a pimp, I have a husband. I want him to love me so I make the most money I can for him. The more money I make, the more time he spends with me.

"When I first hit the streets, I was only seventeen. I felt dirty about everything sexual. I had masturbated and was guilty about it. I had fantasies about having sex with three guys tying me up and whipping me, and I thought I was sick in the head. I was a real martyr, felt I had to serve someone, had to be used, to give constantly. I wanted to eliminate all my bad feelings about myself. With my pimp, I could. I got more and more into performance. And that blotted out everything else. If my pimp wants to watch two women making it, I compete with the other woman. I perform with my tricks. Yes, I even perform with my pimp.

"And all the while I feel nothing, and that is what I want."

I had read that Charles Manson, of the Sharon Tate murder fame, had learned the technique of controlling women from black pimps in prison. I had always been fascinated about this technique, and asked Dolly what it was.

"It's a challenge. It's like a game of Russian roulette. A pimp has a price, just like whores do. He can be bought. Most pimps are black, and they learn the rules of exploitation when they are very young. As a matter of fact, a lot of the women on the street are southern white women, which I think is really strange. They have been brought up hating blacks and here they are hustling for black men.

"With a trick, you're completely in control. They want sex so much that they'll do anything. With a pimp, sex means nothing. You can't get to him sexually. The only thing that works with him is money. So he keeps you in your place."

Another way pimps keep prostitutes in their place is by threat of violence. Dolly nods sadly when I mention this. "It can be dangerous not to have a pimp," she says, her voice resounding with the first emotion I have heard. Before this, the tone of her voice was smart-ass. Now, she is feeling something real.

"I have a friend who's been trying to work without a pimp. She's taken four or five terrible beatings. The pimps are hysterical because inflation is killing everything. So they're really bad news nowadays. My friend is going to have scars for the rest of her life. She was found unconscious on the street, kicked all over the place. It was really bad."

I respect this tragic tale with silence, but Dolly cannot feel anything for too long, especially anything this bad. She brightens up, utters a laugh, and swigs on the gin bottle, which is almost empty. She then informs me I have to pay the management twenty-five dollars for the use of the room. "I get fifteen, the hotel gets ten. My pimp gets everything," she says almost cheerfully.

"What do you get out of it, Dolly?"

She puts down the empty gin bottle and picks up her cigarettes, her small radio, the earrings she has taken off in preparation for leave-taking, bored by my question. Then, suddenly, she decides to deal with my naiveté. "Look," she says to me harshly, "most street whores think of themselves as victims. Money can change that. If my pimp has a Cadillac, it's a symbol to me. I can get anything I need with money. I can get a nose job. I can get silky clothes. I can send money to my mother. You can create a whole aura of sexuality with money—a nice apartment, velvet cushions. The tricks really get off giving you cash for their kicks, and that's sexual, too."

I look about the bare room and think it would never in the world turn me on. What is this primitive thing that turns on tricks?

"I get a lot of guys who want me to piss on them," Dolly says sarcastically. "They're such eager beavers. It's easy for me to get rid of them. I piss on their face, and it's over in a few seconds.

"At least I don't have to handle their cocks. The first time I saw a cock I hated it. I still do," says this fantasy lady of male desire.

It seems that most of Dolly's real feelings about life are negative, and in an effort not to feel them, she has shut everything else out of her life. I have no moral attitudes toward prostitutes—it just seems that their life is very hard, with very few enjoyments. It's unfortunate that the one virtue of that life, making money, has to be taken from them also by a man who gives them very little—their pimp.

Sexual performance has no class authorship it seems. An upper-class woman I interviewed seems to enjoy her sexual performing for men, perhaps because she is doing it only for her own pleasure.

Patricia

Baroque music is filling the airwaves, suiting the nineteenth-century atmosphere of the parlor we are seated in. Tapestries line the walls, there is an antique desk in a corner with a quill on it, holding a long lavender feather. Gilded engraved editions of classics line the walls and family portraits complement them. Outside, a lovely pregnant garden is blazing in Baltimore's southern sun, an artist's palette of color.

I sit upon a red brocade loveseat, too small to be comfortable. Facing me is Patricia, the mistress of these rooms, who swings back and forth on an old rocker which seems to be out of place.

"When I see a Nazi film, I really get excited," Patricia explains, picking at her low-necked T-shirt which reveals her full breasts. "That's because as an American diplomat's daughter I grew up in Paris and was very susceptible to those gorgeous six-foot, blue-eyed, blond Vikings when they took over the city. Wow! They were really impressive!"

"Has that affected your sex life?"

She laughs. Her gusto does not seem to fit the room or her background. It is a lusty laugh, the laugh of a barmaid in a French countryside inn, serving weary travelers. "You mean sadomasochism? Not really. I've read a lot about it." She pauses, fretfully. "Although there have been some times—when, for one reason or another, I haven't had sex for a long period of time. That's when S/M can be very exciting because it gets to your nerve endings quicker. But, generally, plain sex satisfies me."

"Plain sex?" I laugh. "What does that mean?"

She laughs with me. "To me, it means swinging, lots of men, women, nudity, anything!"

My eyes travel about the room as she speaks and notice that most of the furniture is covered with hand-crocheted coverlets. Although Patricia is not a formal person, the setting of tea service, china, and silver seems ready to be used, almost as tokens of a past life. She explains that they are remnants of her father's estate. Next to me, near the window alcove, is a flat foam-rubber mattress, a jarring note in this formal setting. I ask what it is for.

"For sex," she replies quickly. "It's a foam-rubber mat about five inches thick. I've covered it with heavy cotton. It's good for sex because it's harder than a mattress. It doesn't give. Beds are usually too mushy. Also, I hate to redo my bed every time I have sex. So I just throw a towel over this, and it's whoopee!"

At forty, Patricia is a well-proportioned brunette, with friendly eyes and a ready smile for every question. As we talk, customers for her lovely floral decorations arrive, are introduced informally, pick up her beautifully hand-created designs, graciously paying her for them. When I remark that her attitude is open and friendly, she tells me it is one of the things she learned as a child in her diplomatic and wealthy surroundings. "I was always exposed to many people and taught from childhood to elicit the best from other people and to show them my best," she explains.

"What's your sex life now?"

"I've got five or six regular boyfriends who come up and have lunch, dinner, drinks, or to go to a concert. I don't date men who just come here for sex. They have sex, stay a half-hour, and say 'thank you, bye-bye!' That's a very ugly kind of thing."

"Does that happen a lot?"

"In swinging it does. I've been rather disappointed in people involved in swinging. In Europe, it's a white, society kind of thing. Here, it's blue-collar. The swinging clubs advertise and get a vulgar type of man."

"What else don't you like about swinging?"

"Sometimes it's unfair. I'm sick and tired of having to indoctrinate, having to persuade. The husbands always say the wives have to be shown how to swing. That makes me feel like I'm an unpaid whore."

"Why do you do it?"

"Well, you sometimes meet very interesting men. Last month, I invited a couple to swing, over the phone. I opened the door and the man was so exciting I practically came. But his wife was frigid, and my partner was disappointed. This happens very often in swinging, where one person doesn't like sex, or can't do it, and they swing for the other person. There are a lot of *impotent* men who hide themselves at swinging parties. They go from one room to the other and when someone asks them, they say, 'Well, I've just done it.' Meanwhile, they can get vicarious thrills."

"How else do you meet men?"

"Well, I sunbathe on the terrace, topless. Yesterday, there was somebody waving to me from the roof of the next building. I waved back. He signaled about a drink. We met downstairs, he turned out to be charming, and we made love that evening."

"Will you see him again?"

"It depends. You see, I think sex is below the belt, and love is above the belt. Even with love, it doesn't last very long. The longest a love relationship has ever lasted for me is three or four years. After that, the sex gets boring."

We are interrupted by a very large man who has come to pick up a huge floral bouquet. Although his appearance is a bit scary (he looks like a humorless Sydney Greenstreet), Patricia treats him with royal manners. When he leaves, business over, she offers me a special coffee liqueur which a Brazilian planter brings her from his estate. He is one of the best lovers she's had, and she's had him sporadically for five years. I remark she seems to know many wealthy men.

"Money is not the attraction, but, generally, men who have degrees and are involved with foundations and big business do have money. I'm attracted to them because they are mature. The struggle weeds out the boys."

The liqueur is indeed delicious, conjuring up fantasies of soft, tropical breezes, banana trees, and tall, dark men on wild horses, riding over the Brazilian plains. "What other ways do you meet men?" I ask, coming back to reality.

"When I'm waiting for the street light to change—I'll stand there, and often there's a man crossing from the opposite side of the street. I'll look straight into his eyes as he's approaching me, and I'll smile. Then I'll say, 'Good morning.' It's really a great opener."

She gets up from the rocker and walks over to the large dining table where a half-dozen beautiful floral bouquets are awaiting their pickup. She touches one, turns the leaves on another, caressing the blossoms as she passes by.

"Do you enjoy sex?" I ask her from my far side of the room.

She turns and pivots like a chorus girl. "I love it," she says in her upper-class accent. "I've been a nudist all my life. In fact, I used to love going to a nudist camp in the country where I was sure to be able to just screw my head off. But then people got into drugs and became impotent. There's nothing like drugs to make men impotent. They think they're having a good time, but I'm not."

"Are you good in bed?"

"Men tell me I'm an excellent lay. I'm considered absolutely tip-top. If I'm properly stimulated mentally, I don't like foreplay. I like getting down to brass tacks right away because I'm so excited. A man penetrates me and I'm ready to come. I can't wait through all that fingering and eating. In fact, it turns me off because I have to hold back. If a man enters me right, I can come by the third stroke, and then I'll keep coming every few minutes. Then, the second time around, I'll give him all the foreplay he wants.

"There's two things I like stiff—one of them is ice cream and the other is penises." We both laugh at this absurd comparison. "I have vaginal orgasms from stiff penises. I don't like to get into clitoral excitement because it takes away from the vagina. And the vagina is where I have those wonderful, marvelous, compulsive orgasms. Do you know the kind I mean?"

I nod from wonderful memories. "What happens to you afterward?"

"I get completely dry and rough and tight, and I don't want sex for two or three weeks," she says, astonishing me.

I ask her about her bisexuality. "Sex with women is an appetizer. Men are entrees. I like the meat and potatoes men. I've gone to bed with hundreds of men and I prefer them. I'm a really liberated person, the most liberated person on this globe. But I do have one rule: I only fuck married men who commute, so I don't have to meet their wives."

"You seem to meet an awful lot of men. Do you enjoy them all?"

She sighs. "No, about twenty-five percent of the men I make offers to don't respond. And another twenty-five percent are entirely uncreative and just want to get laid. And another twenty-five percent are married men who want you to make love to their wives.

"But," she adds, her eyes snapping, "the other twenty-five per-cent are wonderful."

Patricia is a sexual performer; there is no doubt about it, for she never talks about her feelings, only about her enjoyments. But she is a sexual performer who seems to be enjoying it, whether it is because of her highly social upbringing, or her inability to expect anything from men. Patricia has learned to take care of herself and therefore can limit her sexuality to the area of fun and games, which works for her.

Often performance sex is just considered kindergarten games, and the performers wonder why people get so vulgar about it. This is very often true of the Sixties hippies, who couldn't under-stand what the furor was all about when they took their clothes off, made love in groups, etc. Laura, who appeared nude in a stage revue, spoke of this attitude.

Laura

Laura is slim and sexy, and speaks in a soft, sweet voice rem-iniscent of leading ladies of former times. Although she sings and dances in the nude, she says: "I really like the show—but it's not erotic, it's just fun!"

To rehearse the show the cast decided they would have an orgy. Laura attended with her boyfriend. "Nobody could take it seri-ously. The men couldn't get hardons. Nobody had orgasms, and my boyfriend and I just laughed."

When she leaves the stage door entrance, men from the audience are waiting for her. "That's when I get so many propositions from the men who have seen the show. I don't understand it. The show is fun. Sex is fun. There's nothing wrong in running around naked. Why on earth do the men in the audience think they can fuck me?"

"How does your boyfriend feel about that?"

"He always meets me but he can't really be unpleasant. He doesn't want to offend the producer. It's a rotten way to live."

"What is your personal relationship with him like?"

"Well, he and I are pretty monogamous when we're both in town. When one of us is away, we don't talk about what goes on. I feel like I'm being strangled, always being with one person. I can love more than one man. I can sleep with more than one person. I can love women, too.

"As a matter of fact, with the same sex, he doesn't get jealous. We do a lot of *ménages à trois*, but always with two girls. He wouldn't be comfortable with another man in bed with me.

"I'm jealous of him sometimes, but I tell myself I have no right to be. Last time I was away, he was seeing this other woman who got really serious about him. When I came back, she sent me a lovely gift. I met her and liked her and we all made love together.

"Our sexual life is a lot of fun. It's not on schedule. I don't like to make it at night, after the show. I like it in the morning, in the bathroom, in the kitchen, in the subway. The show doesn't arouse me at all. As a matter of fact, it depresses me, turns me off sex.

"I get upset when I see all those men getting excited and wanting to fuck me. Instead of wanting to fuck me, *why don't they go home and get it on with the lady of the house?*"

Laura's question is a good one, except when we realize if the males in the audience go home to get it on with the lady of the house, there's much more vulnerability and emotion attached to sex. Instead, the image of Laura, nude and free on the stage, seems a much more exciting proposition to them. They won't have to love Laura, they think, all they would have to do is fuck her, and that prospect is very exciting. It is interesting to me that Laura, the provocateur of these kinds of sexual ambitions in the show, sees it all as just childish fun and takes no personal responsibility for turning on her audience, a feeling shared by many other sexual performers.

Very often a sexual performer is not only not turned on by her male audience, but is turned on by an entirely different sex. Carrie is a case in point.

Carrie

Twenty-four-year-old Carrie looks like a college freshman, with her long, straight, blonde hair, her tiny body, her freckles, and her buckteeth. She lives in a very small, but very elegantly furnished, apartment which is decorated with theater posters, books on acting and the theater, and a wardrobe for any occasion.

Carrie, who has two college degrees, is an aspiring actress, taking lessons regarding her craft each day—singing, diction, dancing, etc.—and supporting her studies by working as a go-go dancer in Chicago five nights a week for fifty dollars a night.

"I wear pasties and a G-string when I'm on stage, but when I have to mingle with the customers, I put on a skirt," she says very offhandedly.

Carrie is very, very cool about the fact that she gyrates for money every night in the week. "I work from about five or seven till three-thirty in the morning—half-hour on the stage, half-hour off. When I'm off, I've got to mingle and get the men to buy booze. The management wants to sell drinks, so they don't care what you do. Even if you punch a guy in the nose, it's all right as long as he buys champagne. As a matter of fact, some of those guys love it when you're mean to them, when you give them rough verbal treatment.

"They bore me to death because they want to talk about sex constantly. They want to pick me up and fuck me. Last night, I was offered four hundred and fifty dollars for a fast fuck." She says this very coolly as she drinks apple juice. With no makeup, Carrie gives almost an obscene impression when on the stage because she looks like a little girl.

"What do you think of when you're dancing?"

"I think of the next scene I have to do in class," she says bluntly. "I like to move, like to feel the music go through my body. I'm there to be sexy, so I act sexy. I move my hips in a sensuous manner. I use a lot of eye contact. Sometimes I crack gum and shout, 'Hiya, baby!' I'm a clown. Some of these girls just stand on stage and comb their hair, they're so boring.

"I like to use my imagination. I wear a Girl Scout uniform and do a striptease out of that just to have fun. Sometimes I wear a lot of makeup and a black wig and sleazy clothes, and no one knows it's me."

"Are you ever attracted to the men?"

"No, never!" she says adamantly. "They're mostly white, middle-class businessmen, and they're full of catcalls and mouth gestures. A lot of dancers take speed, and the men just call them names, and they don't even hear it. With me, the men who are attracted to me are older men who want to take care of me because they think I'm a college student."

All kinds of women work at the go-go bar with Carrie—housewives who need extra money, women supporting their boyfriends, abandoned mothers who have children to support. "One woman saves everything she earns for her kids. She's great, even though she's vulgar. She sits on stage and says, 'Hey, you cocksucker,' and flashes her G-string. She's not like some of the other girls who spend all their money on French Provincial furniture and expensive clothes so no one will know what they are doing.

"Sometimes their boyfriends will come storming into the bars and pull their girls from the stage by the neck. We work on tips, too, and a girl will say, 'You want to come and contribute to the pussy fund?' and the guys will get their hands in there and get a cheap feel for ten dollars."

"How do you feel about the job?"

She looks at me impatiently, as if I have asked a stupid question. "Sometimes I feel it is really sick, and I want to get out of it as soon as I can, and other times I don't care and say I've got to make a living some way. Sometimes I get a kick out of showing my body to those guys and knowing they'll never in a million years get a chance to touch it. They come on. Boy, do they come on! I'll be having a drink, and one will say, 'Gee, I'd love to eat your pussy.' I'll say, 'How rude!' and use big college words and act superintelligent, and they don't know how to deal with you. Some guys get drunk and cry into their drinks. The job is part shrink, part sister, part mother, part whore. It's kind of a visual mental therapy, and also seeing if they can score."

One time a good-looking, wealthy guy told Carrie that he

needed a mistress, someone with class whom he could take to cocktail parties and someone he could fuck. He would take care of all her expenses. She said no. I asked her why.

"Because I hate men," she says. "I'm gay. I'm in love with the woman I live with."

"Are you happy?"

A sad look comes over her face. "She's very domineering. She makes love to me the way she wants. My breasts aren't very sensitive, and she keeps kissing them. I'm very emotionally oriented. I don't like sex without feeling. But I'm so in love with her that I fix her meals, clean the house, do all her errands. I've become her servant. She says if I don't like it, I can get out, but I just want to please her. I love her so much." Carrie's whole tone has changed now. Before she was offhand and cool, now she is a sad, pained woman talking about something she cannot control.

"She's not as emotional as I am, also she's bisexual. I'm turned on only to women. I like their softness, their gentleness. The very masculine butch doesn't interest me. She uses a dildo, but it's only because it's her that I like it, not because it's a dildo. She's my princess on a white charger.

"But," she says slowly, "she's draining me of all my energy— the energy I could be using on myself. She's driving me up a wall because she'll shack up with a guy for about three days and then come home to me and say she loves me. When he calls, I freak out. I can't compete with a man."

So Carrie goes from this situation to the go-go bar where she shouts, "Hey, cocksucker, let me wrap my legs around your neck!" while the other girls say, "Hey, cocksucker, I haven't seen you around for ages." But Carrie feels pity for the other women who don't seem to have any other aspirations. "They're there to get a lover or a man, can you believe that? They think they're going to meet Prince Charming in that bar."

Carrie seems to be the classic case of the performing woman who uses her sexuality to frustrate her male audience, and then in turn is frustrated at home by her female lover. It is interesting to me that while she despises her male audience for being macho, she accepts the same kind of behavior from her female lover. It is also interesting to me that the men in the audience get so turned on by insults and by a woman who is out to get them.

Of course, a sexual performer par excellence is the male transvestite, or the transexual who began with another sex and has had to learn the female performance from imitation. Interesting to me is Lana, who has completely changed her life, and her sex, and uses sexual performance to help her ambitions.

Lana

She looks like a large version of her namesake, a Lana Turner who is very, very tall, buxom, and blonde. Her eye makeup is perfect, she is wearing multicolored eye shadow, rouge, powder, lipstick. Her simple, clinging, jersey dress is bursting at the seams, and two buttons have fallen off, showing breasts that look luscious and soft. She is sitting on her chaise longue in a hugely expensive San Francisco apartment decorated with rare Chinese furniture. A satin coverlet covers the chaise as Lana lounges luxuriously against it, not looking at me, staring into space, putting her long cigarette in her bejeweled holder, which I am told later is made of real diamonds, matching the rings, bracelets, earrings, and necklace of diamonds that Lana is fond of wearing.

She is uncomfortable, although friendly, and I am wondering whether she will tell me the truth about the fact that now, at thirty-two years of age, Lana has only lived ten years as a woman. Before that, she was imprisoned in a man's body.

"I know that I was psychologically and spiritually one sex, a female in every way," she says. "When I was five years old, I remember wanting to play with dolls. I had dreams of growing up and marrying and having children, just like you did." She darts a glance at me through her long, long lashes. "Then, when I became an adolescent, things got as bad as they would ever be. It was hell! Absolutely hell!" Her husky voice breaks a little, and she steals another fleeting look at me, her blue eyes frightened, wondering about the impression she is making.

"Nobody understood me. My parents loved me, but they were

confused. But I was rescued from the horrible limbo when I was twenty. I met a doctor who specializes in transexuality, and he began giving me the hormone treatments, and then I had the operation. He said I was a classic transexual and never would need psychiatry. I felt so calm, I felt beautiful, that the road's bend was open. Then I became a woman, physically and legally."

Lana's definition of a woman is someone who gives birth. "I can't have children, that's my only sadness," she says. But in every other way Lana feels that she is a woman. Since penile skin was used in the lining of the vagina she was given, she feels there is definite sensation when penetration occurs. However, her sexual life is much different now than when she was a man.

"My sex drive is different, lower from a physical standpoint. I feel that I'm very mercenary because of that. I go to bed with men to better myself. I go to bed with men to assure myself that I'm attractive enough to get any man I want."

Lana never, never initiates sex. "There are certain looks that are inborn in every woman. I wait. I'm very passive and wait for the man to make all the moves. The only thing I refuse is anal sex. I was much more romantic ten years ago, but now I control my romanticism. We have to protect ourselves in life, and it's too easy to get hurt. But I love men telling me that they worship me.

"I still think that love is something that lasts forever and ever and that it's magic when you find someone. But I've suffered greatly more than once. I was taken advantage of by men whom I loved. And in weak moments, it can happen again, but if things are going great, I can't even remember suffering."

Things are going great for Lana, for after working seven years as a prostitute in Japan, she has amassed a fortune. "I have to go back three months out of every year," she says in a depressed tone of voice. "But I can make the fifty thousand dollars I need to live here in style."

One of the things that Lana did for that kind of money is work in the Japanese version of a massage parlor, where she blew one man every fifteen minutes, a task she found very, very easy and which gained her the reputation as the only white woman who could work in that system.

"I've made enough money to live well and travel. I'm probably much more realistic than romantic at this point in my life. I pay over a thousand dollars' rent, have my servants, like diamonds and good clothes. I travel in society and keep things very under-cover. I have a very large group of friends and admirers both here and in Europe—doctors, lawyers, businessmen, corporation presidents. I have never been rejected by any man!"

"Never?" I was interested in this phenomenon, for every woman I have ever met has been rejected at one time or another.

"No, I mean I just sense it. You can feel whether a man wants you or not. I'm very choosy about the people I spend time with. Why, I could go downstairs tonight and I could have ten men who would pay me, and I could surely have ten men if I didn't want any money. Frankly, I have just never found anybody par-ticularly that attractive who I just had to run over to and ask him to go to bed with me."

As she keeps flicking her hot, red ashes in various ashtrays placed about her, Lana's rings shine in the subtle light, as if each of her sentences has diamond exclamation points. She is beginning to look at me now, where before her glance was always to another corner. She cuddles her body, puts her feet up, and her face gets a baby look, the look of an overgrown baby doll.

She says she is happy that she doesn't have vulnerability in sex-ual needs, for she can control her life better. "If I were married to someone, I'd physically have to have a certain amount of sex. I can be much more cool and distant without needing it." As a result of this coolness, Lana admits to using the power of sex over men and manipulating them to get what she wants. "That's femi-ninity, which is a woman's psychological role. I know how to handle a man, how to get what I want out of men. I know that I'm stronger because I'm a woman, but I don't have to throw it in their faces and beat it over their heads.

"I don't love emotionally," she goes on to say, "but there is a part of me that would like to marry a millionaire, and yet, there is another part of me that just wants to meet somebody who will appreciate me and whom I can share my life with. I can give love, and would love to meet a man who could give me the same."

She turns to me, suddenly more comfortable. "Can you see any-thing? Anything different about me?" she asks anxiously.

I tell her I can't, although I have entered the room knowing that Lana is a transexual and have noticed her large bone structure. But I do not want to hurt her feelings, because Lana is doing something rare for a transexual: She is actually telling the truth about her sexual feelings and emotions.

"I think I still have a lot of hang-ups about my appearance. There's still a little girl in me, a little flicker of flame. I dream tomorrow I could meet someone. I think my soul is beautiful and wish I could go around without makeup and still feel I'm a beautiful person. But I can't. I'm meticulous with manicures, pedicures, makeup. My body is very feminine, but I have a large hip development. But I guess everybody would like to make improvements."

Although Lana claims to feel limited sensations with male penetration, limited sexual needs, and no orgasms, in her personal life she has trouble giving a definite no to a man. "I find I make excuses. I put him off. I think deep down I can't say no to men. You know, I'm a very strong woman physically, and the men who are attracted to me aren't the type who are going to push themselves upon me. But in the past they have been weak men and they have drained their strength from me. I'll always attract the wrong kind of man, but now I think I've gotten to the point where I can control them."

She tells me she has a dinner date and invites me into her bedroom-dressing room. It is a room decorated like a Thirties film, with satin curtains and long, tasseled drapes. Everything is nude satin—everything, that is, except the furs showing from her closet. She walks behind a gorgeous Chinese screen to dress. "I'm not flamboyant," she says. "I dress conservatively, but I take a lot of pride in jewelry and clothes."

She is now wearing a hand-embroidered Japanese robe to sit in before her vanity mirror, repairing her already-perfect and voluminous makeup. "I'm not going to say, 'Oh, Prince Charming is going to come along and carry me away on his galloping white horse,' because I know that's not going to happen. I just want to be appreciated, and if a man has money, that's fortunate."

She begins to dress. A long white satin gown is selected. "Men look at me because I'm gorgeous. I'm statuesque. I have the ability to carry it all. I'm very chic, very sophisticated, very European."

The gown is Grecian, matched with a jersey cape, trimmed with fox. "I know that when I walk into the restaurant tonight every man in the place will stop and look at me." She adds more diamonds to her already plentiful supply. "You see, if we know each other when I'm fifty, you'll see that I will never have wrinkles. My skin will sag, and then I will lift it. I've had extensive plastic surgery on my face. I've had my nose done a couple of times. Silicone injections on my cheeks, my forehead. I've done something few people have been able to do."

She pauses, turns to look into a large floor mirror, staring at herself intensely, pursing her lips at her reflection. "I've been able to create. Yes, because this is my power and I have created it." She turns, looking at her reflection from the rear. Then turning again, facing me, she says haughtily, "You see, I have created . . . Lana. . . ."

Lana has become the stereotypical extreme of what the glamorous sexual performer is. Yet she admits to a compulsive romanticism which she fights by controlling her sexual performance with wealthy men who will be generous to her. There seems to be no middle of the road for Lana. She sees sexual relationships as one of two extremes: love and suffering or, preferably, performance and wealth.

This extremist point of view exists in most sexual performers. Where Lana at least is controlling her relationships with wealthy men and making her life more comfortable, there are many less fortunate sexual performers who have Lana's attitudes but have not made the big time. Caroline, a street hustler, is a case in point.

Caroline

She walks into my apartment, breathless, sweaty, immediately asking for a cold glass of water. "I asked several people where your house was, and they looked at me like 'What the hell is she doing, coming into this neighborhood?' "

"That's crazy," I respond. "This is one of the most cosmopolitan neighborhoods in the city."

"No, no," she insists as I show her into my study. She sits on the couch, trying to catch her breath. She is dressed for a courtroom appearance: tailored clothes, no jewelry, little makeup. The tone of her clothes and her skin is reddish brown, and she gives the appearance of warmth on a sunny day, which her genuine smile confirms.

"I can't believe anyone hassled you," I remark again.

"Well, they did," she says, and we begin the interview.

During the first few minutes, I am astonished that only a few blocks from my house is Caroline's street prostitution beat, Fourteenth Street and Third Avenue. I am also amazed that any woman who worked that route could be acting like a frightened little girl.

"I've been a whore since 1958," she tells me, wiping the perspiration from her face, turning on her transistor radio next to her for comfort and security. "I've lived with my old man almost all that time."

"What's it like, using sex for business and then using it for love?" I ask the eternal question.

She looks shocked at it, indignant. "Come on, baby, if you're any kind of a good whore, you never *ever* enjoy it, even if they go down on you. You just never enjoy it! My usual thing is to work midnight to six in the morning. I just stand there. One thing I pride myself for is that I never *ever* went up to a guy and said, 'Hey, baby, you want to go?' No, that isn't my stick. I just stand there, and if a guy sees me standing there like a normal person and if I look all right to him, he's going to come over. If I look good and clean and wholesome, someone's going to say, 'Hey, baby, you want to go?' " She laughs heartily at her statements, and says them with pride. I offer her a drink, but she says haughtily that she doesn't drink or smoke.

"I've been very lucky because most white men like big breasts," she says, laughing and shaking her entire body. "They come over and say, 'Hey, I want to suck on your bust,' and we go to a hotel nearby. I feel that even if they do the actual sex act, they do it because that's on the program. Most times they really just want to caress my bust and put their penis between my breasts and just get off like that."

Caroline looks at me closely, then grimaces. "At first I felt disgusted, but then after a while I thought, *Oh, my God, well, you know people get their kicks that way*."

"You mention white men, how about black men?"

"Hell, I don't dig black tricks," she says with anger at her own race. "They have a tendency to rip you off, or if they're not going to do that, they're going to try to force you to join their little set. Hell, no way in the world am I going to give my money to a man. This is mine, I wouldn't have a pimp." Apparently, Caroline's determination to be a free agent works, and she has never been brutalized for it, refuting other prostitutes' testimony.

After a night's work, Caroline goes home to her old man. "My usual thing is to take a bath and take a douche. Then I hit the sack. We might get it on about noon, that's early morning to night people. Then we get up and eat, just like a real family."

I ask her if she gets very tired on the job.

She giggles. "Not really. Those johns are really funny. They tell you all about their problems. You've got to listen about their wives, whom they lost in death, what business problems they have, what they did and shouldn't have done. Oh, man, they just keep rapping to you! It's really weird, because a lot of black broads don't even know what they're talking about. They say, 'Hell, I got to sit there and listen about the stock market!' It's funny. It's absolutely ridiculous."

The tricks of her trade are many. For one thing, she doesn't like or trust other prostitutes, says they are not honest. "I like women who are outspoken, who say things for real, not phony broads who say, 'Oh, God, you look simply boss.' If they're whores, they've got to be liars."

Earning from ten dollars to fifteen dollars a trick, Caroline has learned how to rip off customers. "The first thing a whore learns is how to hide her money, and not to let the person whom she's participating with in the sex act know where the money is. First of all when a whore picks up a cat, she has to see how high he is. If he's very high, he's easy, because johns are not going to get an erection if they've consumed a considerable amount of liquor. So often, they're asleep as soon as we hit the room. And I take all their bread. I always leave them carfare, though, because I don't want them to get mad at me."

She grins widely. "They come back, and they tell me, 'I know what you did to me the last time, but you were great, because shit, you left me some money to get home.' So we do it all over again, and I rip them off again. A lot of them want me to eat and drink with them then, they think of me as an old friend. Then they get into bed and fall asleep, and the same thing happens. Sometimes I run into a john who doesn't have enough money for the hotel, so if he's a nice guy, I take him into a hallway and save him money. Then I have to go to a bar and use the ladies' room to clean myself, because I'm a freak for cleanliness."

Although some of Caroline's attitudes seem to confirm the classic conception of the generous whore, she says her feelings are not in her job at all, that while working she feels like she's in outer space. "I'm not there. My body is there, but I am in space somewhere. I can't really explain it to you, but I know when to say 'hmmmm' and when to make noises and scream. I give them their money's worth."

"But do you have trouble turning off?"

"I don't. I'm very cold, really a cold person, sexwise," she says, with tears in her eyes. "I'm a very frigid person. I don't know why. I don't have any feelings about it. I'm the type of person who can just cut it, just like that. I've never had an orgasm in my life."

She turns off the radio now, smooths down the wrinkles of her dark brown dress, and I tell her she looks lovely in her outfit. She is pleased at the compliment, and her voice throbs with emotion as she says to me in despair, "I want to find a guy who really cares about who I am, not what I look like and how I dress. I dream about a superstud sometimes, and when I walk down the street, I look at men's flies and wonder.

"But," she says quietly, "I don't really want a superstud. I just want a man who knows all about the dumb stuff."

Caroline is a very moving example of a sexual performer who absolutely believes in romance, and never has experienced it, and has never even considered it might be her choice of profession that has prevented this. Her profession was not an economic necessity, for her parents were middle-class and could have sent her to college if she wished. But for some reason, Caroline chose the life of a street hustler, the hardest life of all for a woman. It is amazing to me that she has the ability and the courage to show her real feelings and her vulnerability to me, even if it was for only a few seconds.

The strain of romanticism exists in all sexual performers. It feeds the extremist point of view that sex with feelings is painful, and sex without must be rewarded. But a person has only so much sexual energy, and when it is spent in performance, it is not easy to invest in vulnerability. Charlene, a young, energetic stripteaser, is a case in point.

Charlene

Charlene's offstage personality is so totally at odds with her onstage performance that I smile to myself as I watch her. Frizzy-haired and babyish, she is touching her crotch as she talks to me. She is wearing a strapless leopard affair on top of worn dungarees. We are in her Nevada hotel room, where the remnants of her silver sequins and plum feathers, used in her act, are in evidence. I have just seen her performance on stage. She is brash, she is coarse, she is funny, and she is very, very overt in her sexual come-ons. When she touches her crotch on stage as a stripper, it is not done to comfort but to titillate. Here, in her hotel room, she touches herself to comfort.

I watch her getting ready for our interview, getting into a cuddly and sleepy position, her fresh red cheeks blushing as she tries to find a comfortable position on her hotel bed, moving this way and that, her huge breasts popping out of her tank top, the nipples showing through. She keeps complaining about bronchitis, and I wonder at her manner of dress, but she says it is the most comfortable thing she has to wear.

At eighteen, Charlene is a cross between a comedienne and a stripper. Making jokes, she takes off her clothes to the beat of the drummer. She is very serious about what she calls her "acting" performance.

"I do my job as an actress. In one of the songs I begin to take my clothes off. Then I tell stories. I work it through an acting beat. When I get off stage, I'm a very sexually oriented person who has been affected by my performance. It's like working in a bakery, you see the bakery goods and you don't want to eat. The intimate physical interaction makes me less sexual. It's the most unerotic feeling in the world, so to speak. It drains me of sexual energy. It affects and dirties my sexuality because of the intimate contact with the audience."

Charlene has bitter criticism for the audience. "They are very, very subjective and not artistically oriented. As an actress, I look out on the audience and see a nondiscriminating group. Very frequently, they'll applaud things that aren't refined. Their reaction when I take off my clothes, rather than correlating it as an intelligent motive within the context of my skit, they just relate it to tits and ass, just flesh. This attitude makes me feel that it's the artist versus the commercial world."

I cannot believe her jumble of half-intellectual, half-theatrical concepts, and try to get her to talk about something without using this esoteric vocabulary. So naturally, I ask her about sex.

"I'm basically monogamous, and I'm looking for a husband. I'm mentally and emotionally tied to the idea of a committed sexual relationship, although I must admit"—she purses her lips like an infant waiting for Pablum—"in this search, I do have exceedingly strange tastes. You see, I have this Pandora's box and I don't want to open it."

"What's in the box?"

She looks at me guiltily, and begins to pick her nose with her tiny pinky finger. "I am exceedingly sexually attractive to women. But I will not give in to it. If I were to be with a woman, I would have to give up forever the idea of security, emotionally and financially. You see, I want to marry a Jewish doctor or lawyer," she says very matter-of-factly.

However, in her pursuit of this very conventional goal, Charlene has made very strange bedfellows. "I have taken the ball by the hand. The other night I went up to this man and asked him if he'd like my phone number. Of course, it's very pathetic because he thought of me as aggressive. He felt I was just this little wild, brazen thing, and I must be doing this with everyone. Of course, I did give him my slinked-out, cross-eyed, do-you-want-a-cigarette-too number, which is my way of cruising!" she admits.

Not too successful with heterosexual men, Charlene has had two long affairs with homosexuals. "I can feel free because there's a lack of male chauvinism, a weakness. I can be aggressive and gentle. I can be a man and a woman. Men who are soft, small, and very sweet-looking are terribly attractive to me. Of course, we were monogamous. No more men for the men I live with.

"I would initiate our lovemaking. I would take off his shirt, kiss him, hug him, stick my tongue in his mouth, touch his genitals. We were so totally in love."

But the relationships broke up when these homosexual men went back to loving men, leaving Charlene very sad.

On the rebound, she receives calls from a famous actor. As she tells me this story, she begins to dance around the room, giggling, playing an imaginary piano with her fingers in the air, taking up her plumes, waving them. "He's sooooooo gorgeous. He's soft and sweet, with curly brown hair. And talented. Turns me on every way. Emotionally and intellectually. Makes me feel totally beautiful. Sends me flowers. Calls me and says, 'I can't help thinking about you.'"

"Do you want to marry him?"

A frown comes over her impish face, and she shakes her head in the air as if she is talking to someone other than me. She puts her thumb in her mouth, stares at the ceiling, and looks like a baby who has just lost her candy.

"No, it wouldn't work. He's constantly on the road. His life-style is totally untuned with mine. I want a nice marriage. A very pretty house. You know that play, *The Doll's House*. He loved her so much. I'm basically an old-fashioned girl." She sucks her thumb constantly now. "I know I've been promiscuous, I've been with over a hundred men, but I'm really trying not to." She begins to blush, looking so guilty I wonder what on earth she is going to say. "Besides, the actor is married"—she pauses, looks out of the window with a hint of tears in her eyes—"to my best friend, and I feel very, very guilty about it." Then she turns around to me, and I am to hear words of utter disaster from this eighteen-year-old child.

"I'm so tired of it all," she says listlessly. "Sex just isn't worth it."

All of the women in this chapter have chosen to act at sex rather than to feel. Although this strain of performance runs through everyone's life, these women have made it their profession.

Their illogical attitudes toward what they want and how to get it, the tremendous strain of Rachmaninoffian romanticism—loud chords on a grand piano—their lack of responsibility for their sexual professions, all of these things prevent them from a greater happiness in life, with or without love.

Five

❀ ❀ ❀

THE EROTICISM OF
OLDER WOMEN

Older women always complain that they are not represented in books about sexuality. When I interviewed them for this chapter, it was easy to understand why. I found that older women simply do not like to talk about sex, because for them sex is incorporated into that old structure of marriage and romance; it is usually a duty, something to be borne. Only when women go through an entire change of role identity due to their menopause do they sometimes change their attitudes toward the sexual part of their existence.

When I asked several older women about sexual pleasure, these were the kinds of one-line answers I received:

"I never said no to my husband. I never said I had a headache. When my husband stopped at seventy, it didn't bother me one bit."

"When my husband ejaculates semen, that's my orgasm."

"When I saw my husband nude, I was disgusted. It was the ugliest thing I'd ever seen. When he showed it to me, I said to myself, *Well, you'd better wake up. This is going to be part of your life, as it was in your mother's before you, and your grandmother's and everybody's down the line.*"

"My husband and I have sex once or twice a week, although he's seventy-eight. I used to have orgasms when I was younger, but I don't have any sensation now."

"The best part is to tell one another we love each other, better than intercourse itself. You just don't get the same satisfaction from sex."

These negative attitudes about sexual enjoyment lead to all kinds of misinformation. One common mistaken belief—that masturbation leads to blindness—was repeated over and over to me, despite all the new information being published recently. One story about masturbation that absolutely terrified me was the apparently common practice of using a light bulb to replace an absent penis. One woman was rushed to the hospital, all cut inside, and no wonder. When I asked how this could possibly happen, I was told that artificial fruit was the usual thing used, but light bulbs were more readily available. Keeping sexual information in the background, in the closet, led these women to improvise and, I might add, to improvise dangerously.

Although these older women's interviews are not highly erotic, I find them incredibly humorous, and sometimes surprising. One woman who is very, very unusual is Edna.

Edna

Edna is a jolly, pleasant, intelligent, overweight woman who, at sixty-three years of age, is a consultant educator. She has an active sex life, and her favorite lover is a glamorous figure of the theater, a handsome, charming, virile man of fifty who I think is super.

"I'm very attracted to physically handsome men," Edna says. "His voice, his beauty, his kindness will turn me on."

Edna has known since 1933 what turns her on. "I was taught early in my life that the most sensitive spot in a woman's body is just north of the clitoris and that stimulation released by the tip of the finger or the tongue can beat plain fucking. It's my spot with a capital S, and I have multiple orgasms," she says breathlessly. "I also have the atom bomb orgasm, which is as complete an orgasm as you can have, with all the bells ringing and the lights going on and off. They last for a long time."

Although her lover's environment is the sophisticated center of the theater where good-looking women and men dominate, Edna met this handsome man at a nudist camp. "We were lying in the sun, and I started to massage him. He made a move. I was surprised. I didn't think we would become sexually involved because of his fame. . . . We weren't in an entirely private spot. But I told him what I want and what I like, and I got my complete orgasms of satisfaction before there was any penetration at all. He figured it out quickly."

This affair has gone on for four years, although both of them travel a lot. I asked Edna how a woman of her age came to be so free about her sexuality.

"Well, when I see my ex-husbands, I realize what my sex life was with them and how much I've learned and they haven't. During my marriages, all we did was fumble around. I knew what I wanted, but I didn't have the guts to ask for it. In 1933, I was taught to use the vaginal muscles before women knew what they were. I still use them, and they are in good condition. I've also had a lot of success with impotent men. I know how to relax them so that they regain their prowess.

"I tell them to sit in a chair, with their feet flat on the floor and hands on thighs. Then I tell them to think about every spot in their body, every toe, every finger, and to breathe deeply and expel the tension and the anxiety. Then I have them do it all over again and this time to breathe in dynamic energy. It works every time. They can get erections and make love."

Edna describes herself as a grandma, short, fat, and indifferent about her flesh. "I have certain indulgences. I've always been turned on by the cerebral. My current lover is a Renaissance man. I've done a lot of things, like swinging, which bored me terribly.

"I've always had a happy life, because I have an open mind. In 1927, my college professor said have an open mind and displace the barriers between you and what you don't quite know or what you've been raised to be prejudiced against. I'm a very happy woman and have a happy life. My sex life isn't as busy as it used to be, but I have a secret. . . ."

"What is that?" I ask.

"My vibrator," she sighs, glistening with happiness. "I bought one last year and I really enjoy it. I read my favorite detective stories, or I do my crossword puzzles, and enjoy the sheer pleasure of the vibrator's stimulation. I have a lot of orgasms with it. I think it's such fun. I travel with it. I do it a couple of times a week. I've recommended it to everyone.

"I call it Mother's Little Helper," she concludes.

Edna is unusual, because sex has always been a part of her active life, rare in a woman of her age. I was happy to meet her and hear that she was enjoying her erotic life, with, and without, a man.

An older woman who has the most unusual orgasm I ever heard about is Clare.

Clare

"I've worn flimsy dresses with nothing underneath and have had a lot of one-night stands." Clare, a pudgy woman wearing a too-short skirt and a Jackie Kennedy pillbox hat which she is thirty years too old for, is talking to me in a whiskey voice, her green eyes glinting. "I'm a pretty easy target because I'm lonely, and it shows. I'm also a crotch-watcher. I walk down the street and watch crotches. And I like nice asses, too."

"Have you ever run into any trouble?"

"A couple of times. A black guy once beat me up, and I had to call the cops. This Sicilian I'm seeing now gets funny every once in a while. Incidentally, he has small feet, and the cliché doesn't hold. He's well hung and very versatile in bed.

"I have a few old friends whom I can call and say, 'Let's have sex,' but generally I like to cook dinner for a man and spend the evening discussing my work, and most of those guys are married. I work very hard at my pottery, and it's very beautiful. I like it when my work turns a man on."

At fifty-eight, Clare has had two husbands. "I'm sorry they're dead, but I was never satisfied. In fact, I'm still not satisfied. I masturbate all the time when the guy leaves. It's the only way I get my rocks off."

"Who is your fantasy man?"

"Young men. I'm shy with them. One night last week I was thinking, *Gee, what a fucking bore to go home alone. I'd really enjoy having a drink with a man. Cooking dinner. Going to bed with him.* I saw this young guy with a great crotch coming toward me. He stopped a second. I saw the look on his face. All I had to do was make the first move, and it would have fulfilled a lot of fantasies for me. But I *couldn't* do it. And he *didn't* do it. And I said to myself, *Jesus Christ! Why don't you do it? Because you didn't meet him at some kind of lousy party? Because you're too old for him?* I turned around and looked back, and so did he. But we never got together."

"What's the most erotic experience you've ever had, Clare?"

She sips on the ice cubes, remnants of the tall bourbon and soda she has gulped too quickly. "I had several orgasms at the dentist," she says, laughing.

"What?" I shout, for dentists and doctors seem to be getting all the action.

"No, it wasn't with him. It was from a root-canal job. I had an orgasm that was so intense that I passed out. He was digging down through my tooth, and it went right to my cunt. It was so real. I was in that chair, I had had some gas, and I fantasized that the instrument was a prick, and it somehow went down and down and down to some place I had never felt before. There was pain, but there was also this intense feeling of pleasure. It happened three times during the treatment, each time he did the root-canal job."

"Did you discuss it with the dentist?"

"Yes."

"What did he say?"

"He said it was a very unusual reaction!"

Clare was unusual because, although she was melodramatic about her life, she had an obvious sense of humor. Try as I might, and I did try, I couldn't identify with her root-canal orgasm, but I absolutely believed she had experienced it.

More often than not, older women fell in love but did not like sex, even with their husbands. Anna is one of them.

Anna

"I'm separated thirty years from my husband because he ran away with another woman and because I didn't like sex," sixty-five-year-old Anna says, wiping the tears from her eyes, remembering her trauma. Plump, frowzy, bucktoothed, wearing a loud, bold-striped dress with gaudy jewelry, she describes her younger self as "beautiful and shapely."

"He was crazy about me, and I was crazy about him. He was so tall and handsome and warm, but I just couldn't." She wipes away her tears as I drink my cup of instant coffee.

We are in her small apartment in Brooklyn, radically clean, decorated with chrome and plastic flowers. There is a large double bed in the bedroom, covered with a pure white silken spread, reflecting its disuse except for sleep. On her bureau is a gaudily mounted photograph of her wedding taken forty-three years ago.

"What happened?" I asked quietly, feeling compassion for the terrors of the older generation which has never learned to enjoy sexual activity.

"It was because of my mother. She had ten children, and she used to say all men were animals, including my father. She said that's all they wanted.

"I used to look at my husband, and it was a very sad thing, because he was a loving, gentle man. He wasn't that way at all. But just the touch of him would send me going. I would try to bear it, but when he got all red in the face, I would actually see an animal, and I would beg him not to do it anymore. I said he was a mad dog. I hurt his feelings.

"When he just held me and kissed me, it wasn't bad, but when it got to the point where he had no control, I would get all tight and scream. He would say, 'Don't be frightened, you'll come around.' And I would say, 'Why do you have to change? Why does your face get like that?' If only he could have looked normal.

"He pleaded with me. He said, 'I'm a good man. I don't understand it. Other women find me attractive, and you push me away like a dog.' Then he'd go out and have a couple of drinks and come back and wake me up and ask, 'Is it possible you want to be raped? I can't do that, it's not in my nature.'

"So he started to drink, and he started to gamble, and then he went to women, and that's the way my life went." She dabs at her eyes as she speaks, to soak up the ever-present tears that are still there after thirty years of separation.

"How long were you together?"

"For thirteen years. Then he met a woman who was very aggressive. He said, 'Anna, it's not that I love her more than you, but it's just that I know she would do anything for me, both sexually and otherwise. I'm thirty-five years old; I can't play house anymore.' "

Her voice gets hoarse as she says, "It's like a part of me died then. To this day, I don't need anybody, and I hate myself for it."

"Have you had other boyfriends?"

"Today, I get very uptight if I thought anybody was going to share my bed. When I was young, I felt so much love, but I couldn't do anything about it.

"Nowadays, when I go out with a man, the conversation is awful. I have to make believe I didn't even go to school. There's nothing sexual about stupidity. I have to stay with this man for four or five hours and say yes to everything he says. On my last date, the man talked about how many gallons go into his car, all night. I really did try to like him because he looked like John Wayne. But I didn't really find him attractive after I dated him."

"Who's attractive to you?"

She pauses, licking her lips, her eyes glinting, and says, "I have fantasies all the time about Robert Redford. I like a good-looking man. I look at the back of a man's head. I look at his hair. It's very sexy to me. I look at Robert Redford, and think, *What a wonderful man!*

"I'd like to go to bed with him," she admits.

Like most older women, Anna has learned to joke about the sadness of her erotic life. Yet when we think about these women's lives, lived without the pleasure even of marital sex, we realize how fortunate the younger generations really are.

Sometimes, because of a lifelong devotion, a change takes place when the wife becomes older. This is true of Milly.

Milly

"I was brought up without the mention of sex, and I guess I never got over it." Fifty-five-year-old Milly is dressed in leopard-spotted chiffon as she drinks from a can of beer and munches potato chips. The yellow satin drapes match the couch cover where tossed stuffed animals impart a feeling of Hollywood decoration. Milly's apartment is very high up in a Miami Beach high-rise, and everything looks as if it were just purchased yesterday.

"If you ever brought a fella up to the house, you had to marry him. So you used to sneak a lot, sneak long walks by the waterfront where the neighbors couldn't spot you. After a while you'd get tired of the guy because he had a runny nose or might have bad habits, and boy, were you glad you didn't introduce him to the family. Who would want to marry that?"

Some beer spills on the plush carpet, and Milly wipes it with her lace handkerchief. As she bends, the foam rubber couch moves with her, and her face is flushed when she rises.

"Everything was whispered about, and nothing was out in the open. I remember when I got my period I thought I was dying. Where was the blood coming from? I got my father's old, long underwear and rolled them up under my dress until they were bloody, through and through. Then I stole my brother's BVDs. Finally, I started using my own panties. My mother walked into the house and asked why there was so much underwear on the clothesline. I had washed out everything so there would be no evidence. Finally, I told her what had happened. She said now I was a lady and would have to change my life. From what to what, she never said."

Milly chuckles as she tells her childhood tale. She is a large woman, fond of wearing large rings on her fingers, but her wedding ring is a simple gold band.

"Whom did you finally marry?"

"I married Mike, my neighbor. Our families used to summer in the country at the same place. Mike and I would go down the hill to the village dance every Friday. My mother gave us a kerosine lamp to carry so she would always know where we were. One night, we ditched it and I heard her screaming, 'Milly, Milly,' all through the woods. She finally caught us behind a big rock, kissing. So we became engaged."

"Just like that?"

"Just like that! But even then we could never be alone. Finally, I learned how to swim so we could go to the beach and swim out far. My mother used to stand on the shore, yelling, 'Milly, Milly!' One day the sounds came nearer and nearer. I turned and there was my mother. She had hired a man to row her out. After that, we got married."

"Had anything sexual happened between you?"

She walks to her brand-new refrigerator and gets another can of beer, offers me one, but I am dieting. She says she should too, slaps her hand on her fleshy thighs, laughs, and continues to speak. "Are you kidding? I was afraid of everything. My mother wouldn't even let me sit on his lap. That's why, when we finally got married, I was hysterical."

She pauses. Then she opens a tiny golden heart she is wearing about her neck and shows me a picture of a handsome, virile-looking man. "That's Mike," she sighs wistfully.

"Well, the night we were married, I was scared. We went into the hotel room, and I wouldn't undress before him. I felt terrible. I asked Mike to let me go home. Finally, we had sex, and it was bad. It went on all night. All I heard was a banging in my head. I thought, *One or two times, but he goes at it all night.*"

"Even at sixty-five?"

"Now it's worse. Now he never stops because the kids are married. When they lived in the house, I used to plead with him not to do anything because our bed creaked."

"Did you ever talk to anyone about this?"

"There was no one to talk to. One time I mentioned it to my

doctor. He said, 'Wait until you're forty, you'll begin to enjoy it.' I complained to him my husband wouldn't leave me alone. 'Do you have orgasms?' he asked. I told him I didn't know. He said, 'If you had them, you'd know.' What does he mean? Do you know?"

"Have you ever enjoyed sex?"

"Well, nowadays, it's a little better. You see, I expected romance and candlelight, not his all-night stuff. I love my husband, but I don't get anything out of it.

"But now, we come home, undress, watch television, and cuddle. If I tell him I have a headache or a backache, he massages me.

"It's nice!" she concludes, smiling.

Milly is lucky because her husband is still around. Often a woman is widowed after a long marriage, looking for love, trying to change her sexual identity, and confused at what comes about. Rosalyn is like that.

Rosalyn

She is very petite, wearing golden eyeglass frames matching her golden jewelry, an attractive accessory to her beige pants outfit with matching beige leather bag and shoes. Her name is Rosalyn, and her house in Pennsylvania is decorated with the precision of a woman who knows her own taste. It is sparse, comfortable, perhaps too eagerly artistic with its paintings by friends of the family.

Newly widowed after a twenty-three-year marriage, Rosalyn describes herself as a "Jewish grandmother."

"At the beginning of my marriage, it was great. It could happen every night, sometimes in the afternoon if we had the time. Then it suddenly stopped. . . ." She looks at me sadly as she mentions her dead husband and sex.

"Did something happen?"

Anger takes over her expression, and confusion, a look I recognize and that I have seen many times before. "Yes. My daughter was born. We had had two years of sex. After that, the rest of the years, twenty-one in all, we lived without sex."

She stumps out her cigarette, the sparks flying. I sympathize with her feelings about motherhood robbing her of her womanhood, but it seems to be fairly consistent, especially in the older generation of marriages. If she had been born fifteen years later, she would have been groomed into the era of the "female orgasm compulsion," which took place in the Fifties.

"What could I do about it?" she says to my unstated question, the rhythm of her question soap-operaish. "I was afraid to leave him. I couldn't tell anyone, even my closest friends. How would it look if they knew I wasn't having sex? So I started masturbating in the bathtub, like I did when I was a little girl."

I look at the displayed photographs of her children, healthy and happy, and wonder whether they know what they cost their mother. It's no wonder that they probably felt the flinch of her sarcasm when they were growing up. I wonder what they have to say about the fact that two months after their father's death, Rosalyn made love to the second man in her life.

"My husband had affairs, but I didn't think I had the right to," she says, illustrating the definite difference between marriage then and marriage now. "So, I'm making up for lost time," she says, with a sudden twinkle in her eyes. I am again witnessing the change that comes over women when they talk about sexual pleasure, and as always, it delights me. I giggle and ask what she's up to.

"I've had seven lovers in six months," she confesses breathlessly. "And I've also been in a ménage à trois." The words coming from her seem to outrage Jewish motherhood, and I can hardly believe my ears.

"This old friend of mine and I were up in the country and met a young man. He came over to dinner and we began talking. Then it started to rain. We drank wine, smoked some grass. He began to massage my friend's back. They began having sex, and I sat by and masturbated, watching them."

What a wild experience, I can hardly believe it! But I try to keep my journalistic composure.

"How did you feel?"

"I was a little jealous, but it had a good effect on me. The next week a nice man walked into a restaurant where I was eating. He was wearing a ruffled shirt, dark trousers, like a musician at a bar mitzvah would. I talked to him, liked him, and gave him my phone number. That's the first time I did that in my entire life. It was very, very daring!

"He called the next week. We went to a concert in a park. Afterward, we took a walk and began to kiss. Then we lay down on the grass, and I started to fondle him. I said, 'Let's go to your place.' He said, 'Oh, it's a mess.' I said, 'I won't look.' So I put on my dark glasses, and we went to his place and fucked."

I am getting increasingly optimistic about my old age as I listen to Rosalyn. "I've been pretty lucky since I've been single. I've had more dates than a lot of women my age. Everywhere I go, I meet men.

"But, there's only one problem." She looks at me sadly. "I'm having really bad luck."

"Doesn't sound it," I remark.

"Well, it is in a way because . . ." She pauses, slightly embarrassed. ". . . because they've all been impotent." She takes off her glasses, and I see her eyes are filled with tears. "Tell me, you've been single a while. Is that the way it is?"

Rosalyn is like the many women who, because they have changed their attitudes, think things will go smoothly. However, I must say I wished they would for her, with only two years of married sexuality to remember.

Rosalyn was lucky that her children were married and out of the house. Not only men think mothers shouldn't have sex; children do too, as in the case of Hortense.

Hortense

At fifty-five years of age, after raising four children in Providence, widowed Hortense suddenly realized that all her life she never had time to devote to herself.

"I was a teen-ager when I got married. Now I'm practically living alone and a free agent."

The only hitch in her life is the fact that her eighteen-year-old daughter is still living with her, which makes it difficult to take her dates home.

Finding dates is also difficult for Hortense, who is an attractive, older woman, brunette, slim, chic, with a nice personality. I wonder why.

"I finally had to join a computer-dating service," Hortense said, the wrinkles under her eyes getting deeper, not matching her youthful appearance. She gets very nervously animated when talking about men. "I felt like a nut, but it worked. I started dating." Finally, one man turned her on.

"I went out with him for six months. I wondered how to get him to go to bed with me. I wasn't experienced in these matters. Sex was always a routine thing in my marriage, like my other housewifely chores. There was a time for sex and a time for cooking and a time for shopping. I never in my life had an orgasm. It was nothing to look forward to. It was just one of my duties."

But Hortense used her imagination, and giggles when she tells me what she did.

"We had two apartments and a house between us, but his daughter was in his house and his sons at his apartment. So I said, 'Between the two of us, we can't go anywhere for privacy.'

"The next date we had, he drove me to La Guardia Airport. We had dinner, and over cocktails he said he would arrange for a room. I whispered, 'Great.' But I was nervous. It had been years since I had been with my husband.

"Well, when we got into the room, I just dropped my bag and started to kiss him. Then it got very exciting, and we were very, very close to each other. We stripped. In bed we petted. Then we screwed." She giggles some more. "It was terrific."

She runs around the room, happy that she had this experience. "I told him I hadn't liked sex with my husband. Later he said I was wild. Just think," she says, with a lovely softness to her voice. "Me wild? You know when a man looks at you that way, you feel like a . . . a . . ." She can't even find the word for how wonderful she felt.

"I hate the fact that I can't bring him home. But I can't sleep with a guy with a teen-ager living in the house."

I ask her why, since she is single.

"It's inhibiting." She shakes her head firmly no.

"I'd love for my daughter to move out," she says bluntly. "I want my privacy."

Hortense was very, very lucky that after a boring life with her husband, she finally is having a good time. It's about time, and I agree that her daughter should take off and let her mother enjoy herself for once in her life.

Sometimes when women become older they feel they have nothing to lose: They've been married, they've had their children, they can't get pregnant because of menopause, so they might as well live it up. Often, they are startlingly surprised when the behavior of a lifetime as a lady, assumed to be the proper behavior, changes to the behavior of a sexual woman and that this behavior is very popular with men. Adriana found that out.

Adriana

Stockbroker Adriana looks like a voluptuous Gertrude Stein, an intelligence behind her eyes contradicting the soft smiles and little giggles occurring as she speaks about her young sex life.

"When I was a little girl, I used to get this rash between my legs from eating strawberries, and my brothers always wanted to help put on the baby powder there."

"How's your sex life nowadays?" I quip.

"I have three or four lovers all the time, because I have a high-powered sexual energy. In fact, I masturbate when the man leaves." She answers the loud whistle of her copper tea kettle as I look about the room, decorated like a pink boudoir with handsewn covers, pillows, embroidered nature scenes in handsome frames. Even the plants are pinkish in tone: violets, forms of wandering Jew, begonias—everything here on Seventy-second Street is pink, pink, pink.

Adriana returns to the room with a waddled walk, as if she is in pain, but denies this, although her face is gaunt as she busies herself with the task of tea-making, which for her is ceremonious. I watch her as she spoons the black tea, pours the water, stirs, and the famous Picasso portrait of Gertrude Stein, predicting the writer's appearance twenty years in the future, comes to my mind.

"How do you find so many lovers?"

She giggles, pouring the brew into a handsome pink china teacup. "It's because now that I'm fifty-four, I've changed."

"In what way?"

"I tell them what to do, give them specific orders. Last night I said to a very successful hundred-thousand-dollar-a-year executive, 'Put your hand on my left shoulder and move it up and down my body very slowly.' It excited the hell out of him!"

She leans back, her flowered pink caftan merging with the Rousseau-like couch-cover pattern. I have the feeling that she is a water lily, slowly drifting down the exotic stream in the middle of a tropical jungle, reaching for the waterfall to orgasm.

"Were you different before?"

Adriana's smiling eyes are sad now, contrasting with her severe nose which is like a sculptor's mold. She moves her lips, biting, licking, as if she is harboring a painful secret. The tea brew smells like incense, adding to the portrait of the mysterious Cheshire tiger Adriana communicates.

"When I care for a person, I can't ask for sexual things. There's something about caring in that old romantic way that jails you, binds you. You think about him instead of yourself."

I nod in agreement knowingly.

She continues. "Now I meet men who used to make me tremble, and I'm very casual. There was one man who turned me on for five years, and we finally got together. He was just about to come, and I told him to hold off, to get a towel because we were lying on my new bedspread. I could never do that years ago."

"How did he react?"

"He grabbed me on the floor and fucked me for an hour he was so turned on by my demands!"

"Why do you think a demanding woman turns them on?"

"They know I don't want to trap them. I've been married and had children and love affairs, and all that. I don't believe in monog-

159

amy any longer. I only insist on one thing: When a man is with me, he has to give me a lot of attention. I have to be the center of his focus. When he leaves, it's good-bye till next time.

"The other night I opened the door for one of my lovers, and he was standing there, jerking off in the hall. I knelt down and immediately began sucking him off. He came as the elevator approached our floor. So we rushed into the room and giggled like two little kids.

"I'm very sensitive around the rectum and like men to lick and suck me there. But I can have a very good time, have a lot of orgasms, and still masturbate when they leave. I masturbate by rubbing a towel or the bed covers between my legs. I lie face down and sink deep into the pillows. Then I put the material between my legs and rub up against it. I don't even touch myself."

"You have a good sexual appetite; do you resent the fact that men don't fulfill you?"

She smiles graciously. "My energy is higher than most people's, so it's hard to find someone to match it."

A few years ago, she had found the only man in her life who could. "The orgasms I had with him were exquisite. He had a lot of stamina so we would go to bed very early, about eight, and make love for two or three hours. He used to numb me with pleasure. There's something that happens to you when you've had a lot of sex, you get so relaxed. We'd sleep for two or three hours and start again. By that time, I was so full and relaxed that it was like a whole different kind of orgasm. Every part of me was totally open. There is an orgasm that comes from hunger, and then there is this kind of orgasm that comes from being satiated. I stayed with him for four years because of those orgasms.

"We wouldn't stop for anything. One day he lifted me with himself inside of me and had to pee. We went over to the sink, and he peed into the sink, and then we went back to making love. We used to sweat a lot and had a beach towel on the bed."

She pauses. "I sure would like to work up another sweat like that before I die."

Every woman would like to work up a sweat like that, whatever her age. If there is anything to learn from the older women in this chapter, it is that it is never too late to become erotic. If younger women would take heed from their elder sisters and shoot for the moon instead of worrying about who wants them and what they can get for it, maybe, like the older women, they will start enjoying their lives with a greater sense of humor.

Six

❀ ❀ ❀

THE EROTICISM OF AUTHORITY AND VIOLENCE

Although the element of authority and violence has been developed in previous chapters, in most cases the women were involved with the *illusion* of both. In this chapter, the women are involved with actual authoritarian eroticism and actual acts of violence.

When women are frustrated in their attempts to make an impression on the world, ambitious and adventuresome women have always aligned with powerful men. These women are erotically turned on by the leadership quality of these men, the power they wield over others. When the powerful man shows his erotic vulnerability to his woman, it turns her on. It is exciting to her that this leader of men turns to her in a soft, vulnerable way and makes her feel powerful. It turn her on almost as much as if she had his leadership status herself. The dictator's wife or mistress is revered by all almost as much as he is. She is "off-limits" and, as in the case of Eva Peron of Argentina, even elevated to sainthood. She is the inspiration for his greatness, and it is her duty to keep him well and happy. More than just married to one man, she is loved by his entire corps or country. It gives her the sense of power that nothing else she can conceive of does, and thus she fully recognizes his authority.

Conversely, the woman who is subjected to the authority of a man who does not have leadership avenues for his ego very often is subjected to violence, brutally and directly (as differentiated from the S/M activities). These women, frustrated in their attempts to deal with these men, often take abuse to the point of no return and then strike out with unpredictability. Since women are not allowed to experience rage directly in our society, they must sublimate their anger into depression or masochism. (Evidence of this is the policing authorities' consideration that the politically violent woman is the most dangerous of all.) Thus, women take abuse until they are pushed to the breaking point. It is then that they may commit acts of violence against their abusive husbands, their authority. Most women who commit acts of violence against abusive husbands and lovers are not sentenced according to male standard punishment. But women who attack society directly in acts of terrorism are.

"Careful" women will be turned on by being a powerful man's woman, enjoying all the supportive power of his status, yet not having to be one iota responsible for this protection. There is something about a powerful man that makes a woman feel more vulnerable. If a man has power in the world, status in the world, a woman feels he has the right to power over her. Most women feel a surge of pride when an escort commands the respect and attention of a restaurant's maître d', so one can imagine the turn-on when a man gets the respect and adoration of an entire country.

Most women who have this admiration for powerful men look for rich business executives. One of these women is Olivia.

Olivia

"I only like rich and powerful men because I want someone who will go along with me, as I plan to retire from business when I'm forty and go into politics." These determined statements about her interest in power and leadership come from Olivia, a twenty-seven-year-old divorced mother who says that any man is within her reach. And when she gets him into her reach, these are the things that she likes to do with him.

"I like to really turn him on, to make him want to *come* so badly and not let him, to tease him until he wants to get in, and say, 'No, no, not yet. . . . Gee, I need a cigarette . . .' to cool him off for a while."

Olivia's cold-hearted technique matches her bare and undecorated apartment in Washington, D.C., which she has lived in for a while. But when I find out about her fill-in erotic turn-on—a fill-in until she meets her rich and powerful man—I understand why there is no commitment to her surroundings.

"I like one-night stands," she says softly. "I go to bars and pick guys up, and it's great . . . somebody new with no entanglements. I usually sit next to the one I've picked out and tell him that someone else is bothering me, and that brings out the Sir Galahad in him. He usually buys me a drink, invites me to dinner and his hotel room."

I think of Judith Rossner's best-selling book *Waiting for Mr. Goodbar*, and wonder what Olivia gets from these encounters. "I learn a lot of different things," she explains. "One night last week I was with a cowboy from the rodeo, and I learned all about his life. I think the more experience with different people you can have, the better a lover you will be."

At her current rate, Olivia is learning fast. "I like somebody new all the time. Most men have just one song and dance, and I get bored. I was with only one man, my husband, until I was twenty-five years old. I worked to put him through graduate school, and he left me the day he graduated. My marriage has made me very, very aggressive," she says bitterly. "I've been through about seventy-five men in these last three years."

Well dressed and coiffeured, with very large breasts for her very short body, she surprises me by sitting in an unladylike cross-legged position on the couch, and I can see up her skirt while she smokes long, thin cigars. I surmise from her tailored outfit that she does not sit like this at her company's business conferences.

"I meet guys at bars, on the street, at church, and very few are invited to my home. Last week, a terrific-looking guy came up to me on the street and said, 'Let's play hooky!' " Her eyes twinkle as she says she did just that.

"A classy lay turns me on the most. I spend a lot of money on clothes, and I like to be picked up because I'm classy. When a guy takes out a book of poetry while he's eating me, that's classy. I'll reward him by rubbing his penis, or turn around and let him play with my anus. I like to be eaten, but I don't like to blow guys because I have a false pride and don't like to bend over. It's all a big game, anyhow—a game plan."

The most important part of her game plan is the meeting of powerful men, and this is where all her fantasies are centered.

"I do like the element of excitement and danger. At the office, we have these accordion, plastic doors. I always want to pull in one of the directors and make love to him while everyone is walking past. I conceived my child in a swimming pool in a luxury hotel while people were about. I love to make it on planes—first class, of course.

"I like it when a man strips me as soon as we get into a room. I love it if he gives me an expensive dress and rips it to shreds so I am naked. I like men who spend money. Last week, one guy flew all the way from Toronto, and it really gave me such a feeling of power."

Thus, power seems to be Olivia's real turn-on. "My career is the most important thing in my life. I don't date colleagues. If a male executive screws around, he's considered a man, but if a female executive does it, she's considered unprofessional."

But the professional tensions of her thirty-thousand-dollar-a-year job drive her to frequent encounters with strangers of the opposite sex. "I need a lot of emotional support. I don't have time to make commitments right now. If somebody tells me I'm good in bed, it gets me through the next week.

"If I don't pick somebody up at least once a week, I get upset with myself," she concludes.

Olivia's turn-on is fascinating because it illustrates the connection between power and self-abuse. While she plans to be with a powerful man, she abuses herself with one-night stands who will never see her again, at her own wish. It seems that women who like power always tie it in with some kind of violence toward themselves.

Patti is an excellent example of that combination.

Patti

I am in Oakland, California, sitting in a dark room with a light bulb in the far corner, and cannot see a thing. The door opens and a huge, shadowed woman enters and sits opposite me. On the table between us is a tape recorder. She feels about, making sure that is all I have with me.

I cannot see the woman's face clearly in the darkness but do recognize that her silhouette is very, very strong. But her voice is young, and I estimate her to be in her early twenties. All these precautions have been taken because Patti, as I will call her, lives with a member of a motorcycle gang, and has agreed to give me an interview about her sexual life as his old lady. She has selected a rented motel room and surrounded herself in darkness to protect me, so that I will not be able to identify her even if I want to.

An ominous atmosphere obviously fills the air, and I ask her why she has decided to talk about her experiences. "I'm not worried," she says in a low, husky voice. "I'm not going to say anything bad about them. I think they're the only *real men* left in this world, and I'm proud of them."

She then proceeds to tell me about the assemblage of women in this motorcycle gang and what their sexual customs are. "Well, there are the old ladies and the mamas. Now the old lady is her old man's property. They can't screw around with anyone else. They have to take care of their old man and his kids, if he has any. The mamas are different.

"The mamas are very often prostitutes. Now, say I'm an old lady and I'm not in the mood to be eaten, well, my old man can go to the mama. She's there for the sexual satisfaction of the entire group. Even the women," she adds quickly.

Astonished, because of the notorious heterosexuality of the club, I ask what she means. "Well, if a dude is out of town on business and his old lady gets hung up, she can have sex with the mama with no repercussions. But always the mama makes love to the old lady, the mama satisfies her."

I am amazed that a homosexual activity does not threaten these marauders of purple passion. "What about male lovers?" I ask.

"Nobody is permitted to touch an old lady," she states harshly, like a political sentence. "If an old lady takes a liking to one of the other guys while her old man's away, and she makes a pass at this other guy, the old man will be told when he comes back by the other old ladies or old men, she's the type of girl who's never satisfied with what she has." Apparently, heterosexual activity with someone other than her old man means she's not satisfied and that is not accepted; homosexual activity simply means she's frustrated, which is acceptable. The other acceptable custom is that only the unfaithful woman gets beat up, the male intruder does not. "The guy who actually did the screwing just took the initiative, the girl presented it to him," she states flatly, viewing it all as absolutely fair.

Sometimes a member of a rival motorcycle gang rapes someone's old lady and then there's a real kickoff. One time, some local thugs grabbed one old lady in a supermarket and threw her into their car, took her home, and had her. The motorcycle dudes found out who these thugs were and tore the house apart. "Any man worth his salt is going to fight for that girl." She bangs on the table to emphasize her point, and I catch a glimpse of a ring with a tiger on it; the tiger has one luminescent green eye.

For all this old-fashioned protection of old ladies, the mamas get none. "A mama is usually initiated by the men, with the rest of the group watching. My old man found a mama who was a Berkeley prostitute and brought her back to the club. I immediately read him the riot act for doing it, because he was mine. But he reminded me it wasn't for him. We were short of women at the time; of the twenty-one guys in our group, there were eight without old ladies.

"So we all got together, and all of the guys screwed her in every way they felt like, and they made her perform all different types of sexual acts to prove that she was worthy of becoming a mama."

"What makes her worthy?"

"Obedient performance. Like if an old lady isn't into giving her old man a blow job, or eating out his asshole, the mama is made to do it. Also, she does all the cooking and cleaning, and if we need a baby-sitter, she has to do that too. She is literally a slave."

When the clubs have to raise some money, they often sell their mama for a night, for a month, or forever. "She literally has no say in the matter. She has to whether she wants to or not. Also, in one group, there was a bust for dope and the mama had to take the blame. She went to jail for the club."

Female mamas are most common, but there are some male mamas, too. "A lot of gay guys really get off on the toughness of the men, like the gay leather clubs. The men call them every degrading name a homosexual can be called, and those gays love every minute of it."

I am surprised again by the homosexual element of the gang's activities, since I thought any deviation from male/female fascism would threaten them. But apparently it does not, since it is not taken seriously. Only the old man/old lady relationship is serious to the gang's ego.

The couples live in a big house with the single men. Most of the couples sleep in a large room, with blankets separating them. "There is no such thing as privacy. When the guys are in the mood, they just drag their women down. Sometimes they perform specifically for the purpose of exhibiting their skill. Sometimes an old lady nearby will say to her old man, 'Why can't you do things like that?' Everybody screws at once, but there is no switching, *not ever!*" Her voice gets heavy to make her point that this is not a swinging club.

Although in public Patti never argues with her old man, whenever they have the privacy of a bedroom, she power-plays head games with him. "The standard old lady is quite content to lie in bed and let her old man screw her, usually in the old missionary position. When it is all over, she sighs a sigh of relief. I was never satisfied with this. I spoil my old man rotten, but when we are alone, I get him so high on me that he usually begs me to make him climax. I give him this super backrub—there are a lot of nerve endings in a man's back—and he begs me to go down on him. I say I'll do it later, when I'm ready. The first time I did this he really thought I was going to let him hang like that and he got really super mad. But when he realized that he could screw the life out of me when I was ready, he liked it. I like him to beg for it, especially because he is such a big huge man. He's over six-foot-six."

The obvious S/M power play to this activity delights the old man only in private. In public, everything is different. "Sometimes I tease him so much when we are eating dinner. We all eat together, and I say, 'Gee, I wonder whether he's going to come tonight, to do it. He's been so lenient lately I think he's getting old or something.' Everybody knows I'm teasing him. But he has to show them that he's top man, so he grabs me and rapes me right then and there. And I love it, every moment of it."

Often the old ladies fight for their men. "In a bar once, we were all sitting and drinking, and a local gang decided to hassle us. So I went over to their leader and said, 'Look, man, I don't want my old man should dirty his fingers . . . I'll take you down.' I was big, and the other girls were very small, and the guy laughed and said, 'We're not going to fight ladies.' And I said, 'Yes, you'll fight us because we won't let our old men dirty their hands.' So we started to take the motorcycle chains from our waists. The old ladies usually wear these when the bikes are parked," she explains to me, "and if you get those swung at you, I don't care how strong you are, you're going to go down. Well, they gave us the respect. They walked out, and all our dudes broke up laughing at what I'd done." I am startled by this resemblance to the Mafia's beliefs of respect; the only difference is the Mafia would never let women do their work for them.

Although chains are a normal weapon in gang fights, the men do not use them on the women. "They don't want to mar the merchandise," she explains. "The only times I've seen motorcycle chains used on women have been by other women in a rival gang fight."

I tremble at the image, but Patti moves her chair, and I sense she is getting impatient to go. I ask her about the club's garb. She tells me the men wear "colors," which are denim cutaways, sleeves cut out of the jacket and the back of the jacket embroidered with the insignia of the club. In addition, there are all sorts of added medals.

"There is an initiation for certain people. It's like the Boy Scouts or Girl Scouts earning certain badges. During the times when a girl has her period, it's a sign of courage to eat her, and a guy can earn a medal that way. Some medals mean the guy has eaten a black chick out on her period. There are very few guys that can honestly say that because the idea of eating a black chick out turns most of them off."

Generally, black women can only be mamas, although there is no strict rule against their becoming old ladies. "Black mamas and black gay guys are allowed. But there are never black male members of this group. If a black man says he's a member, he is lying," she says staunchly.

I ask her why she thinks her club exists. She explains that most of the men join the gang for love of motorcycles, love of partying, love of women. Women are definitely property, for their enjoyment. If a woman complains about her lack of sexual pleasure, and her old man believes he is a superstud, she will get smacked in the face.

However, Patti claims it's all an erotic turn-on. "There's something about the restlessness and recklessness of these men that brings something out in the women. It's like the women who used to fall for the gladiators back in the days of Ancient Rome—the same type of superman with the brutality aura which turns most women on. And the macho image. Like when the club walks into a room wearing their colors, the entire room stands at attention not knowing whether they're going to fight or smile. *That kind of power is thrilling.*"

A woman is allowed to leave her old man only if she explains her dissatisfaction to him and he agrees. "Sometimes the tension of feeding his friends and cleaning up after their parties can be a pain in the neck. An old lady might say, 'I want to visit my mother for a week,' but she has to have his permission. If she just up and leaves, it's an affront to him. You have to give a man a little common courtesy and not hurt his pride," she says softly. The old ladies hardly ever leave for sexual reasons, for if they do not like something, like anal sex, it is traditionally practiced on the mamas.

Patti feels that her club represents the All-American Male. "They feel this is our country, and we got to live here. They're anti-Communist. They wear the swastika, but it is only about physical supremacy that these men are supermen, and their women are very, very female. They hate dykes. They respect their old ladies, and they want respect back."

I felt Patti was very honest about her erotic turn-on and her respect for the men in her club. Although women do not have many privileges in this all-male society, Patti had learned how to get her own way. She is clever enough to know that if she absolutely respects her man, she can tease the life out of him. This gives her power over his emotional vulnerability, an obvious sexual thrill for her.

Often when a violent man does not have an impressive place in society, or does not have the illusion of power which joining an all-male club like the motorcycle gangs gives him, he takes out his violence upon his woman. Often, the woman accepts his brutality, until one day, having experienced much too much, she erupts. This is what happened to Doris.

Doris

"I married my best friend. During my first marriage, he helped me so much. I had no money, and he used to bring food for the kids. So when my husband died, he proposed. He kept rushing me. Kept hurrying me to get married, so I finally gave in."

Doris is a soft, pretty, black woman in her late twenties. Speaking in a lovely manner, she tells me she is uneducated and unskilled for the job market and has spent most of her life since she was fourteen having babies and working in laundries.

"When I was pregnant with my first child, I didn't even know where babies came from. I had only lived with women during my childhood. My mother died when I was born. My grandmother had been abandoned by her husband, and my great-grandmother, who owned our house, waited for her husband to return to her, although he married and had another family. It was all very romantic in that house, with all women, but definitely a fantasy. But black women very often live on fantasy," she says softly.

Doris speaks compassionately and not out of self-pity as she describes the way she was brought up. There was no fantasy in the way she was always, as a girl, put in her place. Her brother, the first son of five generations, was spoiled and catered to. Thus, Doris was taught since childhood about what men in her family expected from their women.

"When I married my second husband, at first he spoiled me terribly. I thought, *Oh, good, this time I have a good man*. My first husband was not good to me. He didn't beat me, but he always went out with other women and never left enough food for the kids. This time I thought, *I'll be happy, it'll be different*. My second husband gave nice gifts to the kids. He was terrific to me, called me his 'brown sugar.' So I married him, without too many reservations."

As soon as the wedding ceremony was over, her husband began to change. "I don't know what happened." She looks up at me quietly, wondering whether I can tell her what did happen. "He made things unbearable for me. Nothing I did could please him. He kept telling me things were wrong with me. That I couldn't hear right, couldn't speak right. He kept complaining about the house, told me to quit my job. When I did, he told me to get another one. If I came home ten minutes late, he'd accuse me of being with another man. I told him it would take more than ten minutes to find a place and take my clothes off."

Doris smiles pleasantly as she tells me of her tragic second experience with marriage. She is a very warm woman with a pleasing disposition, and I have the feeling she does not feel she has a right to criticize. She confirms this as she tells me how she responded to her second husband's behavior toward her.

"I told him I loved him. I believed that if you treat somebody nice and kind, they will come around. I did everything he told me to do. You know, I was happy being single for that short time between husbands. But I wanted a family, a husband, a car, a house —things like that. Maybe it all was a fantasy, but the other women I know felt the same way. I know, I asked them."

Even while her husband was treating her badly, they had sex every night, which Doris enjoyed. It was traditional sex, with no variations. Doris said her husband was very gentle in bed. "I used to go to bed angry, but I thought, why should I stop doing something that felt so good. One part of my body had nothing to do with the other part. So we would have sex and then I would turn around and tell him I was still mad."

Although she had sex since she was fourteen, Doris had her first orgasm at the age of twenty-eight, only a year and a half ago. She describes it as a warm feeling all over. "He could always get to me if he did things like hold my hand or call me his sugar fox. I never could keep being angry at him."

All her unexpressed anger erupted one night a year ago when Doris had friends in for drinks. "He never wanted me to see my friends. We had gotten new furniture, and I wanted them to see it. After all, I had worked in a laundry to pay for it. When they arrived, he told me to tell them to go. I delayed, coaxed him, and said, 'Why don't you enjoy them?' Then he started to beat me with his fists, so my friends left."

Although I am amazed that her friends did not try to interfere, Doris approves of their behavior. Even though she was being beaten into a bloody pulp, she feels people should not interfere in a marriage. "My kids were tugging at my husband. He started choking me and I blacked out. Then he pulled me across the floor. He said he wanted to kill me. I saw the gun he kept on the bureau. I lunged for it and fired. He fell. I said, 'Get up, honey.' I thought the bullet went into the wall. But my baby son turned my husband over, and I saw the blood and said, 'Oh, God.' "

Today Doris reprimands herself for not doing what her husband said instantly, for then he would be alive today, and she still hasn't reconciled herself to the fact that her anger would have built up in another situation. I asked her if there was a way to have avoided the tragedy.

"Yeah, if I could have beaten him up. Black men are always beating up their women, and the black women stand for it. Black women say whitey treats their men awful and the black men have to take it out on someone. The black women don't want to marry out of their race, so that's how it goes. If you're a black man, you think you can do anything."

I ask her whether she could have called the police if she was fearful. "I couldn't call the cops!" she shouts, animated and angry for the first time in the interview. "Oh, my God, you don't call any cop on a black man. It would be terrible. He would have killed me as soon as I put my hands on the phone." She pauses, calming down. Then I ask Doris what turns her on. "When I get seriously involved, I get weak, I give too much. Then he's able to wrap me around his finger. I'll do anything he says. I love him and love him very hard. I try to please as much as I can. I think, *If you're good, he's going to love you. If you're bad, he won't.*

"When a man starts being bad to you, you don't care what happens to you," she says sadly.

Doris was able to keep her eroticism separate but like many poor women, did not really enjoy sex. This is true of the poor of any color. The poor live so close to survival that the frustrated men of this economic class do take out their violence on their women, finding this violence erotic. And the women are brought up in a tradition of not fighting back. They take this abuse until it builds up, and often in an act of violence the women have to pay for it. If the women could be lucky, like Julia was, and take steps before the final trauma, then poor women might have a chance.

Julia was lucky. She took steps before tragedy occurred.

Julia

For years, tiny, pert twenty-four-year-old Julia would get up in the morning and work eight hours a day, come home, cook dinner, and take care of her two small children, aged now two and six. After dinner when television shows got boring, she was regularly beaten up by her husband who was five years older than she.

"Beating up on me was the only way for him to feel that he was a real man. He hated all women. He's even abused his mother. I would never allow my son to talk to me the way he talks to her."

Julia has no religious affiliations. Her husband, from a Catholic family, would not let her use birth control. He would search the house for these devices, and one time when he discovered birth-control pills, he threw them out, violently assaulting her again.

Julia withdrew. "I always loved to read, but he forbade me to. He beat me with his belt whenever I did. I found he would pick fights with me for any kind of reason. He tried killing me, choking me. His mother said, 'He's your husband and you're his wife, so if it's bad, it's bad. If it's good, it's good.' But I withdrew every way that I could."

One of the orders Julia was given was to go down on her husband. "He told me I was stupid and ugly. I refused to blow him, so he would rape me. But it started to become more and more physically painful. He was insistent that I was unfaithful. He asked me what I did, how many times, how often? I would deny it. Then he would beat me. It was so awful. I had to wear long, long dresses and a long, long coat to the office so people wouldn't see the bruises."

Julia smiles timidly as she tells me her horror story. She is so very, very fragile, and her two children reflect her. They look like they will break into tiny pieces.

She tells me about her childhood. "I had an awful lot of hate in me, and I took it out on my doll. It frightened me because I destroyed her. There was no one to tell me how to be angry, so I just kept it bottled up. I kept it bottled up when he beat me. But when he began beating the children, that was it."

Her cool manner, which has been surprising to me, now turns into harsh emotion. We both look at her children, both too quiet with the horror of their experience. They are breaking my heart with their wide, dark eyes filled with terror at being in my apartment, in a strange place for a reason they cannot understand. They have been almost too well behaved for children of their age, watching and waiting for . . . I wonder what. When my dog barks at the little girl, her older brother, aged six, defends and protects her. It is obvious that he knows what violence really is, and Julia confirms this.

"He began hitting the boy with a coat hanger. Then he would give him a penknife to play with. He also had guns around the house, which the boy was encouraged to play with. One day, one went off."

Although her husband forced her to have sex, even raping her when she was sleeping, beating and abusing her, it was not until her children were threatened that she made a move. She called the police. Her husband retorted that he could rape her right in front of the cops and they couldn't do anything because she was his wife. Thus, she began to lock herself up in the attic with the children.

Her husband walked around the house, naked, with a large erection showing. He would masturbate with his pornographic magazines, then try to break down the attic door. She called the cops every night.

"My mother told me I was wrong, that my husband absolutely controls me. But I took him to Family Court, and now, although he hangs around the house, I have an order of protection. But . . ." she pauses, looking at me terrified ". . . I have a long knife beside my bed. If he comes in, I will use it. There will be no playing around. Of course, I'm hoping he doesn't come because it is a life-and-death situation. I wish I could rely on the police, but I have to protect myself.

"But if he kills me, what would happen to my children? They would go with him, or my mother, or his mother. One choice is worse than the other."

Although Julia's life has no eroticism in it, it is an example of how violence replaces eroticism. Julia's husband gets turned on by beating her and forcing her to have sex. Julia, unlike Doris, did not separate the sexual part of her from the other parts of her, and suffered from not being able to express her feelings of anger, being afraid of them—and that is where her passion truly lies.

Sometimes violence in a poor woman is so direct that she becomes a criminal, usually through a man's influence. This is the case with Connie.

Connie

The prison walls resound as a large, brusque, black woman, only twenty-six but in prison the fourth time for assault, tells me about her sexual activities.

"In this place I'm not sexually stimulated at all. I'm totally turned off because the women here take sex as a joke. I mean, to me, sex is like a religion. It's not something to bounce around like a ball." She giggles heartily, showing that a couple of teeth are missing.

I ask her if there is a lot of sex in this women's prison.

"Sure, it happens all over the place. When I first came in this time, I had one sexual experience because, although I like men, I like women also. But it has to be done real sneaky, and I got caught." Her face looks like a naughty little child's. "And I wasn't even doing anything. I was sitting on the toilet."

"Was it worth it?" I ask her, laughing at her description.

She laughs, pounding her large fists on the window bars. "No, I'd rather masturbate than have sex with one of these women. But if they find you masturbating, they send you to the psychiatrist and then it's all over the campus."

"Campus?" I do not know what she means.

"Yeah, that's what we call the prison."

Although I had never thought of that description before, it absolutely fits because the guards' uniforms of white shirts, blue ties and skirts, and brown oxfords remind one of schoolchildren.

Connie continues her tale: "If a guard sees you masturbate, she'll go to the afternoon coffee klatch and tell the other officers. Then they'll tell others, and before you know it, the whole campus will know. By the time the story gets around, they'll say I had a dildo."

"Do you use one?"

She giggles again and asks me to turn off the tape recorder. "No," she whispers. "But we stole a vibrator from the beauty parlor, and we passed it around. It was great!"

Again a loud giggle, and a guard comes to see what we are doing. Satisfied, she leaves. Connie continues. "I had fantasies of a water bed, black lights, reefers, the Holiday Inn, a penthouse, a tub of water, all with men and women together. Shit! I have way-out thoughts."

"Do you have a constant man in your fantasies?"

"Yeah, it's the old white guy who used to live in my neighborhood. The women in the fantasies change, but the men are always this guy. He was an actor, and he had a lot of class. I like class. I never had an orgasm till he taught me about oral sex. He was seventy-seven years old and had a bad ticker, but he made me have an orgasm. No black man ever made me orgasm from sex. They're all too interested in themselves. All they want to do is bang. I haven't met one yet who's tender."

Connie then describes how she feels when she is erotic. "My orgasms make me feel weak. I don't know what's happening to me.

I feel as if all my pores are open. It's great. Too bad it took such a long time to feel it. For a while I thought I was a frigid, cold-blooded person. I hate to admit it, but sex was my weapon because men are so weak. A piece of pussy just turns them right on. You'd be surprised how you can string a man out like that. A man would actually take care of you and your entire family, just for a night in bed."

I ask Connie what really turns her on.

"*The Godfather*," she says, meaning the book by Mario Puzo. "Boy, did I like that book! I could really dig it. When I read that book, I woke up and had wet dreams. I got pregnant right after that."

"Didn't you use birth control?" I ask innocently.

She looks at me angrily, gets up, decides she doesn't like me any longer and that the interview is over. "That's genocide," she says, with an ugly look on her face as she stalks out.

Obviously the product of poverty, Connie has acted out her violence in brutal acts which guarantee her a life of prison. What startled me was, though she had the usual criminal's rip-off attitude toward men, she actually liked this old man who introduced her to sexual pleasure. But poor women do not protect themselves, as illustrated in Connie's attitude toward birth control.

As a backlash result of macho behavior, changes are occurring among women even in poverty cultures. Billi, a daughter of a laboring family, who dropped out of high school to go to Hollywood, has gone to quite an extreme to get away from the macho male.

Billi

Billi sits on her couch, touching her vagina. Slim, wearing a cheap Indian shirt and men's dungarees, her hair is dyed very, very black, highlighting the soft hue of her blue eyes. She seems very vulnerable and open for a seventeen-year-old movie extra, and I wonder how she gets along in Hollywood, U.S.A.

"I'm in love," she says happily, her face breaking into a wide smile, her green nail polish blending nicely with the silver jewelry she is wearing.

"We see each other three or four times a week, and we have sex six or seven times each time. When I first met him, I was so intrigued. He is a transvestite. I got very turned on. He was all dressed up with stockings and a garter belt and a bra with falsies in it. I proceeded to put the same stuff on myself. I got turned on because he wasn't the ordinary man, the macho man. It's his femininity that turns me on.

"Sometimes I put a wig on him and call him Elizabeth, but he's getting sick of that name because other people have used it. So I renamed him Heather, because it's very feminine and sweet and soft. I call him Heather, and he becomes very girlish. I'm very dominant in our sex life. I tell him what to do and I push him around. I lay back and command him to eat me out and he does. It's heavenly," she sighs happily. "Sometimes I tell him, to put it bluntly, to fuck me because I need something inside of me. It's not always the tongue that turns you on, you know. Sometimes I'll use a dildo on him. I'll put it on and pretend I'm the male. I never knew how much it would turn me on."

She is giggling delightedly, and I am captivated by the sweet and loving way she is telling this very bizarre tale. Billi doesn't seem to worry about the impression her story is having on me, as so many other less way-out women do. She is just telling me what turns her on, and I can take it or leave it.

"You know, I've read that women are supposed to have penis envy. I guess it's kind of true in my case because I always wondered what it was like to be a man. But he has the opposite of penis envy, or whatever you call it. When I proceed to screw him, he acts like a woman. He whines and screams. He doesn't have a vagina I can fuck, but I screw him in the asshole, and while I'm doing this, I make like I'm a man and he's the woman. I say, 'Oh, your cunt feels so good and this and that,' and he gets more turned on, and so do I. I can't have an orgasm like that because I just get excited, so I start rubbing my breasts against his cock and then after a while he feels so much like a woman he starts to come, and I get very turned on. Then we turn it around and either he screws me or eats me, it goes on like that."

Sometimes Billi puts on male underwear, BVDs, shirts, or pajamas. "I get sick of being too feminine, so this is great."

Billi started her sexual activity when she was fourteen and an extra in a film. "I asked this guy to screw me to get it over with, and he did."

After that, she turned on to women and realized she was dominant.

"I don't get turned on by masculine chicks. When I started making love to a girl, I thought I would be submissive, but I went and turned it around and started the whole scene. I was shocked, but I had a nice time."

One of the reasons she thought she would be submissive was that she was always that way with men, macho men, who seemed to abuse her.

"They always pulled tricks on me, and I had to kiss ass. They really screwed my head up. One guy used to beat me up and I'd forget and, like an asshole, come back for more. Macho men are very demanding. I hate to be on a show, hate to play games. You have to do what they like. They're the men, and you're the woman, and you're nothing but a bitch to them."

So Billi started to run around with gay men, to gay clubs, and felt they knew her very well. Now, she and her lover still go to gay clubs. Her lover dances with men, but when guys try to pick him up, she just walks over and says something like "He's mine, honey, so keep your hands off!"

"Gay men can be very snotty when it comes to that," she comments.

Her lover does not dress up in women's clothing in public. Billi really loves him and wants to live with him. "I think we should wait awhile, though," she said to his invitation to share his house. "Because we love each other so much, I want to see if it lasts."

Billi begins dressing to go to her lover's house, and I see a horrendous transition. She puts on a scarf dress which is very, very low and very, very red. With spike heels and false eyelashes, she looks completely different. I ask her how she feels about the way she looks. "I wish I had more money, but I don't give a shit. If I want to dress like this, then I say, 'Fuck you, people.' But if I had more money, people wouldn't treat me so bad. They're always thinking I'm going to steal something. I've never taken money. I've never even taken money from a man. Some girls grab and grab, but that's not for me.

"Guys are always bumping into me for a quick feel. I hate it. My fantasy is to be a man. I've been brought up to think that guys have it made. If I was a guy, nobody would walk over me," she says defiantly.

In her sexual fantasies, she has variations on the dominance theme. "In one fantasy I'm lying on the bed and there's an older woman, very shapely with a typical hour-glass figure. She has full lips, and long, mangelike hair. She tells my boyfriend to eat me. He's in woman's garb and he obeys her. If he doesn't do it right, she hits him.

"There's another one that I'll never tell him because you know how men are about women's fantasies—they get very jealous. In this one, I'm making a dirty movie, and this very dominant guy, very dark, with a moustache, is telling me what to do. He doesn't look like anyone I know, but he reminds me of an Italian lover I once had. I could wear a turtle-neck gown loose to the ground and he'd want to fuck me. You know how those Italians are."

She pauses for a minute, polishing her green nails greener for her date. "As a matter of fact, when I went with macho guys, I used to have fantasies about thousands of women making love to me, swarming over me, making love to me orally. But since I met Paul, that's gone. As a matter of fact, I'm not into women, unless he wants one for a one-night stand.

"I feel very secure with him. He's my Prince Charming, and he's my queen. He's every girl that I've always wanted and every guy that I've ever wanted. He's like me in many ways, that's why I love him so much. I love getting dressed up like this and being very feminine and very sexy. I like wearing sexy clothes. My boyfriend loves it when I look very sexy and get dressed up and we go out, because he feels proud of me. It's like saying 'She's mine and she's looking good.'

"We never fight, because I'm very, very forgiving. I'm a very soft, very mushy person. I can't stay mad at a person for a long time. But I'm trying to learn not to take shit from people. You know, there are so many people you have to take shit from in my business. I still have to kiss ass. I make nothing, working my ass off, but I have to do it to get experience.

"Because of my boyfriend, though, I'm not going to anymore. I'm not going to kiss anyone's ass but his," she says happily.

In her search for tenderness, Billi has found a man whose role changes in the bedroom give her the opportunity to act out her anger toward the macho male and the macho society. Billi convinced me that her relationship with Paul has softened her, and instead of heading for a life of a street criminal she will be able to save herself from that. There is no doubt in my mind that Billi would have ended up in prostitution had she not developed this relationship.

Unexpressed erotica results in violence, whether it is the unexpressed violence of S/M, the expressed violence of the poor man with his macho attitude against his wife and women, or the expressed violence of prostitutes toward all males. While the criminal and wife-abuse elements mostly occur in poverty environments, where the forces of women's liberation have not made any perceptible inroads, most of these women simply accept rather than rebel against their life of abuse which turns their male partners on, but, unlike their S/M sisters, does not turn them on. Because of their lifelong abuse, poor women know better than to enjoy violence.

Thus, the development of female erotica has a political element in it. For women have to be armed with decision-making options in order to explore their erotica. And, unfortunately, in today's American society, decision-making only comes from the reality of being financially independent.

It is sad to me that there are so many women who do not experience their own erotica. Even in nonabusive, poor family situations, wifely erotica is simply not explored. Sex is simply a woman's duty, something she has to perform very often affectionately for her husband while allowing him to ogle girlie magazines.

Poverty strikes women, then, on many levels. It is amazing to me that poor women have carried on so well. But, as illustrated in these interviews, most of them have repressed their rage and thus have repressed the development of their erotic lives. More than any other group of women in this book, poor women's erotic lives are not their own.

Seven

❀ ❀ ❀

THE EROTICISM OF
LESBIANS AND
BISEXUALS

I remember in kindergarten class a close-knit group of girlfriends often hid out in the girls' toilet. Standing almost in a circle, we felt around each other's genital areas, telling each other what felt nice and what didn't. It never occurred to us to let those dirty boys— who told dirty stories and whose fingers and faces were always dirty—near us. They could not be trusted, those boys. The way we liked things, sweet and pretty, they liked them loud and vulgar. The way we liked to be in our rooms, playing house, reading, listening to music, some of us playing the piano, they liked rough-housing, using swear words, and tearing each other's clothing. The way we liked lemonade and cake on holidays, they liked to scare everyone with thorny firecrackers.

Yes, indeed, we girl chums decided the boys were definitely ugly, and to be ignored. And we did ignore them for the next few years.

Then suddenly everything changed. The boys began cleaning up and acting nice to us. They gave us gifts, flowers, golden crosses at Christmas, spoke politely to our mothers when we met in the street. What had happened to those ugly little urchins? And what had happened to us? Because all of us, to a girl, began preferring this boy and that, getting crushes, and going steady. We still liked each other, too, but now our friendships were expressed by holding hands, talking in whispered tones about our boyfriends, and lending each other forbidden lipsticks and special clothing. We had forgotten all about our sexual exploration of each other's bodies, and when we remembered, we were not embarrassed. That was kid stuff, we told each other.

Yet, when as an adult I met various lesbian members of the women's liberation movement (the first time I had made acquaintance with a large group of lesbians), had I told them this story, they would have said that we girls were all lesbians and afraid of exploring this. This contention causes me much confusion and pondering. Are they indeed right? Does the sexual attraction of a female body mean that one is lesbianic? Yes, say the lesbians. I tend not to agree.

For me, lesbianism has always seemed an expression of affectionate love between women, somehow translated by these women into a form of sensuality. There are all sorts of theories about why this is so, but no psychoanalytical theory is accepted regarding this custom. Yet, in the women interviewed for this chapter, there seemed to be two existing elements in their lesbianic relationships: One is that they all endured a great hatred of men; the second, which is connected to the first, is that they all assumed that their erotic relationships with women had none of the difficulties that heterosexual relationships endured. Yet, from the interviews, it seemed obvious that the homosexual female relationship had all of the elements working that the heterosexual relationships have.

Lesbians are alternately passionate and faithful, promiscuous and violent, jealous and full of despair. Although the lesbians of the women's liberation movement would swear to me that being with a woman was somehow easier than being with a man, that there was a softness to their relationship, an understanding, it turned out in interview after interview that the contradictions and complications of the involvement with the erotic loved one was very often imitative of heterosexual conflicts.

Lesbians were also the most difficult people to interview because of their sexuality. Yet, I can certainly understand the maternal aspects of a woman's breasts, comforting and soft, having been breast-fed by my own Italian madonna mother. This breast eroticism seemed to be the dominant element in lesbianic lure, the erotic interest in the vaginal area a secondary one and one very often pierced by imitative genitalia à la the dildo.

Which brings me to a point that has always confused me. If, indeed, as modern lesbians claim, female eroticism is quite different from female/male eroticism, then why the use of the dildo? Although I must add in haste here that many lesbianic women refuse absolutely to use one, it certainly is an accepable sexual ingredient in most lesbianic relationships.

I have read lesbianic poems and lesbianic novels, and it seemed to me that they were honest explorations into emotion. However, today we have a new kind of homosexual woman whose choice is political, not emotional. Thus, her lesbianism seems fraudulent to me, for eroticism must be organic or it is not eroticism at all. I disagree with these lesbians of the women's movements and their claim that heterosexual and homosexual women are indeed alike and have the same ends, for the political motives of the homosexual women are of a separatist nature, while the heterosexual women's motives are of a merging nature.

As to the organic sensuality of the lesbianic world, it seems from my research that it is centered on a combination of, first, affection, and then secondly, narcissism. Most of the lesbians told me they liked being in the company of women, that it was more secure for them, nurturing. This affectionate nature of women is interpreted as sensuality, with the added narcissistic element of making love to the same kind of body. But there does seem to be evidence of erotic unfulfillment in that the women do take on male and female roles in the absence of a male body, as if organic sensual eroticism must *absolutely* contain male and female characteristics.

Homosexual women have various methods of handling this male absence. There are the macho lesbians—the extreme of these women are the bull dykes. Although modern lesbians are attempting to do away with these stereotypes, in the women interviewed, I found these extremes still to be true. Many fragile, young lesbians are coupled with the macho, older lesbians. When asked, these young women will admit that if a man acted like their lesbianic macho lover did, they would not stand for it. It is curious then that the macho behavior, so threatening in a man, seems not to be as threatening when expressed by a woman.

As to the reason bisexuality is combined with lesbianism in this chapter, there is a simple explanation. Although bisexuality has been documented as a valid life-style, no bisexual woman in this chapter remained bisexual for long after my questioning. The information given me was that the so-called bisexual woman was really a lesbian who used men as a power play toward her lesbianic lover or for a vessel for her hatred/revenge toward men. All the bisexual women said men were sexually attractive to them, but they felt no emotional response to them. Emotion was always reserved for the women. Thus, if eroticism is emotional and vulnerable sensuality combined, then we can make the assumption that *these bisexual women are using men for the same reason that they have accused men of using women: simply to get off*. Bisexual women play the stud role in reverse: They imitate the Don Juan playboy, the man who has done in women. Another way to look at their behavior is that it is kind of playing the middle from both ends, a sort of double insurance, a sort of double incest—bisexuals end up with mother and father, too. As a result, their life-style seems to be inorganic and weak because of the indecision that seems to consume their lives.

In our modern society, which seems to be all about *not* being vulnerable, bisexuality has become very chic. All young people who are hip (and some older ones) claim bisexuality is the natural state of woman and man, completely ignoring the fact that traditionally (although this tradition has been used for enslavement) the natural state of man and woman is begetting children. When we back away from unwanted traditions and become free of them, I constantly wonder why we can't simply enjoy that freedom. Why does our culture have to invent a new, so-called natural state? Everything is natural if it rings true for the two people involved. *But is it erotic?* For getting past all the political garbage, when a woman speaks about her vulnerable feelings for another human being, whether this other human being is male or female, there is an erotic reality. It is only when the bisexual or lesbianic coupling seems to occur out of hatred or for political reasons that it gives a cold chill.

This modern trend toward bisexual chic is another expression of sexuality upon cultural demand. Like Victorian sex, it does not ring clear and true. A woman loving a woman is erotically true if these women experience erotic vulnerability. Just like women and men who follow the heterosexual life-style because it is expected of them, lesbianism and bisexuality experienced as a radical lifestyle, rather than springing from the depths of a woman's erotic soul, are as ambiguous and artificial as a calendar pin-up in drag. Sometimes when I am in lesbianic company, I am reminded of my girl chums from kindergarten class. Often, from their conversations, I suspect that lesbians still regard men as those "dirty little boys telling dirty stories," not contemplating that those little boys could possibly have grown up to be warm, affectionate, compassionate human beings just like the little girls.

Our childhood teachings of old-fashioned decision-making have been soiled by the Freudian idea of regression, destroying our ability to be erotically responsible and erotic, decision-making human beings. Do we really get closer to the truth if we let it all hang out? Decisions are seen as a puritanical repression rather than a responsible process of desire.

The most responsible woman is not the woman who in her dissatisfaction with men turns to women for love. The most courageous woman is the woman who brings all of the feminist insights into the male/female relationship, thus working for the humanitarian end of changing the heterosexual relationship. Lesbianic relationships, although erotic and human experiences, do seem to be another trend towards separatism, with its ultimate aim perhaps being a separated society.

At the beginning of the political women's liberation movement, many feminists were touting that men could not be acceptable sexual partners. In order to be a true feminist, the propaganda ran, one had to turn from men erotically and focus on women. I was very uncomfortable about this idea, even though many of the "new" political lesbians erupted from my heterosexual friends of many years, friends who had shared with me the dissatisfaction with women's rights and privileges.

I became ostracized among these women and was thought of as a "traitor" because I could not make this proper transference. Although I explained many times that I felt sexual eroticism should be organic to the person and not politically decided, and that I had no prejudice against people who were organically homosexual, I was looked upon with suspicion and distrust.

Many lesbians chose coincidentally to confide in me, and I heard again and again, from their passionate outbursts, how women loving women was the same as women loving men; the sexuality was different, that was all. The same kinds of insecurities, role problems, jealousies, indecisions and distrust existed. Thus, I came to the conclusion that all that liberation propaganda was just that—propaganda.

Because of this, I have chosen to contrast two partners in a lesbian relationship, showing the keen differences in observations of both these partners.

Zohra and Poppy

Zohra, the older woman in the relationship, was born in this country, but spent a dozen years in Israel. Returning, she established a successful film career. Since her commercial work paid off so handsomely, she built a lovely house at the seashore, where she writes. In her barnlike rooms, we talk about her erotic life, which at forty has produced only women lovers.

"I've only necked with men," Zohra says. A small, dark woman, she is half-child, half-woman when she speaks about her personal life. "Although emotionally I prefer men. They make better friends," she says.

Zohra has had only thirteen lovers, and currently is in a two-year relationship with Poppy. She tells me explicitly how she enters relationships with women and what happens.

"I choose women who like me to be the aggressor. I pay for everything—dinner, drinks. Then I create a situation where the person believes she is seducing me. I am passive. It's kind of teasing. I usually drink a lot of wine because it is very hard for me to have sex without it. I provide everything—atmosphere, music, conversation. I have to be very sure the person wants me.

"The seduction is mental. I talk about how much I don't want sex. I'm the opposite of what the situation really is, and I'm entirely negative. It's like I'm saying, 'Let's see what you can do about this.' "

The women Zohra usually seeks out are usually dependent in bed, very aggressive out of bed, very intelligent, and have just come out of another relationship. She finds them with an uncanny skill.

"Finally, she will go into the bedroom, and say, 'I feel better in this room. I want to lie down. It's so comfortable.' She thinks she is the woman who can seduce me, that I am falling into her trap. But I really took her there."

As I listen to Zohra, her kohl-tinted eyes begin to seduce me. She speaks very slowly, reminding me of everyone I've ever seen in a Buñuel film because there is pain in her honesty, in her revelation about her need to control.

"I almost picture a spider and a fly at that moment. I approach her. She has fallen into the net. Then I am very sensual, not sexual. It takes a very long process to get to know each other. I take her clothes off. We talk, but not about sex. I play music. I delay and delay. Then, in my mind, I become a male. Before this, I am female. I become male when I start to please her. I touch her all over her body. I watch the excitement in her, and that excites me. I like to produce excitement more than have it myself. I continue to give her pleasure. I go down on her, and she will climax. Then I will have my first climax, and it has to be mine, given to myself by myself."

Zohra talks about the tremendous power she feels when she makes her lover climax. "I feel very close to her emotionally then. Then I let her go down on me and I will climax. When I climax, it's very private and very lonely. Then I get angry."

Zohra's anger starts with her first, lover-given orgasm, and although for the first month of the relationship everything seems to be high and exciting and all sorts of wild things happen sexually, Zohra begins to withdraw and starts getting bored. As she speaks, I am aware that she is talking like the cliché male playboy.

"I start getting bored after the whole conquest has been completed. Then I feel trapped. Although my feelings for the woman are nice, I cannot recapture the sexual feelings. I usually remain with the woman but feel tremendous guilt about it. I never verbalize it. My behavior is not that nice. I become hostile. I feel like punching her all the time. Then she usually complains, 'You were so nice to me. Why are you so nasty now?' "

"Why are you?" I ask, puzzled.

She pauses as if it is an old story. "Because it is incestuous. As soon as I start liking the person, they become very familiar. It is something that happened with my parents. . . ."

Then Zohra proceeds to tell me a tale of parental incest like no other I have heard. "When I was a child, my father wanted me to be the boy. I was the oldest of four daughters. So he dressed me up in boy's clothes. He also took me to bed with my mother. They would put me in the middle and play around. They teased playfully. Then he would throw me onto the side of the bed and have sex with my mother. One, two, three. It was brutal. I was very upset about this, and I felt terribly guilty about it.

"As a result, my only fantasy is a man and woman making love and my watching. I have this fantasy when I masturbate, but I have never had the courage to act it out."

Because of her firsthand knowledge of her father's sexuality with her mother, Zohra decided all men were brutes. "Although I imagine there are men who are extremely sensitive, I have a block about this. Now that I am forty, I have thought of having a young, beautiful man as a lover, someone who knows nothing about sex and whom I will teach everything."

As is common in lesbian circles, Zohra usually uses dildos in masturbation and in making love. "I like penises. I will surprise a woman with a dildo when I know she is ready to be penetrated. But they usually get angry because I have not told them I intend to use it."

Although Zohra has been a lesbian all her life, she does not like lesbians. "I find lesbians are antimale, very sexually oriented, and practice very much what they criticize in the male. They say a man doesn't take time before intercourse. Well, many lesbians don't take time either. They are extremely fast and extremely insensitive."

Zohra likes to make love half-dressed, only with her pants on. She likes to rip the woman's clothes off in almost a rapelike situation, a fact that turns her on, even though she is deadly afraid of being raped by a man.

She says that the first person is the male in her and the second the female. "I'm trying to get both parts of my personality together. I'm tired of being a male publicly, in business and in lesbian circles, and privately being a female with my books, my music, my paintings. I want to be a female in the outside world, too."

Zohra has been seeing a young, twenty-five-year-old woman for two years. Poppy is from a wealthy family. She is slim, chic, and bisexual. She works as a typist, as she struggles for an acting career.

Where Zohra's tones were melancholy and passionate in their insecurities and honesties, Poppy's are fragile and trembling as she tells of their relationship.

"I'll always remember that first night," she says, smoking a long, thin cigar and looking like a French film star. "I was very aggressive with Zohra. We were both rather shy, but I pursued the relationship. I made the first move. We had dinner several times, but I set it up so we had a late date where it was obvious we could do nothing but have sex.

"We took bubble baths separately and put on robes. It was all quite ladylike. When I realized she was self-conscious of her body, I was shocked. She is such a professional lesbian in public, and privately she was rather shy."

Although Zohra indulged in oral sex, she did not like to be penetrated with Poppy's hand or finger. "It was nice being with her, and I was eager to get close to her. She didn't like her breasts touched. It was as if her body was cut in two; the top half of her torso was the feminine which did not turn on sexually, and the bottom half was masculine which did turn on. I found myself puzzled because before we had sex, she had the kind of attitude that she'd take care of everything. She opened the door for me, paid the check, got my cigarettes, but intimately, she was very shy and retiring."

Poppy said the first months of their affair were terribly exciting and terribly frightening at the same time. "The only thing we disagreed on sexually was that she wanted to use a dildo. I let her, but I was uncomfortable. It was such a bad imitation of a heterosexual relationship. If I wanted a man, I'd go out and get a man."

Poppy did just that and taunted Zohra with it when Zohra began to withdraw. Although Zohra saw other women, the threat of a man was more dramatic. But when I referred to Poppy as a bisexual in view of her sexual behavior, Poppy was very, very upset.

"Bisexuality makes me nervous. It's like I'm indecisive. It's easier for me to achieve sexual satisfaction with women. It's safer. . . . Yet, there's a strange sense of fusion which is bewildering because I can't see clearly where I end and Zohra begins."

With men, Poppy feels much more comfortable sexually. "I feel much more centered because I'm not eager to relinquish my identity as I am with Zohra. Sexually, I have to work harder for an orgasm with a woman. But there's a great risk with men, too."

Poppy cites the risk with men as beginning when she slept with her wealthy father when she was sixteen. Before that, she was not attracted to girls, and had only been sexually active with boys. "I wasn't that hot for my father, but I was needy as a child for his love. I was coquettish and provocative. We were kidding around on his bed, and suddenly my hand went to his crotch. He then penetrated me. Part of me just thought this was a game. But then when I began being aroused, he withdrew, which was very painful. I think he was just about to ejaculate."

Poppy then recited a long list of obscenities that she had shouted at her father. "I called him a faggot, twinkle toes. He got angry, and I ran out of the room to the phone. He took the phone from me and threw it at me and hit my back. I fell and broke my nose."

Poppy was taken to the hospital for her physical injuries, and fortunately, a sensitive doctor also prescribed psychotherapy for her. But she told no one what had happened. She just lay there sullen and uncommunicative. "I never went back home again," she says sadly. Instead, Poppy got an apartment by herself and started to work as a call girl at seventeen years of age.

"I felt a terrific power because I could evoke from these men all kinds of things that I would never allow them to get from me. I was incredibly angry at men, and this was a perfect outlet. They came to my apartment, paid me a hundred dollars an hour. The woman who helped me get the johns knew I wasn't into freaky scenes so the johns were mostly conservative conventioneers and commuters whose wives must have been totally asexual. I was aggressive with these dopes. I usually offered them something to drink. I was very cool. They liked to talk a lot about their wives and kids. A lot of them seemed to want to talk more than get laid.

"Then I would make a subtle move, and we would fuck. It was a big con game."

After a year of this experience, Poppy began to make love to women. "All my relationships have to be sexual. There is a sexual tension I love. It's exciting." And after making love to more than one hundred men and a half-dozen women, Poppy says she feels like an animal, a teen-age adolescent who is a victim of biological functions she can't control.

"Remember those kids in school who would get excited and mess themselves up and run to the bathroom to jerk off because a girl turned them on? Everyone in school looked at them with a mixture of contempt and compassion. Sometimes I think I'm just a young boy or a man who is highly aroused and can't control himself," she says.

Here, we have a love relationship with all of the misunderstandings and ego conflicts that we find in a male/female relationship. Zohra and Poppy see their relationship and the power according to their own individual needs. Poppy can threaten Zohra with her bisexuality, her ability to make love to men, which Zohra is not able to do. It is interesting that Poppy needs absolute control over men, but in her relationship with her woman lover, she gives the control to Zohra. Zohra appropriately imitates male behavior, the macho behavior Poppy hates and is disgusted by in men.

Both women's experience with incestuous fantasy and incestuous reality is not uncommon in the homosexual world. Many women report this to be a dominant factor in their choosing women to love, as if their fathers proved to them at a very early age that men cannot be trusted.

Many women who married and raised children at an early age and were then divorced or widowed, instead of continuing to love men, with their new freedom and consciousness choose to love women, something they have always wanted to do. Mary, married twice, is a woman who, although she still has male lovers, calls herself a lesbian.

Mary

Mary is slim, taut, and middle-aged. A doctor living in Tampa, Florida, she has been married twice, but for the last ten years of her life has made love mostly to women.

"I was very happy when I discovered that my making love to women did not turn me off men. Although I prefer women, my entire sexuality has benefited. When you make love to people of your own sex as well as to the opposite sex, I think you are sexually a more complete person."

Although she did not act on them until she was thirty-five, Mary's fantasies were always only about women. "In my early childhood, all my fantasies concerned women and breasts. In the fourth grade, I used to draw them. I was at a very strict convent school, and my teachers called in my parents to reprimand me. I never could fantasize about men, even through my two long marriages." After those two long marriages, and bearing four children, Mary turned to loving women.

"I think sex is probably the most wonderful thing in the world. I have a hard time in the summertime when I have to choose between having sex and going swimming, because I also adore swimming."

Although Mary has had lots of sex, she has never fallen in love. "People say when you're in love, there's an addictive quality. It seems to be monogamous, and I don't like that. In fact, I will go out of my way to choose a woman who will not fall in love with me. And it's hard, because people respond very passionately, and men and women get crushes on me."

Mary is soft-spoken and comforting, and I can see why people would be drawn to her. She represents, it seems to me, the eternal mother. And what is better than the eternal madonna who likes sex?

"I don't go along with the myth that all sex is marvelous with a woman because she is a woman. I think it depends on the sensitivity of the person." In fact, recently, she had an evening with a man. "We were on the couch and both were naked. We had been kissing and fondling and had had intercourse once already. We both love music, and I asked him to play Bach. He said, 'I can't really fuck to Bach.' I said, 'I'll bet you can.' So we put the Brandenberg on and started to make love, and we made love for hours and hours. He had five orgasms. He said, 'Now I'll always fuck to Bach.'" She smiles as she retells the story. "His body is very spicy and pungent, and I love to go down on him because he has an absolutely intoxicating smell in his groin."

Since that sounds pretty erotic to me, I ask Mary why she calls herself a lesbian and not a bisexual. "Because I prefer women. Now a night with a woman is different. Last week, there were four of us having dinner. We were hugging and kissing each other. One of the women had simply gorgeous breasts, and we all said that we thought it was simply shameful that she kept them all to herself. So while we were eating, she took off her blouse and sat there with these two absolutely sublime, mind-blowing breasts. She let us play with them while we were eating. It was sweet. We were eating and talking and swapping recipes and playing with each other, in the genitals, breasts, and faces.

"It was a hot night so we decided to skinny-dip in her pool. Two of the women were a monogamous couple, and when we said we wanted to have an orgy, they said no. But we sat in the back, waiting for it to get dark so we could swim naked, and there was honeysuckle and roses, and we drank fruit drinks and kissed." Mary pauses a moment, crinkling up her nose, looking like a woman who would crochet a comforter in a painting by Hopper and not at all like a woman who would skinny-dip.

Finally, in the pool, Mary sat on Joan's shoulders and had an absolutely electrifying orgasm. And then they all took turns. Finally, they retreated to the two bedrooms where the couples made love. Mary and Joan made love till nine o'clock the next morning. "We found parts of our bodies we never knew existed. Under the toes, between the fingers, the back of the neck. Joan likes finger penetration. We've never used apparatuses. In fact, I had a vibrator and gave it away.

"One thing I have found is that there is a real difference between making love to men and making love to women. With women, there's always more leisure. There isn't that terrible urgency to get right into orgasm." I have heard this many times before from lesbians, who claim the orgasm is the least of their pleasure. "Sometimes when I'm with a man, I suddenly laugh about something, and it absolutely destroys the poor man's erection, but women seem to go along with these changes."

Mary describes orgasm in exact terms. "It begins almost with a convulsive feeling in the pelvic bone area. I feel I won't be able to stand it if it continues. And I feel I won't be able to stand it if it doesn't. Then it spreads until the whole genital area is throbbing, then travels to the groin, down and up the legs, and through the back. I always break out into a terrible rash which is a dead giveaway, and I can never fool anybody. Then it goes to the top of my head, and then it's just waves and waves of energy. It just goes zap and stays there. You think it can't possibly get better, and you take a breath, and then it starts again. It's marvelous for any physical problem. I have a circulatory problem, and it gives me the most intense relief."

Because of this, Mary masturbates every day and tells me the amazing fact that midwives used to masturbate women in labor to ease their pain. Mary is matter-of-fact about masturbation and doesn't use a fantasy, although she does admit that she has a rape fantasy.

"In mine, it's always the Nazi war movies. One of my friends has it, too, only with her, the Nazi falls in love with her and becomes a different person."

Mary feels that everyone in love becomes a different person, and it is one of the reasons she avoids serious love affairs.

"People have been very hurt by life, and when they fall in love with me, I can't say no to them. They frighten and threaten me. They feel rejected if I don't want to see them. I cannot return their feelings because I think people in love do not relate to another human being as an equal but as an object.

"I just can't be that much to somebody. It's too much of a burden. So I will try to find somebody who is more open sexually and who enjoys sex for sex's sake. People who regard sex as something very mysterious and marvelous think of it as a challenge. It's very hard to find someone who just thinks it's fun." But Mary has been lucky and says she has two absolutely exquisite male lovers and three female lovers who answer this description perfectly.

Although she does not believe in love, she does believe in passion. "Passion is something that moves us beyond reason. I eat with passion. I fuck with passion. I swim with passion. I walk with passion. I listen to music with passion. I write with passion. I'm a very passionate woman," she says adamantly.

Mary, a woman who finally has given herself the right to her personal freedom, refuses to fall in love because of the demands it puts upon her. Yet, she claims she makes love with passion, analyzing passion as that which moves us beyond reason. She is right in her definition, but the fact that she cannot fall in love means that she is limiting her sensuality to only the physical part of sex. It's as if she knows, after two long marriages and four children, that she doesn't want the responsibility of caring that much for another human being again.

Falling in love in its popular conception does unfortunately focus responsibility away from pleasure to commitment, and it is interesting to me that with this attitude, Mary prefers women. Her sensuality with her women lovers and with her male lovers seems enjoyable but definitely without commitment. Perhaps bisexuality exists only where there is a lack of any kind of commitment to another.

Bisexual women usually feel that they can commit themselves personally only to women, but do admit that sexuality with men is more erotic. It is almost a contradiction in terms, but Betsy explains it well.

Betsy

Her fragility is the first thing that strikes me, and it does not match the portrait of herself that Betsy is conveying. A small-boned, fragile, red-haired woman who still has traces of tomboy-ism in her appearance, with her Huckleberry Finn freckles, her shy smile, and her slender body, Betsy calls herself an assertive lover, the aggressive partner in a female couple. "I tend to be more aggressive," she says when she speaks of her behavior to women. "I reach over and kiss my lover, touch her, manipulate her breasts, kiss her on the neck, get to know her and what pleases her. Some-times I use a vibrator, although I don't like them for myself. We are very affectionate, kissing and touching all parts of the body, including genitals. My physical relationship is always good with women."

The last long-term lover Betsy had was someone who became very clinging and dependent and wanted to know everything Betsy was doing. "She had to work nights on her degree so she was always questioning me about who I was with, and whether or not I was faithful. It got so that I stayed home every night just to get her call. I became very frustrated and angry at myself, but I needed to be close to her. I thought we could get over these hurdles, but we never did. It's funny, I was the more aggressive and bossy one in the relationship, but she entirely controlled me in the end. Of course we broke up." Betsy's eyes are filled with sad tears of longing, as she tells me of the ending of her two-year affair.

I ask her what her relationships with men are like, since she has had over four dozen lovers and has made love to only ten women. "I would never have stayed home for a man. Men have always been imprisoning and restricting to me. I tend to be more free-spirited with a man than with a woman. I'm much more in-volved with a woman, much more emotional and dependent. The intensity with the woman threatens me, but with a man, I have more sexual freedom."

One of the ways Betsy denies herself this freedom is that, al-though she wanted more than one orgasm with her woman lover, she never asked for it; yet, if she had been with a man, she would have demanded more. "With a man, I would have said, 'Hey, I want more.' With my lover, I never asked her to continue. She would give me one major orgasm and then stop. On the other hand, I would give her multiple orgasms, even though it took some time."

Betsy thinks her relationship to women is more sensitive and sometimes filled with deep insecurity. She traces this to her relationship with her mother. "My mother used me as a punching bag. It's as if she never wanted me. As a matter of fact, I was a change-of-life baby. My sisters were much older, and my parents really wanted a boy. So my mother was very frustrated and filled with hate. She would pull me out of bed and throw me on the floor and start punching me and wouldn't stop. Wham! Wham! I was black and blue all of the time."

Although Betsy sees her father as a compassionate and warm man, she resents him for not intervening when his wife beat her. "I finally told him one night when I was twenty-three and she was beating me up. Can you imagine? I had gone away to college and was engaged to a man . . . and she called me a rotten son of a bitch, a selfish thing. She said to me, 'You were never any good, you never will be any good.' She grabbed my hair and my throat and started choking me to death. I had to use my feet and everything else to kick her away. Meanwhile, my ostrich father is sitting there, and I am pleading with him to get her away from me. Finally, I got her off me, and I said to my father that I was leaving for good and asked him what kind of a man was he to let this woman abuse her child the way she did, to deprive her child of warmth and love. How could he sit by and watch this?"

As she speaks of her mother, Betsy still speaks with fear, although it has been ten years since this traumatic scene, ten years in which she has not only built up a career as a sociologist but has furnished her own luxury apartment on Chicago's south side and has had several affairs with women. The one she remembers most is the first one.

"She was my best lover—brilliant, affluent, lovely, charming, romantic, decisive, strong, loving, gentle, and harsh. The relationship went on for two years, but I grew too close to her. She was a closet gay woman and wanted eventually to end up married. So she began pushing me away. She eventually pushed me out the door. I think of her as my Princess Charming."

Asked if she has a comparable Prince Charming, Betsy gets up from her lounge chair, puts on a rock-and-roll record, touches several books in the bookcase, gets a bottle of wine and pours two large glasses for both of us, gets another pack of cigarettes from her table, and begins smoking furiously. I wonder why the question is so potent.

"Yeah, I met him once." Her voice now has lost its educated, intellectual tone and has become a street voice, the voice of a street whore, the voice of a bitter, despairing woman.

"He was playing a game," she begins her harsh story, puffing furiously on her cigarette and drinking large gulps of wine.

I am astonished at this transition and feel now that I am talking to a bull dyke in the old sense of the word.

"He was charming. He had a game. It was to sweep me off my feet and charm me . . . to promise me everything. He doled out love, and when I began to respond, he just suddenly disappeared. He doleth out love and he taketh it," she says, laughing bitterly to herself as if this is some private joke.

"Why does *he* disappoint you so much more than *she* does?" I ask her.

She looks at me furiously. "She was cruel, and there was that mysterious quality about her. I never knew if she was going to be cruel and demanding or loving and warm. Like . . ." she again has taken on her soft tone ". . . like my mother. As a matter of fact," she whispers to me in secrecy as if someone else were in the room, "she reminded me of my mother more than anyone I've known, and I loved her madly.

"I'd do anything for her. With men, I just want to fuck and get up and go home. They disgust me, especially when they want oral sex. If they demand that, I just get up and get dressed and leave. They get angry and plead. But I can't care. They can fuck me, but if they become too demanding or physically aggressive they disgust me. As a matter of fact, they often squeeze my breasts too hard. And when their sperm runs on my body, I want to throw up. I like sperm only in two places—on him or in me. I don't want to see it anywhere else. I can take men or leave them."

I point out to her that it seems to me that she is imitating behavior from the worst kind of men and ask if she is aware of it.

"Well, they've outnumbered me for many years . . . and it's time for Montezuma's revenge, it's time for my revenge. It's a man's world, and women have been used. There are many women who feel as I do."

"If you feel like that, why aren't you a lesbian? Why do you call yourself a bisexual?"

She answers in her tough voice, the voice she switches into whenever she talks about men. "I like to leave my options open. Sometimes I want a cock, but not very often. Sometimes I spend days walking down the street looking at cocks. So I have one. I go to a bar and pick up a guy and that's that.

"There is such a difference between female and male that I think they are very separate." She is now using her feminine tone of voice and has leaned back, putting her cigarette out, and has squelched her aggressiveness. "It is inconceivable to me to expect fluidity between a man and a woman. It's easier to love one who is closer to you, woman to woman or man to man, than it is to cross the barrier of two sexual opposites, male to female. I think it is almost impossible."

I tell her that this is straight lesbian propaganda and wonder whether there is any man that she admires.

"Jesus Christ," she says with laughter. "I have an image of him as a strong man who is able to lift a child off the ground and wipe the tears from her eyes. I see that as a quality in men that is very human—one I don't find."

"But if you refuse to invest any kind of emotional vulnerability with men, how do you expect to get close to them emotionally or spiritually?" I ask quietly.

She looks at me for a long time as if I have said a dreaded thing, something that is defeating to her, something that is threatening. Then she clears her throat, and says, softly, ever so softly, "You have a point there."

I wait in silence for her to speak again, for I can see she is in a tremendous amount of pain. Then she says, still more quietly, "Sometimes I think being gay was just all a fantasy, a rebellious experiment . . . and that the experiment went too far." She wipes a tear from her cheek.

"Sometimes I wonder where the rebellion leaves off and becomes one's life." She looks at me for understanding, and my heart

breaks for her. *"Because if you've lived it for a time . . . it be-*
comes you."

Betsy is representative of many lesbian women who will give
understanding to a woman's behavior, but not a man's. It is interesting to me that Betsy was aware enough to tie up her lesbian
eroticism with her rebellion toward her family and the roles they
played in her life. But she obviously could not do much about
this reaction to them.

Here again the male lover is used almost as a recipient for female stud behavior. There seems to be no understanding, no compassion, no vulnerability to the male. At least Betsy was honest.
When I asked her how she expected a man to open up to her
when she was just using him (the same kind of behavior lesbians
traditionally criticize in males toward females), she did consider
my point.

It's as if after all these years of male stud behavior, instead of this
behavior being negated for some women it must now be imitated.
Anne, another bisexual woman, also imitates male studs.

Anne

Anne sits in her large Arizona apartment as if she were
just temporarily renting a corner of the room, instead of being
the lease-holder. In the three years she has lived here, she has lent
parts of the place to friends in need, who are now temporarily
absent. The apartment gives the impression of being an army bar-
racks or a college dorm, for each corner has the personal imprint
of its resident, her taste in furniture, photographs, and paintings
competing with that in the next section.

Anne's space is very, very bare. She is on a mattress on the
floor, covered with a rabbit coat, and speaks of her bisexuality.
Boyish haircut, short gaminlike appearance with an acne complexion, her figure is dumpy, giving the impression of a perennial

teen-ager always eating too much candy. Her voice is very low and very nervous, and she constantly asks me what my credentials are.

She tells of her uttermost fears of the act of love with men. "I'm terrified they'll treat me only as a sexual object."

"What about women? Have they ever treated you that way?"

Looking uncomfortable, she gets up from the low mattress and begins watering her many plants with nervous and edgy movements. "Yes," she says, almost as an aside, "in lesbian bars. The first time a woman came on that way, I was terrified."

"Did you think that women were not capable of that kind of behavior?" The popular gay attitude that women are incapable of acting like men on the make has always amazed me. Perhaps it is because at various times in my life I have seen lesbian behavior that was just as humiliating to women as some male behavior is.

"I didn't think so. . . . I trust women more because women were always more accepting of me when I was growing up. They didn't have high expectations of me. I always had to compete with my brothers and my father."

At twenty-five, Anne jogs three miles a day, swims, and plays softball as often as she can locate a team. She is employed as an executive for an electronic engineering firm. A native of Arizona, she speaks with a slight twang as she fearfully answers my questions about her personal life.

"When did you first know you were bisexual?"

Pausing, she speaks slowly as if she were measuring her answer. "When I fell in love with one of my teachers. I never actually had sex with her, or kissed her, or held her breasts, but I still have lots of fantasies about having sex with her and find the thoughts very exciting. I have homosexual fantasies whenever I make love. Men making love to men, women stimulating women, men being bound by women but being entered by men. I usually don't tell my fantasies to anyone. But I do know that men are very threatened when I say I'm bisexual."

The Arizona sun is turning the room into a desert with its hot, dry light, as Anne continues watering her collection of plants, all large desert cacti, reminding me of phallic symbols.

"Why is that?" I ask.

"Don't know," she answers quickly, pricking herself on a cactus thorn and cursing. "I think they're afraid I'll leave them for a woman. Right now, I'm having a relationship with a married woman, mother of three, whose husband doesn't know. And I'm also having an affair with an engineer I work with."

Anne is busy trying to get the uncomfortable thorn out of her finger by sucking it dry. "With a man, I like touching his penis, but I get a little apprehensive when he enters me. It seems like an intrusion on my privacy. With a woman, my orgasms are easier when I'm being stimulated with her hands inside of me, or pressure from her leg, or oral sex. It's usually gentler."

She grimaces, her acne turning blotchy red. "There's something about being a lesbian that's upsetting. I get depressed about the whole situation when I think of myself as a lesbian."

There are many theorists, especially among radical lesbians, who claim that bisexuals are really lesbians who are trying to hide. I wonder at this and ask Anne about her most erotic experience, totally surprised at her answer.

"It happened in Mexico. I was traveling in a college group, and we went to a fishing village. An American was living there. He was about twenty-five and very, very attractive. He had been drinking beer on the beach, and I began talking to him. When it got dark, we screwed." She pauses, thinks a bit. "It was exciting because we didn't know each other at all, and because it was a challenge. And there was this dynamic and exciting energy between us. He entered me very quickly and made me come very quickly—twice. The second time it was slower."

"What do you think about bisexuality?"

She looks angrily at me. "I don't know. Sometimes I get frightened that I'm not normal, that I should be married and have a family."

"What do you do when you feel like that?"

"I go to a bar in the neighborhood where I can go in alone. I rap with the bartender, have a few drinks, and get pretty high." She stops talking as if she does not want to go on. I wait for her to resume. "Sometimes . . . sometimes I get picked up by men." She gulps the information out in a monotone of shame. "I usually go home with them and then never see them again because I just don't want to. It's just a one-night stand kind of a thing. I guess I'm proving that I'm a woman."

"You mean like some men prove they are men?"

"What do you mean?" She draws a blank.

"I mean the men who treat women as sexual objects, the men you don't like."

"Oh, yeah," she says flatly.

"You're doing the same thing, in reverse, aren't you?"

"Yes," she admits honestly. "I was treating them in the very way that I hated to be treated. I guess," she adds, "I guess, sometimes, I'm really no different than they are."

Anne seems to exactly duplicate male chauvinistic behavior. Afraid of the legend of lesbianism, she forces herself to make love to men. As always, when sensuality is experienced only to prove a point, it is worthless and without much enjoyment.

Some women do not even bother to make love to men, and act out their aggressiveness, in a macholike imitation, with their women lovers. Bambi is that type of woman.

Bambi

"I'm extremely fragile about ever approaching anyone if I feel I'm going to be rejected sexually," Bambi, a young woman with a dancer's face and body, says. "She has to caress me, and if she likes breasts, it's sexually exciting to me." A schoolteacher, Bambi works with other lesbians and dates them. "Sometimes we work until late at night, and then we go home and make love. It's really nice."

When Bambi first entered the homosexual world, she found roles were strictly delineated. "There were butches or femmes—one person who was the aggressor, the other who was receptive. And it was taboo to cross those lines."

At first, she was attracted to being aggressive with women and made her lovers feel very important. Now, she likes to be seductive. "I like to lie there and have someone perform for me. I love to have my breasts caressed. I love to be kissed. I have multiple orgasms all the time, though I need a lot of foreplay." Bambi can even have orgasms just from kissing, but with penetration (with a dildo or hand) it takes much, much longer. "A woman with a dildo really excites me. It is a simulated penis, but it's a woman using it. It's a full circle of fantasy. I'm never unaware that she is a woman, and she can suddenly enter me."

Thinking men's approaches to women were abhorrent, Bambi finds that now she does the same thing. "It's such a silly thing. I used to hate it when men did it, but I have really found myself now looking at a woman sexually, thinking how would she be in bed. But I find that sexuality can be difficult, it's so exhausting. People are so extreme about it that I'm exhausted before I start it. There is so much role-playing, games, seductiveness. It's like a peacock dance, all fuss surrounding the action."

Bambi is speaking to me in a very cold tone of voice. We are seated in her second-floor apartment in Maine, an apartment filled with antiques, plants, and handicrafts. She has trouble talking about sex, and when I ask her specifically what she does, she blocks and avoids the questions, so I must persist and persist. However, I find now she is relaxing and begins to giggle when she speaks of her alternatives to sexuality—her unique way of masturbating.

"I masturbate when I'm driving," she giggles, suddenly showing good humor. "Once a truck driver caught me, and he was so shocked. You see, I love to drive, the vibrations of driving have always made me horny. I love to drive and love to drive fast. Speeding is so sexual to me. It's not the danger of it but the sensation of motion, the rhythm of driving. Often I drive long expanses and masturbate with my hand. Or I pick up beach stones and put them in my vagina. I have long orgasms that last for miles. With the vibrations of the road and with the stones against my clitoris, it's wonderful!" She giggles again. "Now you'll know why I'm anxious to get to the Interstate Highway."

I laugh loudly in appreciation of her secret turn-on. It's always so amazing to me how creative people can get when they are alone. Bambi interrupts my thoughts and tells me of another pleasurable sexual custom, one of childhood. "I was madly in love with a girl-friend who was very brave. I was terribly skinny. She was magnificent. I was terrified of horses, and she loved them. We used to go bareback riding together at night. I'd steal from my bedroom with my nightgown on, and we would ride together in the moonlight. It really turned me on. I was only ten years old."

Bambi's fantasies are entirely of young teen-age boys, of seducing them, having them perform for her, and not allowing them sexual gratification. When they are completely in surrender to her, she orders homosexual men to commit sodomy on them. Then all the men watch her make love to a woman. "In my fantasies, I like to be completely in control. In reality, I like older women. I have a very cavalier attitude toward women. As long as I can masturbate, I can take it or leave it."

Often, in her role as a schoolteacher, Bambi meets heterosexual women. She feels any heterosexual woman has psychological problems because all women should love women. "I don't believe any woman is completely heterosexual, they just have primitive fears that prevent them. All women are lesbians. Everyone is a potential lesbian."

When I ask her to reverse this procedure and ask if she feels that women who block feelings about men have psychological problems, she says that it is not so, reflecting a deep-seated and frequent prejudice of lesbians. "No, women simply are not turned on by penetration," she says. "I cannot be stimulated by penetration. A man has to have an orgasm through his penis. He has to penetrate. Penetration is absolutely essential for men, even homosexual men."

I ask Bambi if she is aware that some women like to be penetrated by a man's penis. "I don't believe that. Every time I make love to a woman who is heterosexual, she says she is getting something from a woman that she cannot get from a man." I suggest the reverse, but she shakes her head adamantly. "When I have sex with a man, I always fantasize that he is a woman," she says, as if judging that every other woman feels this also.

I am uncomfortable with Bambi, for I feel she has a deep-seated prejudice against heterosexuality, a prejudice which heterosexuals are often accused of having regarding homosexuals.

"Are you angry at men?" I ask, trying to break this mood.

"My brother got all the honors," she says bitterly. "I felt I was the black sheep. I get angry at myself at wanting to live up to his achievements," she ends abruptly.

Bambi likes to play pool in bars with men for drinks. One time she had a friend who was a call girl and who used to send her seductive clothing. "She used to give me these great whore's dresses, soft fabrics, lots of period underwear. These were great clothes to play pool with. I would wear my red, thigh-high boots with red stockings. I was a very good pool player and would play for cognac."

She gets more and more animated as she speaks of her fondness for this activity. "I like the company of men, especially in bars. There were women who were seated at the bar, watching me. It was very electric and exciting.

"One night I was wearing this perfectly snug, black dress with long sleeves and a low neckline and two slits up the side. I was winning at pool and was drinking a lot. So I went up to one of the women who had been watching me and asked for a cigarette. We talked for a while, then we went home.

"I loved her because she made me feel free, let me make love to her. I was completely sexually uninhibited and alive. It was over-whelming. I aroused her and sexually stimulated her. I got so much enjoyment out of her enjoyment. We stayed in bed for days.

"It was a complete macho trip."

I'm glad Bambi said it so I didn't have to. It is interesting that she completely glamorized herself in the most female stereotypical clothing and then acted like a macho man, exhibiting the duality that lesbians seem to get turned on by. It's as if they must always parody men, make fun of macho behavior, even while they are turned on by it. There is a bitterness that seems to be constant with lesbians against men, a power play that has to exist for them to become excited.

Almost like the S/M women, lesbians think a lot about directly controlling their partner, another form of imitative male behavior. Abbe speaks about this experience.

Abbe

Abbe, a silversmith, is small, with long dark hair. I would describe her as terribly, terribly feminine and soft except that there is a flippant, aggressive way in which she speaks about her love life.

"I like to be strong and in control. There are times when I sleep with three women a day, but that's just a piece of meat. I get exhausted from fucking. So I like to have relationships with women where we can play at control. If someone is passive, she's dull. What attracts me in women is a sense of bitchiness."

Abbe describes her relationship with men as having this same dullness. "Men are putty. It's always too easy for me with them. If I want someone, I just say, 'Let's go.' I decide everything. I don't make love, I just cocktease. I get them aroused, and they beg, and I stop."

Although Abbe's brutality with men is more obvious, she is equally brutal with women. "If you touch a person hard or hit them and they look at you in a certain way, you know they want it." What she is talking about is "fist-fucking," and she speaks about it with a kind of Mona Lisa smile on her face.

"I gave my little girl a fist-fuck the other day. I did it harder and harder. I knew that she wanted it, and that's what she got. I used my entire fist inside of her, although she is small. I fucked her and fucked her.

"There's tremendous control with my hand. I can be in someone anally, also vaginally, also clitorally. With my mouth and my foot, I can fondle her breasts. But I like to watch her while I'm doing it," she says.

Apparently, this desire to control people sexually and then watch them began in Abbe's childhood. When she was eight, she organized a girls' club. "There was no specific function to the club except you had to go to the thicket and strip and have the other girls watch you." Another childhood game was taking her boyfriend down to the basement and getting him to take his clothes off, then leaving him there naked. "I liked making him do what I wanted him to do."

Perhaps the reason for Abbe's early childhood antagonism toward boys came from her mother's serving steak to her brother, hamburger to her. Her mother explained that her brother had to grow up to be a man. Abbe hated her brother because he was bigger and stronger. Also because every chance he got, he beat her up. "My parents didn't believe me. They couldn't imagine this to be true, so I had to take it, and it was awful."

Thus, Abbe, in adulthood, has decided that vulnerability is not the way to get what you want—strength is. "I like to chase after women. When I get one, I lose interest, get bored," she says, like a Don Juan. She has been checking my expressions with every sentence, watching their effects. Then she looks at me, her tone of voice becomes almost hopeless, losing all of its aggressiveness.

"My life is going nowhere . . . I feel frustrated. When I get frustrated, I become very icy and get into one of my moods." She looks at me harshly. "It's a very dangerous mood."

It does seem that Abbe's homosexual liaisons have a brutal, S/M quality about them. Fist-fucking, another variation of the dildo syndrome, has to hurt a woman, since the fist does not have the penis's sensitivity to a woman's insides. Thus, fist-fucking has always seemed to me much more like the male rape syndrome, something that lesbians would definitely abhor.

Perhaps, in an oversimplified way, the old-fashioned idea that lesbians simply want to be men has a grain of truth in it. Although female homosexual erotic behavior does have elements of softness and sensuality, there does seem to be an overconcern with imitation of men. Sharon talks about the social world of lesbians with this point in mind.

Sharon

"I'm very brazen in gay bars. They're very competitive and superficial. Everybody is going by appearance and available sexuality. How many drinks have you had? What did you play on the jukebox? There are a lot of roles going on, and you have to be very assertive or you'll be destroyed in the situation," says Sharon, a tall, thin, twenty-six-year-old lesbian with long blonde hair.

From Texas, Sharon remembers when she first realized that she was homosexual. "Something used to happen to me every Sunday in church. I used to sit there feeling very physically drawn to my girl-friends. It was very painful. My mother and father never talked about sex. And certainly never talked about homosexual sex."

As a result of her wanting to love women, Sharon came to Los Angeles where she thought she could live freely, working as a secretary, hanging around gay bars at night.

"Timing is very important in a gay bar," she says, putting her hands in her hip-huggers like a Texas cowboy. "I'm very tired of the gay scene. A lot of gay women are asexual, they get turned off to sex. A lot of them want to be the child and want you to be the mother. That's okay sometimes, but I also want the animal feeling of passion, being turned on as opposed to being turned into a mother. Because when I'm somebody's mother, sex just turns off for me because of the incest taboo."

Sharon has a slight southern drawl, and when she uses California jargon, there is a charm about the sound. Although she is very, very soft and pretty, there is a toughness to her which she calls her bravado. "First, you find a woman who is interested in you. You can usually tell that by eye contact. Then you ask her to dance. I always initiate. I've got a lot of bravado. I say, 'How tacky this bar is.' Or gossip about something. If I'm in a gay bar, it's probably because I want to sleep with someone. But when I get them home, I get turned off," she says sadly.

"I still believe you have to love someone in order to make love to them," she says, startling me with her romantic attitude.

One night, about six months ago, she met a woman who was part of a lesbian couple. "Alix went out once a week to gay bars and wanted an aggressive woman for a one-night stand. She'd fuck them and then go home to Toni." But Sharon and Alix became deeply involved.

Sharon is drinking wine from a classical decanter which is out of place in this slightly hippie apartment where mattresses are on the floor. She is becoming quite drunk and begins fidgeting with her many silver rings, looking at them as if her hand is on display, reminding me of showgirls in the Thirties movies showing off their glamorous diamonds. But Sharon is not glamorous; she has the look of the Great American Kid, grown up.

"Yesterday afternoon we were together," she whispers quietly. "Alix was sitting in a chair, wearing a black slip. I began kissing her, bending over her. Then our tongues explored way back into our mouths. She's a great kisser, very erotic.

"I picked her up and carried her into the bedroom. I asked her to take her clothes off, and watched. We lay on the bed, and she wanted to be submissive. I was on my knees and pulled her up, her legs entwined with mine. It was a very special moment.

"I started touching her spine with my hand and then her whole body. She was very pungent, very turned on. Then I lifted her up, and she was sitting across me. I didn't enter her then. I just sort of lay on my side and swung her around, one leg above me, one below, and our clitorises were almost touching. I felt like we didn't have bodies and were floating. The pressures of our clitorises were great. Then we had orgasms. I would have one, and then she would."

Sharon takes the dominant role in their lovemaking. "I say, 'Okay, do this for me, open wider for me.' Then I manipulate her, sometimes with my whole hand inside. She pleads for me to go harder. I use a lot of Vaseline, but one time I scratched her badly. I took her to the hospital, in pain, bleeding. Now we've decided to get a dildo because we must have ripped some tissue, and she is frightened."

Sharon is very nervous as she continues to talk about Alix, apologizing to me, swearing me to change names, places, dates.

"I want so much to live with Alix, but I don't have any money. Toni supports her," Sharon explains, telling me that Alix absolutely will not work. I remark that Alix is acting like a courtesan, and I thought the whole point of a radical life-style was to make one free. Sharon agrees.

"I get very upset about their relationship. They're like husband and wife. I don't want to support someone," she says.

Sharon's and Alix's relationship certainly seems sensual, but it is governed by financial dependency in the future, a common factor in heterosexual relationships. Alix is simply having an affair on the side, like many married women in this book do. The fact that Alix's source of support is a woman and her lover is a woman does not seem to alter the idea that they are living an old-fashioned marital situation.

The most aggressive, traditional, lesbian woman has always been the bull dyke. Although in modern lesbian circles these women are said to be disappearing, when I researched this chapter I found that they were quite commonplace in gay bars. One woman agreed to be interviewed. Her name is Marty.

Marty

Marty is a large woman dressed in trucker's dungarees, which she opens at the fly as she sits on my sofa, confessing that they are too tight. Her workman's shirt is missing a button, and her black hair is cut too close to her head, making her gaunt features look even more drawn. She has chubby fingers, and is wearing boots for a snowstorm, even though it is a sunny day. Her entire manner is clumsy. She looks at me to check my reaction to her costume, her body. She has flung her raincoat over her lap, looking uncomfortable. I have the feeling that the most important thing to fifty-two-year-old Marty, who still lives in Massachusetts where she was born, is the disguise or hiding of her body because she is a "bull dyke," a "butch," and there is no getting around it.

"I've been a homosexual for forty years," she says softly, her voice containing a painful tone which startles me as I realize that inside this masculine appearance is a soft, feminine, sensitive soul. "I mostly initiate. I am the assertive one in the relationship. I like to take that role. I've always been attracted to short, very little women and have felt very much like their protector. I won't allow them to do things. I'm always afraid they'll hurt themselves. It is ridiculous. But I am more comfortable with the more aggressive, masculine role."

Her hands are trembling as she tries to drink from a cup of coffee I have given her, spilling some and apologizing to me.

Continuing her tale, Marty tells me she was the third child of the family. She resembles her father, who dressed her in a man's shirt. Her mother, timid, tiny, weighing only ninety-eight pounds, was always sick, and Marty acted out her first protector role by getting between her parents, especially when her father was drunk. When she was thirteen, her aunts told her she kissed nice, so she went around kissing all her girlfriends and found she liked it. She wasn't ever allowed to play with boys. Whenever her father saw her talking to a boy, he beat her.

"We were so poor I had to stop going to school because there was no carfare. I wanted to be a physical education teacher, but my father didn't want me to. He taught me how to box at home. My breasts were very large, and I didn't like it because they got in the way of athletics. I've always worn a tight, tight bra as a result of that. I hate my breasts."

When Marty left home, she immediately made love to four men. "They were so clumsy. If a man knew how to make love to me, I'd probably be a mother today. All it was was bing, bing, bang and that was it. I like to take time, there's no hurry.

"I spend a lot of time and money on women. I've just squandered money, just given it away." She spills coffee on the couch again and says she is sorry, again, giving me the feeling that she is always apologizing.

Generally, Marty initiates the sexuality and sees sex as very, very tender and gentle. "A lot of women want me to be brutal, and I guess they are disappointed when I'm not. Once I slapped a woman across the face, but I knew if I continued I could have killed her. So I just ran out. I don't like brutality, in bed or out. Even if a woman wants me to be rough with her, I just can't do it."

The "femme" women get the impression that Marty may be brutal because of the fact that she is very, very strong. "I've always felt that being strong physically is the most important thing for me. And"—her voice begins to moan, falling into a lulling sound—"and now that's going."

We wait for a second as I watch this strong hulk of a woman fall apart. As I watch her clumsily moving on the sofa, not wanting to sit still, yet not knowing what else to do, I think about all of the times that I have seen women of this type on the streets and have felt entirely alienated from them with their swaggering walks, their brutish bodies, their tough-speaking voices. It had never occurred to me that inside of one of these "masculine" women would be a woman who had the kind of experiences that Marty was talking about. A sensitive child, an irrational father, an ineffective mother, a totally alien manner of living, a feeling of being too late.

She is quiet, and there are tears in her eyes. "I'm sorry," she says again about nothing, as if she must fill in the silence. I ask her gently what she means about her strength going. She looks up at me, her eyes appealing to me to understand. "I've always had to be strong. I've made my living working fourteen hours a day as a carpenter, always working for someone else. There were many other things I wanted to do, but they seemed forbidden to me. My father never wanted me to be educated, so I feel poorly equipped. As a matter of fact, I have enrolled in night school, but every time I go I get sick."

"You mean with nervous colds or something like that?"

"No," she says, ever so quietly. "Gallstones, cancer, things like that. Every time I go to school, something tragic happens to me. It frightens me. If I'm not strong, if I'm not the strongest, then I'm not anything.

"You know, I had to be strong at home for my mother because my father would beat her. Once, I overtook him physically, and he was in a state of shock. He never thought it would happen. So he beat up one of his friends. He never touched anyone except to be brutal. He never made a pass at me," she loyally defends this ogre, her patriarch.

"I've grown to dislike men's bodies very much," she says, "especially the penis. I saw my first penis at the age of five when a dirty old man exposed himself to me. Later, I was screwing some old man, getting paid three dollars for it. I was living this dual personality of loving women and going to this old man's room. I was a very sexy child, and he loved to touch me. Men used to whistle at me on the street, but homosexual women always called me a dyke, and I didn't like it at all. I don't think one has to parade her bedroom habits." She puts down the coffee cup and it clatters to the ground, breaking, and her face takes on the look of an extremely frightened child. "I'm—I'm sorry," she says as I reassure her that it is all right.

"I've been making love to women since I was thirteen years old. My father made me a homosexual. He gave me all these masculine tendencies and feelings. If only he would have let me go to parties, or play with the boys. If only he hadn't taught me how to box. You know, I look just like my father.

"I know people think I'm crazy when I say this—when I tell them that I love him—I really love my father."

As Marty finishes talking I think, as I have thought so many times in other interviews in this book, how adults still obey their parents, still wanting to be good little children no matter what it costs them in life. Why not simply say to parents "You've won," and go on from there?

Marty's tale filled me with warmth and compassion for her and anger at her father, something she could not express herself. When a father treats his daughter like a son, often in an effort to please daddy, the grown-up daughter does take on this role. For Marty, her father's gift to her, his harsh and brutal treatment of her and her mother, which ultimately killed her mother, set up the situation where Marty was the son protecting the mother. Later in life, it seems that she continued this fantasy.

We are told that family role-playing has so much to do with the eroticism of adults. We are also told that if husbands and wives could stop the role-playing of masculine and feminine images, the children would grow up better.

Thus, I interviewed the wife in a bisexual marriage, for it seemed to me that she would have a lot to say about new roles. What I discovered was fascinating to me.

Adrienne

She is very fashionable with her chic hairdo, her tight, jersey outfit, plaid cape, leather bag and shoes. At thirty-four, she represents the new, modern, acceptable way of living, the open marriage of bisexual orientation, which she has been a partner in for eight years. According to the sex magazines, she has every-thing. But has she?

"When John and I first met, we both worked in the fashion industry. He was a designer and so was I. We fell in love, got married, and entered in a free life-style of swinging. At first, I was apprehensive. Our own private sex was great. He wanted it every night and so did I. We really got along. We both liked oral sex, and that was the way I got off. But suddenly there was a tremendous amount of sleeping back and forth with other couples. At first, I didn't touch the girl, but just made it with the man. I had always had a lot of men in my life, never had to go searching for them, but this swinging was a source of constant irritation in our marriage."

She pauses, lowering a cigarette toward her long, elegant cigarette lighter, and one can see why she would attract many men. Her body is perfect in its proportions, her face innocent, with a tiny nose à la Suzi Parker making her even more chic, more desirable to the ordinary man.

"Well, first of all, I hated the clubs we had to go to, to meet swingers. I really thought that everyone John talked to he wanted us to screw. It was like a meat rack, and I could not handle it. So we fought and fought over it. He accused me of destroying his sex life. I was turning off people, rejecting people. I would kind of brush them off. I never wanted to be a part of it, but I felt I had to be for him.

"What I feared most finally happened. A woman walked into our living room and I absolutely fell for her. It was the first time I wanted to make love to a woman, and I did."

After Adrienne sexually opened up to women, it was her job to go out and find them. "John kept after me, saying, 'You're not seeing anyone, how come?' We had an arrangement where there were certain nights he would have the house for his male lovers, and that was fine. But he wouldn't let me just go out to the movies. I had to be with a woman, or else he'd torture me."

One of the ways Adrienne looked for women was in the feminist movement, at conferences and consciousness-raising groups. "I found that the women were very aggressive. I wanted to be their friend, but they wanted sex. It's much easier for me to go to bed with a man I'm not attracted to than a woman. That's horrible."

However, in this free, modern marriage, Adrienne does not go out with men. "I don't feel I can. I think John would get very upset." So her sex life consists of aggressive lesbians, who don't turn her on, and sex with her husband. Only, since she has not recruited any women for their sex life, John has refused her the one thing she likes: oral sex. "He just penetrates, and I think he's using me. He won't eat me. I guess he's angry."

As for her, she uses a dildo on John because he loves it so much. But she won't use one on a woman. "I like feminine women. I don't want to imitate a man with a woman. I want to be a woman.

"When a woman comes on like a man in women's clothing, I hate it. I don't dig the so-called woman's world, the feminist world. It's the feminist world—the NOW conferences, the consciousness-raising groups—and it's all totally man-hating and lesbian underneath it all. It's antimale, antimale, antimale. I'm always being asked how can I even talk to a male and be a feminist. I'm so sick and tired of being attacked for being married."

I ask Adrienne if she seeks this lesbian element out, because I am aware that a large part of the feminist world is lesbian, but a large part is also heterosexual, and I have many friends who are both feminist and heterosexual. She shakes her head and tells me I'm fantasizing, that she'd love to find a "straight" feminist. Then she goes back to sex.

"I don't like trios very much, but John does. He'll find a girl, bring her home, and we'll have a trio. Then he'll say to me, 'You must see her alone. We'll lose her unless you see her alone,' and I get angry and frustrated. He sees me as going with women as a source for trios. I thought we were supposed to be free and open and dependent on each other, but free. I feel choked. I have no friends, and I'm going mad."

Her eyes are filled with tears, and I point out to her that her supposedly free marriage is very much like the monogamous heterosexual marriage where the man and woman do not allow their mates to be with other people. There seems to be the same kind of strict code, only in reverse: She has to find women for her husband. She agrees and says that recently she has realized all of this and has tried to change her life-style.

"I've begun making friends with heterosexual women and getting less interested in having sex with women. This has led to a very angry confrontation with my husband. He's constantly questioning why I'm not with women, why I'm forming straight friendships. He thinks being bisexual means you're always screwing both sexes. I think being bisexual means you screw whoever you want, whenever you want, whatever sex. I don't like this pressure always to have sex. I've lost my sex drive. It's his sex drive that always drives us." She shakes her head. "I don't know. I think he's afraid to break up our marriage." She sucks her thumb suddenly, and the gesture surprises me. Her face has become incredibly soft now, losing the chicness of before. She begins to fool with her body jewelry, all ornate golden and glittering, and I sense she is nervous.

"What do you think he's afraid of?" I ask.

She looks up at me, her lush eyelashes framing the dark eyes, and says simply: "He's afraid he'll go totally gay." She pauses, picking at her long fingernails. "He can't get into real deep relationships. When you just have sex with people, you avoid getting close to them, really close. It frightens him. He can't relate to straight men and women. We've never had straight people for dinner. He's petrified of getting close to someone without sex. He can understand sex but not friendship.

"I was very into quick fucking. But now I really want to get to know people. John has to fuck first and then have friendships later, but sexual friendships are fleeting."

She begins to mull over what she has just said, and her tone changes to almost a suffering sound, as if she is in terrible pain and very uncomfortable about it. "I want to be free. I want more privacy. I hate his questions. He's always worried."

"What's he worried about?"

She looks at me with hate in her eyes. "He's always worried that I'll turn gay," she says.

Adrienne's description of her free, swinging, bisexual marriage fascinated me because I had always wondered how other people could carry on so many sexual relationships. For me, a sensual involvement, while creating energy, also takes a certain kind of commitment in energy. It takes a person a long time to open up to feelings, to express them, to enact them, to receive feelings back.

How, I had always wondered, did swingers do this so many times per week?

Adrienne confirmed my suspicions that *sex, in their case, was to prevent depth of feeling, not to experience it.* If bisexuality is only a way to keep oneself from feeling open, then it really is antisensuality rather than pro. Although modern hippiedom tells us we can love everyone, can we really? Or can we really love very few people and enjoy them sensually?

With lesbian eroticism, there seems to be much too much imitation, and not enough of what I had hoped to find—an entirely different form of eroticism, experienced by women with women. Although there is a hint of this, female eroticism does seem fixated on the maternal affection for the female breasts. Sucking breasts does not lead to orgasm often, although I'm sure in some cases it has. Thus, imitations of male penis activity must be used. Based on this information, I simply question female/female eroticism.

Eight

❀ ❀ ❀

THE EROTICISM OF THE MALE STUD / PLAYBOY

Ah, men! What can one say about the object of most female fantasies . . . and distortions? For in most of the interviews of the women in this book, men have been represented as: little boys, rapists, clients, nonerotic husbands, endowed lovers, a source of money, wife beaters, only interested in pornography, undersexed, oversexed, impotent, and male studs.

These responses from women are interesting. The one major complaint from most women interviewed for this book is that any act of initiative or aggression on their part produces a limp penis. True, if this initiation is done in a courtesan manner, this does not occur. But most modern women are not interested in the subtleties of the brothel. Most modern women want to be free, to be direct and honest.

Yet, what of men? Is this complaint true? In an exposé in the *National Police Gazette*, the following male fantasies are documented:

"She's waiting for me, sure enough, and she grabs me and pulls me behind some bales of cloth. Then we make love. She tells all her friends, one by one, and I end up with a harem of them. . . ."

"My pet daydream involves two girls who thumb a lift in my car when I'm traveling alone. The girls are always the same, about twenty years old, one blonde and the other brunette. One gets in beside me on the front seat, and as we are driving along, she leans over and starts to caress me. Her friend in the back seat gets very jealous and insists that I stop the car. I drive into a cornfield and make love. . . ."

This same article reports that male fantasies fall into three distinct categories: domination by women, seduction by women, or seduction of a girl who is unwilling at the outset.

Yet, there is a discrepancy: Women say men do not want them to be directly aggressive and seductive. Men fantasize that they are. What, then, is the truth of the matter?

For another opinion, I asked Gay Talese, who has been researching his book *Sex in America* for the last five years.

"Have you ever been the aggressor with men?" he asks me, coming right to the point like the smart and talented journalist he is.

"Yes," I answer honestly. "And I do agree that women should experience asking for sex because the first time I was rejected, I suddenly realized after all these years how men must feel." But even though women's invitations to men may be answered negatively, both men and women should keep trying to bridge the gap between the sexes, so that true passion will result.

Passion is the lost ingredient in most relationships today. Most men tell me sex is quite available to them in singles bars, vacation spots, parties, street pickups. Whereas other generations had to be concerned with sexual activity ruining their reputations, the current generation, influenced by the Sixties culture, gets laid all the time. But there is a problem they report to me: *The problem is not getting laid, the problem nowadays is to feel something.*

Feeling vulnerable, translating sexual "fucking" to eroticism, is the problem. Sadly, it is the man who feels most vulnerable who experiences sexual performance problems. The male stud, always with his large erection, the fantasy of millions of women, reports a lack of feeling. Thus, male performance in sexuality is their single most important concern.

Dr. Martin Williams of the Berkeley Sex Therapy Group reports: "Sexual symptoms come and go, but only rarely does one achieve epidemic status. One symptom which is now sweeping the country has achieved this status. This symptom is manifested as the ability to perform sexual intercourse without being turned on." He goes on to name this symptom "Performance."

> The mind of the Performer is filled with concerns of *doing a good job instead of having a good time. Rather than passion, the Performer thinks of competence.* . . . One can actually become blinded by the performance symptom to the extent that he begins to think it is the *normal form of sex.* . . . An interesting sidelight of this symptom . . . the sex patients we see in our practices are unable to suffer from Performance. They'd love to suffer from Performance, but their reflexes fail them. The goal of the sex patient is, in fact, to exchange his present "disease" . . . for the disease of Performance. Pleasure is not what these patients ask for: *they . . . seek only the ability to Perform.* [Italics mine]

Thus, because of these attitudes, when a man feels vulnerable to a woman, his cock often goes down. This is the real problem in our modern times. A friend of mine, a very beautiful young woman who has men literally at her feet, made a cryptic remark to me recently. "What is happening?" she asked earnestly. "Before, in my life, I didn't talk honestly to men, but we fucked a lot. It was great. I never ran into men with sexual problems.

"Nowadays," she says sadly, "the men want to talk, but they don't want to make love. And when they do, they fail." This woman of twenty-eight repeats the kinds of truths I am hearing from women of all ages: *That, indeed, there is more conversation and closeness of intent but much less action.* Yet, when I interviewed men for this chapter, most of them commented that usually women did not talk to them the way I did, that it was good to be truthful with a woman, it was a relief for them. But I was not sexually involved with any of these men. And the few who did interest me and reciprocated my feelings did not follow through, and admitted later that *I knew too much about their real feelings.*

This, it seems, is the dichotomy between the sexes in this year, 1976. With all of the cultural swings toward honesty and freedom, men want to be more human with women, and women insist upon it. Yet, the Hemingway mystique of perfectionist macho sex persists in the erotic psyche of most men, so when they become vulnerable, they feel they are less of a man.

What is the answer? Perhaps women should be aware of this truth. Perhaps women, much stronger in the ability for emotional expression than men, should understand just how terrifying sensitive and revealing feelings are to men. If they were more realistic about this, *then maybe it would be possible for both men and women to experience erotic feelings on a deep and personal level, without the power-bargaining of marriage, financial security, and/or performance.*

Regarding performance, one popular young man about town made up the following chart for himself and his buddies. Since he is a doctor, he approached it in a scientific manner.

Critical Analysis and Comparative Evaluation:
Sexual Performance Chart

Ratings

1: poor
2: fair
3: good
4: oh, My God

CATEGORIES	GIRL	RONALD [the doctor]	OTHER MEN
Appearance			
Romance			
Conversation			
Verbal Subtleties			
Foreplay			
Penis Size			
a. length			
b. width			
Pubic Mustache			
Irritation			

CATEGORIES	GIRL	RONALD [the doctor]	OTHER MEN

Body Odor
Pre-Coital Wakefulness
Erection Induction Time
Premature Ejaculation
Coital Time Span
Sexual Performance
  a. oral-oral
  b. oral-genital
  c. anal-genital
Orgasmic Intensity
Post-Coital Wakefulness

This chart was Xeroxed and passed on by Ronald to his buddies when they made love to the same woman. What woman looking at this chart wouldn't want to scream "Swine!"? Yet, this clinical type of information seems to be terribly important to the men in this chapter. Ronald and his friends were being terribly honest about this, reflecting the changes in the younger generation of men. Their older brothers would romantically lie to women, even if they were really thinking of all the ingredients on the chart.

It was with great curiosity, then, that I interviewed Ronald for this "stud" chapter, since he had such a creative mind about sex.

Ronald

"I'm good company and I make big money, although I don't spend a lot of money on women," the swinging M.D. tells me in his privately owned brownstone on University Place in New York City. The room is filled with antique masterpieces, beautiful, classical, European paintings, plush, lush carpets, and hanging plants. Ronald, a very prosperous doctor not yet thirty, sits in the center of his living room wearing a Rolling Stones T-shirt and old jeans.
"How do you meet women?"

"At the hospital," he says frankly. "They come in with friends or relatives who are sick and ask me questions, looking for support. Basically, I look for a nonverbal response from them, the kind of emotion where they're admitting they're attracted without words."

"Then what do you do?"

"Then I take them out to dinner, and we come back here, and we generally go to bed." He looks at me sheepishly, as if he is confessing a mortal sin.

"What happens if she says no?"

"If she doesn't cooperate, I don't see her again."

"You mean, you don't see women whom you don't sleep with?"

He shakes his head adamantly, grabs a handful of raisins from a cocktail plate, munches on them, looks at me guiltily, and mutters with apprehension, "I never see women as friends."

Although I find myself becoming angry, I fight my feelings in the interest of research. For whatever Ronald does, it works. I have walked past his house thousands of times, since we are neighbors, and viewed hot and cold running beautiful young women, with naive eyes and sexy bodies, running in and out of the place. In fact, Ronald is the envy of every storekeeper on the block, especially in the summer when they watch his action, muttering to themselves.

"Of course," Ronald adds, "if she's a real dud, even if we have sex, that's it!"

"Why can't you have a nonsexual relationship with a woman?"

"Because it's hard to know someone if you don't go to bed with them. If you know them physically, it breaks down the barriers right away."

I have heard this remark from many men and wonder what they think about the intimacy between heterosexual women. For years I have observed with my family and my friends, and now in my professional research, the special way heterosexual women talk to each other. In fact, they have admitted to me that they can be more intimate because sex is not involved. But back to a man's point of view.

"What kind of women do you like?"

"I don't like aggressive women. I like women who wait for me to make the moves. Most girls I see are dancers, models, actresses, who graduated college and are working as waitresses, waiting for the big break. They need me. The independent woman, like yourself, makes me feel unneeded. I don't like the take-it-or-leave-it attitude. It's as simple as that."

Ronald continues, "I'm not a dyed-in-the-wool male chauvinist pig, but I do feel that men and women have certain roles. A woman should yield to a man emotionally and sexually."

"What does your ideal woman look like?" (I already knew this answer because all of the women I've seen at Ronald's have looked exactly alike.)

"Well, she has to be very young and very skinny. And she shouldn't talk much. There's much more mystery and fantasy when people don't talk."

"Why do you like women who look alike? Don't you like variety?"

"No, it's my style. Like my shirts. They're all exactly alike. My girl has to be sophisticated enough so I can take her anywhere. She has to be able to talk in a crowd, but not step on my words."

"What do you offer these women?"

"My company," he says glibly.

"And what do you offer them sexually?"

"I offer them a half-hour or more of sex where they can have as many orgasms as they like. I like to have sex every night of the week, so if I'm seeing a girl steadily, she can have a lot of sex."

"Do you satisfy them?"

"If I don't, I get turned off."

"What do you mean?"

"If I'm with a woman who is not satisfied in bed after I've had an orgasm and wants to go on some more, I get turned off. I want to rest a while—it's tiring." He gets up from his chair and begins to do pushups on the floor as if he's getting himself into shape. I wonder if he's getting ready for sex.

"What is the most erotic experience you've ever had?"

"One time a friend and I double-dated and his date went upstairs to the bathroom. I followed her upstairs, she was so pretty. I grabbed her in the bedroom, and we made it. It was great except for the fact that my date found us and made such a gigantic fuss." He has been struggling with his words from his pushup position; now he stands and proceeds with an imaginary jump rope exercise for about five minutes while I wait for him to stop. Then he does, looks at me wearily, sits in his chair again, and I can see he is very, very tired.

"Why was that experience the most erotic?"

"Because I didn't know her. It was forbidden because she was my friend's date. It was exciting as hell." He giggles like a kid caught with his hand in the cookie jar.

"Do you have any other fantasies?"

"My great fantasy is taking someone I don't know and forcibly raping her. It would have to be someone who is very high-class, dressed very elegantly, and who is the condescending type of woman. I would force myself physically on her while she struggled."

"Have you ever tried it?"

Ronald looks serious for a moment, and for the first time I see a human expression that is not defensive take over his face.

"Thinking about it is always more exciting than doing it. When a fantasy comes true, it's always disappointing."

"Always?"

"Right. Like the women who come into my office and I fantasize going to bed with them. It might be three years later that we click, and it's always disappointing. Sometimes I think I should forcibly put them on the examining table and just screw them like I want to."

"Have you tried group scenes?"

"No, I don't like crowds. I don't like bars, dances. I like to be comfortable at home."

"Do you want a serious relationship?"

"There's no one I would think twice about not seeing," he says with amazing candor. "I like to see them all, but if something happened, I wouldn't lose a minute's sleep over it."

Dr. Ronald is quite a fellow. I remember, while waiting to interview him, watching a beautiful, young, *thin* woman who had a medical appointment with him walk into his office. After waiting an unusual length of time for her to come out, I complained to his nurse. "What is happening in there?" I asked.

She winked at me. I knew at once what she meant—that the doctor was seducing the attractive patient. When I was finally ushered in, Ronald grinned like a bear and admitted he had just gotten laid. I wondered how often this happened and he said I'd have to ask his nurse, who was *not* a young, thin woman.

A fantasy idol of Ronald's, who is about the same age, has gotten his fame from publicizing his sexual prowess. He is known as the only actor who can stay erect in front of a movie camera for hours. His name is Harry Reems and, oddly, he has a similar attitude toward female aggressiveness. However, Harry does permit women to be aggressive, but only sexually—in bed.

Harry Reems

Twenty-eight-year-old Harry Reems, star of *Deep Throat* and *The Devil in Miss Jones*, is attempting to be normal, or so he states. "I eat pickled herring to keep my erection up," he says, laughing at the image.

Although I have asked a great number of men and women the questions I am asking Harry, he insists on answering in mumbles, looking at me suspiciously.

"People assume I'm a freak or pervert. I don't like making love by frying eggs on someone's stomach. No matter how sane and intelligent I act, I cannot erase the stigma attached to my own name because of what I do for a living, so I'm defensive and frustrated about it. I feel that you're waiting for me to say something abstract, surreally sexual, and I don't have it in me."

When I assure Harry that frying eggs might be sexy and that I do indeed believe that Harry is normal, he begins to tell me tales of the price tag of being a porno star. "Men and women walk up to me on the street and say, 'You must be hung like a bull.' Guys say, 'You have the greatest job in the world.' "

Living in a small room in Manhattan filled only with antique reminders of the past, Harry doesn't seem much like the agile, sexual lover of these films. He explains how he turns on for the camera. "I prepare mentally. You can create a sexual need in yourself.

You have to be turned on by your costar. Everybody has something exciting to them. I have orgasms while I'm acting. Sometimes it's a tedious function. Most times, though, the female star does not have an orgasm. You know, there's no such thing as a good lover. I'm not a superstud. It depends upon the chemistry of people. Sometimes we just fuck each other and nothing happens."

Harry's career, in the course of which he may fuck someone twice a day for six weeks, doesn't affect his personal life, he says. "Sometimes I come home from the set and I'm so frustrated that I masturbate," he admits candidly. "But I only do about six films a year, so there's lots of time for my personal needs." One of the personal things Harry does is go to parties and not tell women what his livelihood is until he has gotten to know them. "I enjoy watching their reactions. They can't believe it. When I try out for a film, they always ask, 'Are you hung? Let's see what you've got.' In my personal life, I try to impress women with my sensitivity. I try to be really honest."

Harry dates three or four girls at a time, going to the movies, cooking dinners, making love. None of these women are from the porno film industry. "I don't mix business with pleasure. I enjoy making my lovers lose control and climax. When a woman climaxes, I feel a certain amount of ego, a degree of pride, feeling as though I have accomplished something. I enjoy oral sex with a woman. I know where the vagina is located, where the clitoris is. Every woman is different.

"Some women enjoy my being rough. I like a woman to tell me what she likes. When I'm doing something wrong, she'll correct me. She'll say, 'A little harder there,' or 'Suck it here.' That's what I call an aggressive female."

However, Harry's acceptance of female aggressiveness does not allow for women to go over to him and invite him to have sex. "When someone walks up to me and wants to get into the sack, it turns me off. I like women sexually liberated only in bed." I infer that means he has to pick them, and he agrees.

"Very few women were like that until recently because sex was a forbidden fruit for them. Now, so many of them are freer, yet some want to be totally dominated. So many of their fantasies are some form of rape in subways, bus stations, or places where there are a lot of strangers, where they are not in control of themselves

231

and are held down and made love to and totally dominated. I've done that to women who have asked me to. A lot of women have wanted to be balled anally, wanted to be spanked. Fine. I can get turned on by that, also."

Harry remembers one experience that really turned him on. It happened when he wired a friend that he was arriving in New York from Europe. "She rented this huge limousine, with a chauffeur. My plane arrived, and I went right into the car. She opened a bottle of champagne, put a joint in my mouth, and did me out sexually, went down on me. It was great. As the car was rolling down the expressway, we made love in the back seat. It was really erotic."

Other things that turn Harry on are aromatic things like bubble baths, making love in Jean Naté with rose petals, and drinking wine in the bathtub with his lover.

But about love, Harry is not too happy. "I was in love with this girl. I knew it because I made sacrifices that I normally would not have made. I spent a lot of time with her. Time is the most valuable thing to me. I was in a web, and it lasted two years." But Harry, who has a temper, doesn't like to argue with a woman. So he refused to talk things out, and they grew apart.

"When I broke up this relationship, I had no desire for sex, even with myself. I guess I don't believe in monogamy. I would only have an open marriage. There's a lot of people you can be in love with at once. I want someone who can be my mother, daughter, sister, lover, friend, all in one.

"One of the things that titillates me still is the danger of being caught. I love to have sex with someone else in the house. I know women who don't want to see a face, they want to see a cock, like Erica Jong's zipless fuck. Nowadays, there's a disappearance of all social games. Women think: I don't want to know who you are, what you do, where you're going tomorrow. Right now, you turn me on, and I want to fuck you."

One time in a movie theater a girl he knew pulled him into a telephone booth and went down on him. "It was fabulous. We both came at once."

I asked Harry what he would do if he was in a room with six closets and knew that behind each door there was a woman waiting to grab him.

"Well, first I would do pushups. I can have an erection two or three times a night, so I'd give it a try.

"I'm behind my prime, though," he says seriously. "I'm getting old. Also, a lot of women are using vibrators, and they are making men obsolete. It gives them the greatest orgasm they have ever had. How can a man compete with a thing whose r.p.'s are incredible?"

But Harry goes on trying. "I find that many women don't like a powerful thrust," he relates. "Others love it. Some women like a guy to ride high up on the clitoris. Some women claim it's too painful, they can't stand it. Some women when they have an orgasm want you to get out, others want you to go in harder, want you to grab their breasts and squeeze them. Some women like me to use my teeth orally, others need to be manipulated around the clitoris. With S/M women, though, I find they have a lot of difficulty having orgasms."

I ask Harry if he feels obliged to help all these women out. "Why will a man drop his pants in front of a nurse and not feel any embarrassment about it? Yes, I help out. I like everything except homosexuality and rape." He moves clumsily now, and I ask him if he is getting tired talking about sex.

"I'm getting very hungry," he says, looking very much like a nice boy whom mama will always love.

Like Dr. Ronald, the swinging M.D., Harry Reems is very desirable because of his fabled constant cock (although a case could be made that in Harry's case it is true). If you've seen any of Harry's films, you will note that he does seem to have a superhuman facility for staying erect. In fact, in New York pornographic film circles, Harry is known as the only actor who "can keep it up all during the shooting schedule." Lights, camera, and crew do not distract Harry from his lustful behavior. Thus, obviously, he is very popular, both professionally and personally.

Both Ronald and Harry are of the younger generation, but older men also mistake performance for sensuality. Often, we see older men with women half their age and wonder what on earth they talk about. The point seems to be that they don't talk. Tommy's relationships with women illustrate this.

Tommy

"She was my fantasy lady, very, very tall, very, very zaftik very, very clean, very, very blonde, and very, very young. I took her to Europe with me, and we made love that first night. For such an attractive, large girl who had been with a lot of guys, she had never gone all the way. We ran into my previous girlfriend, a very, very tall, very, very zaftik, very, very clean, very, very young and very, very red-haired girl named Doris, and they became good friends. With large women, I feel very comfortable. I'm a better lover. I can't hurt them." Tommy smiles. "My father was a great showgirl chaser, and I guess I'm carrying on in his style."

At forty-five, overweight and bald, Tommy sees two or three women a week regularly. Professionally successful and wealthy, he lives a very bohemian life, spending small fortunes in restaurants and bars that cater to artists, with lower prices and casual atmosphere. Tommy covers all these bars and eating places every night that he is in New York. "I spend a lot of time in coffee shops and diners. I like people. I'm too intense with women, have a tendency to go overboard. I like to impress them, taking them to Europe or the Coast. I like tall women. It makes me feel like a hunter, you know. There are some men who go after rabbits and some who go after lions. I like to go after lions, but there's a very good chance of getting scratched." He pauses, scratching his bald spot, and I wonder how these young women can go to bed with him, since his physical appearance is so debilitating. "But there's no challenge in shooting rabbits, is there?" he asks me, grinning. Tommy's lions are always tall and under twenty-five. I have never seen him with a woman who is closer to his age, so I ask him if older women frighten him.

"No, not when I get them inside my territory, in bed. If I'm very attracted to someone, I like to get very close to them. Then they're not dangerous. If I can touch them, I feel secure. But I find that the nicer I am to them, the faster they start to run. You'd be surprised how many women are really interested in *just* getting laid. Women are now keeping score, doing what the men used to do. Older women are angry and dead. They feel they've missed out on something. When I meet a woman who is over twenty-five, I get anxious."

Tommy looks nervous since I am over twenty-five, but I calm him down. "I see women always on their terms. They come to your apartment, they want to see your things, they want to listen to what you have to say. Then they want to leave and come back when they feel like it. I always say to them, 'Why not spend the night?' They say no, they don't want to stay. Usually, the sex is good, but maybe that bothers them. Some women get very frightened when they have a good sexual experience. They're afraid that if they like you they may get involved." I tell him he is speaking about women the way they often speak about men.

"I usually make love three or five times a week, but it's on a hit-and-miss basis. I can't get the new ones to spend the nights. Especially the ones I picked up that afternoon, the ones I'm not crazy about. I can't remember all of them. They're not faceless to me, but I only remember about three or four women." At the rate of twenty-five new women a year for twenty years, he seems to remember very few.

"I once met a sixteen-year-old girl who had been having sex with guys since she was eleven. She told me I was the three-hundred-nineteenth man she had been to bed with. She was keeping score. She was a good lover, but she never wanted to repeat it with me.

"When I go out to try and meet someone, it never works. One time I was walking along the street and spotted one of my lion types. I followed her on the bus. I followed her to Grand Central. I followed her up to Peekskill, New York. I found out where she lived and sent her a dozen roses every day for weeks on end, without a card. Then I called her, and we saw each other for two years."

The new kind of woman, the feminist, seems to terrify Tommy. "Gloria Steinem terrifies me. Why don't you ever see her with anyone? She seems less than human. I saw her once at a party and got no body vibes from her." At the party, Tommy was wearing his cowboy hat and his boots and felt like he was the only man in a crowd of dwarfs.

"Most of the guys around are sissies. I look large around them. I'm always attracted to artists' parties, like painters, sculptors, and potters. They turn me on. But there seems to be a large number of women in this city who are always looking for a better performance. A lot of women don't even know what they're supposed to feel. European women are different, they know their bodies give them orgasms of pleasure."

He smacks his lips as if he has just eaten something delicious. "I have a fantasy of having this beautiful, beautiful house with all these kids running around the lawn, several cars in the garage, my woman in her studio, doing her thing. That's what I think is a sunny life. I get scared when I think of that, though, because I feel then I'm really going to have to be a man. I'm really going to have to do it." When I ask him what he means, he looks glum as he answers. "To please a woman, a real woman."

Tommy thinks women are soft and firm, both in personality and in the flesh. "Women are kind of a warm place for me. I like the peasant quality in a woman, a big, country lady I can take around and show off. Even if they are intellectuals, I like this earthy quality."

But when he finds this perfect woman, he is easily distracted. "When I'm having dinner with a perfectly nice girl, another girl comes in and I look up, and my date gets uncomfortable. My attention always wanders. I'm always afraid I'm going to miss the next trolley car. When I'm with a woman, I should never be let out of the house, onto the street. That's why I fantasize being off in the country with her because I know I have a weakness, and the weakness is to want everyone else I see. I shouldn't ever go to a public place with a woman."

But if a woman did this to Tommy, it would be hard for him. "If a woman walks out on me, I feel desolate. They're so close to me, and I can touch them, but given half a chance, they walk out. I hate it when a woman leaves. I feel it's another defeat, that I should be the end-all. I turn off as soon as I think they're leaving me. I really shut off."

I feel badly for Tommy, even though he has not described an attitude about women that is admirable. "I play a tune and then go dead on people. I don't want to go to my grave before I feel something real," he says softly.

"I hope I can fall in love soon, maybe that'll help."

Tommy seems to be imitating the Don Juan idea, but there is a sadness and poignancy to this man who looks like everybody's father. With his protruding stomach, his double chins, his balding head, can any of these younger women *really* care for him, or is it his money and his contacts that they are after? He is known as "the buffoon," with these younger women making fun of him every chance they get. Yet, it seems that this is what he wants, that it gives him his sense of emotional security. With these odds, I doubt that he will fall in love seriously because of his decadent lifestyle and his illusions about these under-twenty-five-year-old women.

Tommy is an example of an old-fashioned man who wants to be "in." John is a younger version of Tommy, but he is smarter. He keeps one girl for his weekends of old-fashioned, romantic communication, and fucks strangers during the week. But as he speaks to me there is still the same sense of longing.

John

John is tall, good-looking, and lanky, and is wearing a denim outfit, a cross between a hippie and a workingman. "I'm a carpenter today," he says, although in reality he is a vice-president of an industrial corporation. "Depending on the woman, I can be a child, a fisherman, or a super skier, backwoodsman. I play with the kids on the street when I feel like it. I biked here from Brooklyn," he says, as though I am not aware that he has arrived carrying a superspeed bike which is now occupying my entire kitchen.

"How many women do you see in a week?" I ask, wondering if he has any time left over from all his hobbies.

"Well, I sleep with three or four besides Melanie. I see Melanie regularly, but she wants to get married so I feel guilty about it."

"Does that spoil your enjoyment?"

"Not really. Because she loves me, and I guess that's important. She's a schoolteacher. She's probably the only woman I can spend any length of time with because of the very comfortable feeling that goes on between us. I think she is going to be there for me and let me have my other women."

John explains that Melanie and he fuck in cars, on the beach, on the roof of her building, on her kitchen table, and in her bed. "I'm not generally the aggressor. She begins petting me and turning me on. When she reaches her climax, she yells and screams and lurches, and it gets me off. It gives me all the macho ego thing I need. So then, I get off. Afterwards, I feel quite relieved and drained and often fall asleep while I'm still inside of her."

In addition to seeing Melanie two or three times a week, John picks up women in restaurants, at bus stops, in the subway. "I like being with women for the first time. It's fun. But then they always get possessive. They want to move in. They want you to see them more often. I have to keep it on an infrequent basis because I like to have my privacy. I piddle. I read. I screw around with my plants. It makes me feel like a boy, childlike."

Although John, like the rest of us, has only seven nights in a week, in addition to Melanie and the women he picks up, he has two other things going. One is with a divorcée. "Mary is a once-or-twice-a-week dinner and fuck," he explains. And the other is with his married secretary, Ruth. "It happened over dictation. But I'm sorry about that. I lost a good secretary. I got paranoid about our lunch hours together."

When Mary or Ruth ask John to spend a weekend with them or to visit friends, John gets upset, because Melanie is really his girl. "You know, they all have their needs. Melanie is very, very easy. With her, it's very natural. Ruth, on the other hand, likes me to put my finger up her ass and bite her nipples. I don't particularly care to do that. And Mary needs for me to get a baby-sitter for her kids. I somehow have a problem about a woman who needs things. . . ."

In addition to all this activity, John spends some time alone at his house on the beach. One day this fall he experienced the most erotic night of his life. "There was this sweet little girl who worked in a restaurant. We went to a party, and two of her friends came home with us. We started sniffing cocaine, and then we all made love. I actually had sex with two of them. I was attacking the third orally when it all fell apart because my date got jealous." He pauses, scratching his bearded cheeks which are unshaven because it is Saturday afternoon and he is relaxing. "She got possessive like everybody else. She fell in love with me," he says guiltily.

I wait until John has stopped speaking to ask him the most important question of the interview, the answer to which I cannot fantasize. "*John, tell me, why do so many women fall in love with you?*"

"They tell me I'm number one because I'm a nice guy. And when a woman cares, possessiveness goes hand in hand. They say to me, 'If you're not interested in seeing me more often, that's it.' And I definitely do not want to get married.

"I know the best thing for Melanie is to put her out of my life. But I can't stand being the hurter as opposed to being the hurtee." He looks at me with his sad, moon eyes, waiting for understanding. "I just don't want our thing to get any deeper than it is," he pleads.

Poor John looks like someone is choking him to death, while he is enjoying it. I ask him what kind of women turn him on.

"They're generally WASPy. I was convinced I was ugly for the first thirty years of my life until I went on a motorcycle trip and became a different person." He takes out his wallet to show me a picture of the other John.

"All my women look like my sister—long, strawberry-blonde hair, blue eyes, five-feet-seven, slender, Ph.D.," says this thirty-five-year-old man. "I have to learn something from them. The majority of women I come into contact with I don't learn a thing from. After the first time, I lose interest. Men and women are threatened by me usually because I can walk into any situation and take over."

"What about the other kinds of women?" I ask.

"What?" John is suddenly deaf.

"Well, John, I have been interviewing women all over the country, and many of them have absolutely no desire to get married."

"I really don't find those women attractive. I find them unattractive," John says, picking at his nose. "It's something about them that I don't like."

He pauses for a moment. "I guess it's their independence," he says thoughtfully.

Well, John seems to enjoy thinking that all women want to marry him. This is a common fantasy among men. If you are a woman and you enjoy a man, then naturally he thinks you want to marry him. Fortunately, when economic conditions are not involved, this is not necessarily true.

Many men like John get married, are responsible to their wives and family, but one night a week, screw around. Arnold is like that.

Arnold

A forty-year-old stockbroker, Arnold has been happily married for twenty years, with five children he absolutely adores, a lovely house in Connecticut, an interesting job, and a salary of one hundred thousand dollars a year. Every week, though, he screws his current girlfriend, a secretary in a nearby company. Tall, slim, and boyish, Arnold defends his extramarital activities with one statement: "My wife doesn't like sex. She just doesn't want to do it more than twice a month. So I have girlfriends.

"It's not just a fucking situation. I have to be involved. I usually take them out to dinner. We talk. We go to the theater. We go to the ballet. My wife won't go to the ballet. And then I take them home and we make love. It's very, very nice. I always tell them I'm happily married and want to stay married, so I'm honest with them."

His wife is told about business trips that don't take place, tennis dates that are another kind of sport. His girls are told if they are looking for a wedding band, go somewhere else. Half of the time they do. Half of the time they don't. One recent girlfriend made a mistake, however. She fell in love with Arnold.

"She wouldn't see other people. She wanted me to be hers on a permanent basis. I finally had to break it off because it got too intense," he says casually.

About his wife, Arnold says, "Just because my wife falls short in only one area of marriage doesn't seem to be a reason to break up our marriage. She uses the four H's not to have sex: headache, heartburn, hemorrhage, and hemorrhoids. She could write a book on the reasons not to have sex. I don't understand it, though, because when we have it, she usually is multiorgasmic. But she won't do a lot of things. We usually have sex after the eleven o'clock news, and I take a shower and she takes a shower. She immediately wants the lights off so we can't see anything. And she won't have oral sex, absolutely not."

In his social mileu, Arnold is known as a faithful husband. "We have one friend who fucks around and makes no secret of it. So everyone gossips. What they say about me is that I'd like to but I don't have the guts. And I promote that theory. It's fine with me. I don't want to hurt my wife."

In an exasperated manner, Arnold also talks of the possibility of another man's coming into his wife's life. "Maybe he'd bring her out of her goddamned shell. But if she wanted to leave me, I'd be crushed."

Arnold describes his marital life as a series of meetings. Religion, sports, and school demands upon their time are enormous. "I get up very early every morning so I have a chance to think. I think, *Okay, am I for real? Am I a piece of crap? Am I a phony?* I make breakfast for my kids so I can spend some time with them. I love my kids."

Apparently, motherhood is erotic for Arnold, for when I ask him about the most erotic night he ever spent with a woman, he talks about making his girlfriend pregnant. "I took her home from a party, and we started kissing while listening to music. She said, 'We can make love, but you can't come inside me because I don't use birth control.' So we made love, and she had thirty to forty orgasms. We saw each other for months after that. But she became pregnant and had to have an abortion.

"I couldn't be with her," he says defensively, "but I sent her flowers and called her, from a public phone. I really loved her," he adds quietly.

One of the things he liked about his girlfriend was that she did not want to get married or be his mistress. "I can't commit myself to a woman outside of marriage," he says. "If I don't have a girlfriend, I masturbate to the *Playboy* centerfold. It really turns me on. I get a lot of erections during the day, so masturbation helps."

Apparently, his wife doesn't need to masturbate, doesn't think of sex at all, according to Arnold. I tell him about the married women interviewed for this book who are all having affairs with men other than their husbands. Arnold shakes his head and says no, this is definitely not possible in his wife's life. "I know where she is every moment," he states flatly. "She has five kids."

I have the feeling that Arnold is more interested in the kids than his wife, and I carefully question him about them. "I love them very much," he says, and changes the subject.

Regarding his wife's sex problem, Arnold has several suggestions. One, of course, in theory, is a boyfriend who would open up her Pandora's box of sexuality but not interfere with her commitment to Arnold. Another is a sex therapist, whom he says his wife won't go to. Another is taking her away on trips, which would supposedly be sexual. But this is the kind of itinerary he tells me he has made up for their next venture into ecstasy.

"We're going to the Caribbean. We won't leave early in the morning because I want to wait until the kids are safely at school. If anything happened to them, I'd never let her forget it," he says, although they employ a full-time housekeeper. "Then we'll fly out. We have the whole afternoon, and I don't have a business appointment until dinner. Then I have lunch the next day with one of my clients, two appointments that afternoon, and a dinner. Then we can play tennis, and perhaps we can make love that afternoon, although I have a late appointment, then dinner with friends of ours from New York, and an early meeting the next day. Then I'm free all afternoon, and then we fly home that night to the kids.

"I'm sure after we've made love the third day, she'll be open, and we can talk about our sexual problems," he says, absolutely unaware of the fact that he has tried to fit his wife's problem into a very heavy business schedule, very much like her usual schedule of house and children at home. I stare at him, not believing his naiveté about how much time would be needed to break her defenses down, to become intimate. Even sex therapists need two full weeks to begin to help sexual problems, and they are trained for it.

I ask Arnold if he ever had a sexual evening with his wife that was really erotic. "Yeah," he says energetically. "One time when the kids were having dinner. We were both resting, and she was in her bra and panties. I accidentally came into the bedroom. She said, 'What about the kids?' I said, 'Fuck the kids,' and put a chair against the door, and we made terrific love.

"It was great. That night I begged for sex."

"Something else happened that night," I offer. "You put her before the kids."

He scratches his head thoughtfully and looks at me.

"You may be right. You know, they're very important to me. We waited eight years, but we couldn't have children, so finally we adopted them."

He pauses, and looks incredibly green in the face, like he has just had shock therapy. Now, the story is no longer that his wife has sexual problems and he needs to see girls on the side. Now, it is more complex, complicated, and he knows it.

"You know," he says wearily, looking like a defeated man, "maybe that's why she always says, 'If we break up, if Arnold ever goes, *he gets the children!*' "

My God, I thought while interviewing Arnold, *he is probably the husband all the wives in the "marriage" chapter talk about.* How can a woman who has been made to feel that she is a cripple because she can't have children, then made to feel that her primary task in life is the care and feeding of their five adopted children, even with a housekeeper, then made to fit in with a business trip, really feel that she is an important sensual element in her husband's life? If I were his wife, I'd have someone on the side all right, *and she probably does.*

Once a woman becomes a mother, she has her problems with eroticism, but I question whether they are hers, or they are projected upon her by her husband. It's almost as if she becomes everything to the children that his own mother was not to him. Thus, to get excited, he needs the stimulation of a young, attractive girl with no commitments and responsibilities.

Even when a mature man is not married any longer, he likes an attractive, young female companion to make him feel sexy, successful, and desirable. This is true of Bill.

Bill

He is tall and swarthy, with dark brown hair and eyes and a wide smile, an Italian version of Montgomery Clift, my secret fantasy. I am immediately turned on and get increasingly depressed as Bill, an advertising executive, tells me about the women who turn him on.

"Most of them have been models. One is a well-known actress, another a prominent socialite. Often I think, *Why is that beautiful woman looking at me? She has all those men around her.* But I find very often that she is interested in me."

He seems a bit sheepish about the fact that he pursues the classic beauty, *Vogue* magazine-style, and says so. "I'm a real sucker for them. These women are a bit spoiled and selfish because they can get what they want without putting out even a minimum of effort. People are always ready to help them and fuss over them. It stunts their growth, and I know that, and they often know it, and we both don't care."

I feel terribly depressed about the fact that the men I interview are constantly explaining their turn-on as having so much to do with the way a woman looks. Women do not seem to describe their lovers that way, and I wonder why.

Almost reading my mind, Bill tells me why. "I think I go after these women because the culture says they are valuable, because other men want them, because they're beautiful to look at, and because they are a challenge. But," he pauses thoughtfully, scratching his full head of brown hair and looking sheepish again, "often society exacts a dear price from these women because of their beauty."

I know what he means, because very beautiful women tell me

they resent being chosen for their appearance, their wealth, their fame. They want to be loved for themselves. Bill understands this and therefore fathers them. "I try to do everything I can to let her know that I want to know her, know her problems, discuss her life. Often, I feel very protective of them, too.

"I see courting as helping someone see things more positively, helping them change. I become a kind of protective father for them. I guess it's a desire to assert myself and my ego. Women who get to know me seem to say I'm more sympathetic than the average male. I become a big force in their lives, which is probably what I want to be."

Knowing this, Bill dates women mostly under thirty, although he is forty-one and knows many women who might give him what he seems to be looking for: mothering. "Many women are very warm and willing to mother me. But many women aren't. And I don't blame them, but I like women who will."

"What kind of women refuse to mother you?" I ask incredulously, because in my mind every relationship has a little bit of everything in it, a bit of salt here, pepper there.

"Feminists," he says shamefully. "For example, I think a Susan Brownmiller would be a difficult woman to approach. Although I am wholly sympathetic to advancing feminist causes, they all seem to be saying no to giving sympathy and understanding. They make me the enemy and seem to want to make that point."

Although Bill wants to be a big force in women's lives, when he was married for half a dozen years, he found that he kept in all his fury and bitterness at his wife's expectations. "Pat kept telling people what good care I took of her, but when we were alone, it was obvious that she would decide what was going to make our marriage work, that she could not rely on me. But I couldn't get angry with her."

Thus, one day, six years after they vowed "I do," sexually impotent, he left Pat with their brownstone house and all of their possessions, surprising her completely. "In the last few years of our marriage, I felt no sexual desire for her, so I made love to women on the side. I told myself I was being accommodating, but it couldn't last. Although we're still friends, I'm sure she still doesn't fully understand what happened. But because I was so generous, she couldn't resist the move. I knew I had to give her everything I had to get out of it."

Earning over $30,000 a year, Bill has a lot, even now. He lives in a brownstone, occupying the entire parlor floor, in the East Seventies, a house dedicated to a grand manner of living, one block from the park where you never hear sounds of traffic. In his elegant rooms, he has selected a huge brown velvet sofa, with lots of bookshelves and a white shaggy rug, and birch furniture that is handmade and has the look of comfort and caring. Seated amidst huge plants and two white cats, Bill is wearing a peacock-blue bathrobe which was given to him by his ex-wife last Christmas. He looks warily at me, and although we are both Italian, I cannot get into a deeper level of experience and communication with him, so I talk about his anger, which he controls and thus controls the rest of his experience.

"I've tried several techniques to experience my anger because I know if you confront people, it makes life simpler for you. I've learned that in business. If I would be willing to be more ruthless and cold-blooded and authoritarian in my company, I'm sure I could be earning more money. But it's not worth it."

The concept of macho, Bill feels, is still living within him. "I detest the concept and everything it stands for. I don't think men are a superior race." But parts of the macho concept which remain inside him are doled out in his paternalistic concern for the women in his life. For in his affairs Bill makes very sure that he is the stronger person, the giver, thus feeling secure in the relationships in a way he could never feel in his marriage. Thus, in his affairs, he can often initiate sexually.

"Often, women are reluctant at the beginning. Then, after a while, they'll run around nude. And that is an emotional reassurance for me." He finds that most women are open to anything sexual except anal sex. "In Italy, where I lived for a while, I found the women were more open to that, and even had orgasms. There's something about a young, well-brought up American woman that makes her leery of this. It's unfortunate because it's pleasurable for a woman, if I masturbate her at the same time."

Fantasy acting-out also turns Bill on. "I had a rather intense affair once where the woman asked me to be the delivery boy and I'd come into the house and surprise her in bed. It felt kind of silly, but it certainly added a particular spice to our lovemaking. Another time, a woman took nude photos of me, and after seeing them, I had a large erection, and finally we both made love wildly."

Only two things disturb Bill sexually. One is when a woman comes over and says she is attracted to him and wants him. "I doubt it and think it is a put-on. Or I think something is wrong with her," he says candidly.

I get immediately depressed at this thought and wonder whether Bill is picking up my signals, that although I am not a classic beauty, I think he's terrific. And what can you do about it if he doesn't see you unless you're tall, thin, and American?

I ask him if he picks up signals from women easily so that a woman does not have to initiate. He frowns, shakes his head, and admits, "No, I can't always tell when a woman is pleased and attracted to me." *You schmuck*, I swear to myself.

The other thing that Bill is slightly apprehensive about is women who have repeated orgasms right away, one after the other. "The only trouble with those women is they tend to excite me so I come and can't be erect right away while she goes on producing. All women complain about it, and I used to get defensive about it, but what I say now is, 'Wait a half-hour and you'll have what you want again.' After all," he continues, his voice straining, "I can make it two or three times a night." He doesn't admit the afterthought to his feelings, which seems to be, *What else does she want?*

The most erotic experience Bill has ever had was teaching a young woman to have an orgasm. "I bought some wild porno films, got dildos, vibrators, gadgets, put on records of the sounds of lovemaking, and I worked on her all day. Finally, I was inside of her, vibrating her with this vibrator while the records were being played and she watched fellatio on film on the ceiling, and she came.

"It was so terribly erotic," he says quietly. "We had done something enormous in her life."

Bill, like many other men, feels potent when he is in the paternalistic, teaching position. If a woman has orgasms as the result of his patient and tender care, then he indeed feels erotic. What a bore!

But, unfortunately, this attitude is prevalent among men in our society. So while women are learning to be more and more open sexually, when they finally get to the place where they are both initiating and multiorgasmic, they find it difficult to find an attractive man to share their pleasure with who will not be threatened by it.

I have an answer for these women—younger men. It is certainly the pleasure men have been committed to for years—as in the case of Jason who, at fifty-five, falls in love with girls under sixteen.

Jason

In a funky house in San Francisco, there is a large, king-sized bed with a huge penis over it. A few feet in front of the bed are three steps down to a small stage with its own electronically operated curtain. On the stage is a sunken tub, a toilet, and various fancy items indicating a king's bathroom. As I look into the room, I have a feeling it signifies something very theatrical, something to do with sex perhaps? I am even more titillated because in the outer salon, a large room with simple furniture, each wall has a magnificent painting worth a lot of money and executed brilliantly by Jason, a fifty-five-year-old artist who made good from a poor, midwestern family.

Jason is mercurial, his speed legendary. He moves quickly, speaks quickly, and thinks quickly, and I wonder if he ever permits himself the leisure of slow, philosophical thinking. A veteran of four marriages, one still legal, Jason is like a juvenile delinquent, childish and boyish in his attitudes. Wiry, handsome, and genuinely warm and humorous, he tells me about his sex life.

"I see a lot of people now," he says, his eyes glinting. "It's gotten ridiculous. There are four regulars and then some others. I teach a course at a local high school and that's where I meet them," he says in an offhand manner. I am confused and ask him what does he mean. "Well, most of the girls I see are going to high school," he says. I burst out laughing, but then see he is very, very serious.

"When my fourth marriage ended, at least practically ended, I met this fifteen-and-a-half-year-old girl. I was mad about her. She used to tell me about all her other goings-on. She was very, very strange. It got so that I wanted to possess her completely. So for the first time in my life, I was actually monogamous." He scratches his head as if in puzzlement at this extraordinary thing. "I didn't screw anything else for three years. But," he says with a tragic comedic air, "it didn't work. She just didn't believe me. So she kept her activities going, and I, finally in bitterness, went back to mine, but I didn't enjoy it. I was completely hung up on her."

Being hung up on her meant giving her a job in his adjoining studio. It is a huge room with all of the mechanical and technical props of a working artist. Jason used to pay his girlfriend a salary, see her every night, and then drive to high school in the morning on his motorcycle, which is painted Dago green. "I'd pick her up after school, too. Her parents didn't know. Her mother used to call me and tell me to protect her from the boys at school."

Jason still feels a great deal of passion for this girl, who is now twenty-one. Although he does not see her regularly, whenever she needs money, she calls him. Then they bargain, something Jason is good at. "She says, 'I'm broke. Twenty-five dollars?' I say, 'Okay, fifteen?' and then we do *it*. She really acts the whole thing out. She lies down, doesn't do anything. And I do *it* to her. It's great, and I don't know why."

This interchange of money and sex is familiar to Jason. Most of his young girlfriends need money. Most of the time he pays them, giving them odd jobs or whatever. He also supports four households and a house at the beach, and I ask him if he resents paying for his emotional and sexual attachments. "I have the money, they don't. What can I do?" he says. "Okay, no one is nice—really. Sometimes I say, 'Okay, so what?' and live with it. Sometimes it bothers me, but I can't change that."

I thought perhaps Jason gives them money because he can't give them other things, and I wonder what the other things are. I know he doesn't want to marry again, so that's out, but the girls know that, too. I probe into his sex life and how it operates.

"I began to think that men are so limited," he says in such a vulnerable and open way that I am deeply moved. "You know, I undress a woman, intimidate her, and then we go to bed. I have the same pattern. Sometimes I blow a woman. But I don't like to be blown. I lose my erection. A lot of my girls are slightly dull as people. One works part-time as a typist. She claims that I only want to see her to fuck her. She has the most beautiful breasts—those breasts embodied with that mind. I don't know. She's terribly passive."

When a woman . . . (I have trouble calling high-school students women, so I'm going to revert to girl.) When a girl becomes aggressive, which is very, very rare, it turns Jason on. But it has to be a certain kind of aggressiveness, such as his young Mexican girlfriend has.

"She called and asked if she could come over. I was busy so I said no." He seems a bit sheepish, talking about her. "I don't treat her too good. So she came to the door and rang the bell for an hour. I finally opened it, and she told me she wanted to do *it*. I had another date, so I ran into the bedroom and barricaded myself in. She kept pounding and pounding on the door. Finally, I found that I was getting excited. I called the other girl and broke the date. Then I opened the door and I said, 'Okay, you want to do *it*, let's do *it*.' And it was fantastic!"

But other kinds of aggressive or assertive behavior don't seem to work. At a recent societal party of feting artists in San Francisco, Jason said there was nothing but beautiful women in see-through everything. "You know, in the middle of the party, I called up this girl and said I wanted to see her later. What's wrong with me?"

He is joking, but I sense behind the humor is a serious question. I ask him why he doesn't date women who are effective in their own lives, professional or creative women who have their own money, their own style.

He nods his head. "I'm not against it. I'd like to try it. But I never connect with women over twenty-one. I really think there is something wrong. I keep saying to myself, 'I'm tired of fucking children. What does it do for you? To know a child? It can't be about life.' I want to see what it's like to make love to a woman, just to do it for kicks. But I can't do it! It just doesn't happen.

"It could be because I'm like a baby and I'm afraid a woman is going to judge me. You know," he begins to whisper, although no one is there, "I think it's because I'm afraid—afraid. . . ."

"Yes?" I ask.

"Afraid that no girl who was ever with me ever *came!*"

I am astonished; after all, at fifty-five, it is a long time to engage in sexual activity and not know if you have been with orgasmic women. I ask him if he asks them about their orgasms.

He shakes his head. "I asked this girl the other day, and she said, 'Man, don't talk about *it*, just do *it*.' So I don't ask anymore."

So instead, Jason uses a system of bargaining. For an hour-fuck, he will pay so much money, one way or the other. "But it doesn't always work. I have this one girl who comes over and each time she pretends we haven't done *it* before. So I never know if we will. She acts like she's a virgin every time."

Scratching his head thoughtfully, Jason tries to make some sense out of all this. "I think I'm a classic chauvinist. I think I have the Pygmalion fantasy. But girls fight back. They give it to you, too. They think you want them more than they want you. The person with the money has the power. I'm very conscious of power, but I'd like to give it up where sex is concerned. I'd just like to sit down and be interested in someone and talk and then maybe get around to sex, instead of paying for doing *it*."

Jason is a strange combination of boldness and shyness. He is bold in the world, creating beautiful works of art and being successful at it. But somewhere, there is somebody hiding behind that boldness who has never left his small town in Indiana.

"When I was very, very young," he says quietly now for the first time, "I was short and thought I was very, very ugly. I went to a WASP school, and those girls looked wonderful, with their blonde hair and blue eyes, acting like big shit. I thought the only possibility for me was doing *it* with someone who was cross-eyed.

"Maybe that's why I use money for sex? Do you think there's any connection?"

Jason has money and fame and high-school girls, every man's fantasy in adolescence. But even high-school girls rip him off just as his four wives did. He is supporting so many households I couldn't keep it all straight. Of course he is assured an important place in all of them as the wage-earner. But I wish, if he is going to support a haremlike situation, he could at least, like a sheik does, enjoy it more.

A man who has a haremlike situation but seems to enjoy it much much more is Mr. Gustav, a theatrical set designer.

Mr. Gustav

In a ceremonious, James Bond-type atmosphere, a woman's voice over an intercom tells me to take three steps back and go to another door on another floor. I search for this strange door which I cannot find, and suddenly a panel does open, and an African woman greets me, wearing an African robe.

I am ushered into a kind of churchlike atmosphere where models are standing and assistants are pinning strange costumes on them in the midst of an enormous theatrical set. The woman pages Mr. Gustav and he is nowhere to be found. She seats me in the middle of this mad atmosphere in an area where the staff must swelter all day, for it is very hot and stifling. She talks about the set slated for a new Broadway hit, the designs, and Mr. Gustav, and I think she is in love with him. I check my watch and see Mr. Gustav is a half-hour late for our appointment.

"Where is Mr. Gustav?" everyone seems to be saying, staring at me, wondering who I am. I begin to wonder, too, as I wait for the night to begin. I have wanted to interview this man because I have been told that he chooses a different ethnic type or race per week—one week, perhaps Oriental girls, the next, African. I am told he likes variety, and wonder whether there are enough countries to go around—after all, fifty-two weeks is a long time—and if he repeats any race or ethnic type, why and how does he do it?

Finally, almost as if on announcement from the queen of England, Mr. Gustav enters the inner sanctum, kisses my hand, and smiles charmingly at me. He is very, very strong, with a Burt Lancaster ironic expression, and his body is that of a Faustian warrior, all muscle and passion. He apologizes for being late and tells me we must go into his private salon.

When I enter it, I see a space for dream time. One wall is entirely plants, going from the floor to a very high ceiling and on up to the skylight. On another wall there are mirrors, and near them a row of set designs hang. Another room is a kitchen with a bar. Still another room is a seating arrangement, and another leads to a cavernlike room which I am prevented from entering because Mr. Gustav says a leftover, naked luncheon companion is napping there. I suddenly realize that the reason I have been kept waiting so long is that Mr. Gustav has been fucking all afternoon.

He smiles slyly when he sees I have realized the reason for his lateness. Then I am offered wine or . . . ? I ask for coffee. He tells me the work went badly that morning and so he goofed off by having people in for a long, drunken luncheon. He does not mention the sexual part but says gallantly that the woman in the bedroom got drunk and fell asleep. I look at the sexual flush on his face, am attracted by it, and smile. We both know I know.

"Ah, so I am going to be *Playboy*'s Playmate of the Month?" he grins, misunderstanding the reason for this interview. I tell him this is not so and ask him about his sex life, which apparently is in fine shape.

"The first thing in the morning when I wake up, I masturbate," he says shyly. "Of course I have a steady who's very nice, but sexually, it's not too good. I see her about three times a week. We don't have that crazy drive, that excitement, any longer. I can't be honest with her because she gets into a state. She makes me feel guilty. She's so nice to me and wants to be with me so I can't say no because she will get hurt. As a result, I'm very dishonest, and I don't have long relationships with women. Usually, maybe half a year. It constantly changes."

To supplement his sexual time, Mr. Gustav sees women that he "hits on" in bars, at theatrical functions, or simply on the street. "A woman has to be interested in me, she has to be close and charming. Then you touch each other. There!" He reaches out and touches me and positively turns me on. "You see, you didn't move away. That turns me on," he says with a great deal of boyish charm.

"So I try to be honest with women. If you want to ball a woman and take her to the movies and then she says no, you've wasted your whole evening and you're disgusted. So I simply say to the woman, 'Ball with me?' and if she says no, you get another woman. It's so easy, and so you definitely get laid, and everybody's happy."

"How do you feel when a woman says no?" I ask this well-armored man who talks of courting a woman as "hitting" her, a common phrase in male circles, which I abhor because it sounds like such an assaultive act, instead of a seductive, sensual, loving one.

"I don't care," he says defensively, but I can see that he cares very much, and I wonder why each and every woman has to want him so obviously for him to respond.

"Every woman is different—her shape, her eyes, what she says, her hair, her crotch, her feet. Some things are more adorable than others, so you start to touch and play a fabulous game. You begin to know what to do, how to touch each other, how to talk to each other. I used to ball two women for a long time because it is a man's great fantasy. But if the two women are homosexual, it works better because if you are in bed with two heterosexual women and want to ball one, it's a game or a selfish thing, and I feel badly for the other woman. Thus, I often have a man along. I like to ball with two couples in bed."

Apparently, whatever Mr. Gustav's definite armor is, it doesn't seem to be obvious in group sex for he also swings with people he is close to. "I have the idea that I'm very strong, that I am the center of things, that I am the attraction. Whatever happens around me I make happen, so I never feel down or left out."

This attitude is reflected in the fact that Mr. Gustav's penthouse seems to be a center of attraction, with many people dropping by. During this bare hour that I've been sitting with him, the doorbell rings often, which he doesn't answer, and the phone is ringing constantly, which seems to annoy him. "Oh, that goddamn phone," he says of the instrument.

I ask him if he initiates with women. "They usually call me," he says. "Women cater to me. I don't mean they all say yes. Some say no. But the women who stay with me cater to me. I do demand that, I guess. I'm always so definite about what I do and want."

Gustav has never found a woman who equals him in energy, and he calls himself a male chauvinist. However, since turning forty, he has been spending some nights alone in his penthouse, thinking about his life. "I think I'm strong and can handle things. But underneath, I wonder whether something is wrong, whether I'm afraid of something. Maybe I'm afraid of rejection. After all, if someone calls you, I guess they want you and that makes you feel secure. I try to be a happy, jolly fellow, so anybody can do whatever they want with no problems, but underneath, there is a great feeling of having power over women. But then I think I may be getting old and what will happen when I cannot get to my pills and I have nobody to help me."

On some occasions, Gustav feels he can be very vulnerable to women. "I can open myself up to a woman. I can show her my inner feelings, which sometimes goes badly. There are these nights when bodies really melt together, and everything is gone. The whole world is gone, and bodies just move and become one thing, and each movement is like a joy. And you don't get tired, and you want more and more and more, and the woman wants more and more and more, too. It always happens with special women.

"My favorite position is belly-to-belly. Sometimes it's so gorgeous. You just lie there, and you don't know if the light is on, and you don't know if the music is playing—you don't know anything. You just feel each other, and it's nice and sexy, and all your muscles feel this response, a kind of offering up to the other person."

He fondles my arm as he tells me of these sensuous evenings, as if he must hold onto something organic in the telling. I smile at him, for it is rare to have a man describe evenings which I, myself, have experienced and which so often are not shared with friends. I think about my past experiences and feel very close to his.

"But," he says breaking the mood, "my relationships don't work out, because I pick women who cater to me. Even though at first a woman who doesn't think of her own feelings pleases me, later I get bored. Then I tell them to do things for themselves, not to pretend. But it doesn't work."

Gustav has a really interesting attitude toward women who get pregnant. "It's all the same. If I am having an affair with her, it doesn't matter if it's another man's genes. I am responsible, too. It's all the same process of love and sex. I never ask a woman if it's mine or if it is his. I give her the money. She shouldn't have to pay for the abortion, because it is painful enough for her."

Of all birth-control methods, Gustav likes what he calls the little pancake. I assume he means the diaphragm. "I love to put it in, but only after I eat a woman. I like pussies to taste like pussies—nice, slightly pissy sometimes, a little like hair smells, a gorgeous smell. I don't want to put that damn cream in until later.

"Some women have orgasms when I play with them, when I eat them, when I ball them. Some say, 'Oh, shit,' some laugh hysterically, some get spaced out, some get unbelievably noisy and crazy, some shiver all over their bodies. All of it turns me on. I like it."

He smiles as he remembers something that turned him off. "I remember one chick kept saying, 'A little more to the right, a little fast, now go slow, a little slower, a little further up.' That disturbed me. I said to her, 'Hey, hey, calm down. Let's start all over again. You have to relax.' I think communication during sex is good, but I don't like to be told what to do because I might not like it."

The phone rings again and again, and the dogs bark at the doorbell, and Gustav looks very guilty. I wonder at men like him who have completely arranged their lives to be the center of all sorts of attention, thinking that women are catering to them when, in actuality, they are really catering to the women who come to them. After all, at some point, he must have to pick up the phone, must have to leave the penthouse with its waiting women, all waiting to be made special, all waiting to be made love to, all waiting to come to this irresistible, charming, but really aloof, fellow.

"When I'm on the street, I just get horny in the head. I don't get erections until I know a woman wants me. If I feel her crotch and it's wet, it turns me on. But I find most women don't know what to do. They don't grab you and kiss you passionately. They let you kiss them and then wait. That bores me terribly. I like people who touch each other, reach out to each other. I even kiss men on the lips, men who are my friends," he says with passionate fervor.

I ask him if his making his home a center of attraction might be a manipulation. He looks sad as he answers, "My whole act is a manipulation to begin with. I come into a restaurant—I talk loud, I dress up. I don't like to sit in a corner. I must be on top of things all the time. I try to impress people. Every place I am, something has to happen around me. I feel a little bit showy and loud and feel lately that I resent having to do that. It must cover up something.

"I don't know why I need so much sex. It must be . . . somewhere . . . I must be scared underneath."

Gustav, like many other men in this chapter who are successful in business and in their erotic experiences, does spend some quiet evenings at home, thinking about his life. Very often, those quiet evenings are spent with their steady girl, their wife substitute. But they are afraid that if this becomes too enjoyable, they will not have the freedom to ball anyone they want.

Most of these men do not deal with their anger and aggressiveness toward women directly; thus, the reason for the erotic separation—a stay-at-home woman for feelings, a strange woman on the street corner for excitement—resulting in an inability to combine the two.

Regarding anger, it is, of course, always present. But Charles, who feels anger very strongly, has a very difficult time controlling it physically with women he cares about.

Charles

Thirty-two years old, from Arizona, with a successful space-engineering career, Charles becomes very old-fashioned when he falls in love with a woman. "I have constant thoughts about her, and can't wait to see her again. Then I start writing her love letters. When I call, she will usually say that this has never happened to her before in her life."

This romantic, old-fashioned Charles is quite different from the Charles in college. "I would fuck anything that moved, but now I don't sleep with someone unless I feel something for them. I began thinking I was cheating myself when the woman was just a conquest, a lay."

Describing himself as not aggressive and very moody, Charles has trouble with relationships. "They are always power plays. I'm always attracted to intelligent women. They stimulate me. My ideal woman is pretty, slim, and a little crazy. She is provocative, sensitive, and satiric. She sends me a love message, but it's coded and provocative. I'd have to decode her messages."

Charles meets women in all sorts of ways. While working on his antique car, women will admire the car and then he'll drive them to work. "It usually takes me a couple of meetings before I ask a woman out. And she always asks me later why did I take so long? I guess I must be shy or something."

The way Charles likes to entertain a woman is simple. "We have dinner, talk about our days' activities, and go to bed. I put my hand on her hand and make love to her. I can last usually about an hour. Some women tell me their fantasies while we're making love. Others will want to masturbate with me."

Charles speaks of his own fantasies as pedestrian. "They're always reality-bound. If I masturbate when I'm alone, I'll rewind the day in my mind—a woman I've made love to or someone I'd met whom I want to make love to."

Sometimes, accidentally, he finds an unusual erotic experience. "I needed a dime for the meter for my car and was in the loft district. So I knocked on someone's door and they opened it. There were rock tapes blasting. A lot of plastic sculptures were about. Two women were smoking grass. They handed me a joint. Then they kissed me, both at once. I took off their clothes. We switched around. One woman put her index finger up my anus while she was sucking my penis. It was great. We all had orgasms."

Charles can tell when a woman has an orgasm by what he called "the blush." "I've never seen it with a prostitute. It's an awareness not only of yourself, but of the one you're making love with. I love to look at a woman's stomach, see how her hips turn out, make love with the lights on so I can really enjoy her. I like the crook at the base of her spine. I guess I'm an ass man—I don't like big tits."

Charles remembers the first time he was treated to a dinner by a woman. "I suddenly thought about what a woman always feels. *Why is this person doing this for me? What does the money mean? What does he want?* I suddenly understood a woman in a new way."

When Charles falls in love, he feels very, very jealous. "When my lover is with someone else, I always think he is a better man. One time, I found a lover with another man and felt terrible. She said she couldn't say no because she wants people to like her."

Asked what his idea of a man is, Charles replies that he is someone who knows how to cook, how to fix his own car, and who can pick up bleeding people on the street and help them.

Tall, gaunt, with aristocratic features, Charles was teased as a child about his fragility and sensitivity. "I had two older brothers who are very successful now. When we were kids, they were just like my father. I wasn't. So I joined the street gangs in the area. It was great. I was so different from them. The gang was so violent and that was where I got my idea of men from."

Charles has been very violent with women, so much so that they have called the police. "I like strong women. I like mutually supportive roles. When I'm feeling a little shaky, I want to feel I have someone on my side to talk to. That's what I call love."

He looks ashamed when I ask him to be specific about his violence, and begins raising his soft voice as I prod and prod him. I wonder whether he is going to get violent with me. We are seated in his very cell-like apartment, and all the windows and doors are shut. Suddenly, behind his glasses, I see a burst of glinting energy I have not seen before. *Where will I run?* I think. *What will I do?*

"I live with a subliminal rage all the time," he says finally. "My anger and violence come out of situations which I get myself into. Sometimes I can get my anger out in notes and letters. But not always."

One time recently, Charles was washing the dishes after a dinner he had cooked. He asked the girl to help him, and she was snippy. "I turned around and took a quart of milk and poured it on her. I felt good about not getting violent with her," he says candidly.

I inform him that most women are very frightened of male violence because they have been brought up since they were children with this threat in the background. He listens in wonderment, as if he has not even thought of this before.

When I ask him what he thinks of when he strikes a woman, he says angrily, "I think she is very powerful, but at the same time I'm socking her, I'm reaching out with my other hand to comfort her. Of course it's impossible, because the woman is still ricocheting from the shock. By the time they get their breathing speed back, they just want to say good-bye." Charles says every one of his affairs so far has ended this way.

Angry at the women's movement, Charles says he has no idea where women are at. "I don't know about women, because it's not public information except for the feminist politics and these politics suck. Why should they reject me because of some momentary thing? I can't comprehend their fear. It's a very, very unpleasant thing to lose your temper. I can do something in three seconds that would take me two years to undo. Neurologically, I always feel like I have overdosed on some strange hormone."

Charles suddenly looks at me, and asks, "Can you tell me a secret?"

There is a forlorn look in his eyes, a secret yearning.

I say I'll try.

"What are women really like?"